GW01018124

Street People

Street People

Helga Dudman

JERUSALEM POST / CARTA

Photographs courtesy of the families and friends of the
people in the book; others by Werner Braun, Lester
Millman, Zeev Radovan, David Rubinger and Esther
Suffrin; and from the archives of American Colony Hotel, A.
Bonniers Förlag, Stockholm, Keter, The Jerusalem Post and
Historical Museum of Tel Aviv.

Set in 10/11 Photon Egyptian
Design: Alex Berlyne

ISBN 965-220-039-5

Printed in Israel.

Contents

Foreword

While crossing Marmorek Street one morning, I suddenly realized that I must have done just that about twenty thousand times during the twenty years I had been living in Tel Aviv, for the street was on my way to work and to the grocer's. But who was Marmorek? And who were Berdyczewski, Crémieux and Lunz, his parallel neighbours whom I had also crossed so often and so unthinkingly?

So began my interest in streets as entrances to biographies. Israel is unusually rich in this field, being a tiny country with a long past. We have a huge number of forefathers and notables to honour, and large helpings of history, ideology, politics and art which we enjoy commemorating in our often very short thoroughfares. Our main cities today have municipal committees which regularly select new street names from submitted suggestions; they operate under clear by-laws but are under great pressure, political and personal, to immortalize this or that personality.

Tel Aviv alone has over 1,800 streets named after people, and others named after places, things, dates, or abstract concepts. Thus, there is a "Rehov Totzeret Ha'aretz," which is the Hebrew for "Product of the Country Street" — a charming concept expressing a wish for economic independence, but somewhat curious as an address. Then there is "Kaf-Tet B'November," which stands for November 29, 1947, the date of the UN partition resolution, but which today refers to a circle in North Tel Aviv known for its elegant shops.

We also have such distinctively Israeli intersections as the one where Asparagus meets Blood of the Maccabees. But I have resisted all these non-biographical attractions and dealt only with the human stories — the men and the very few women who became Israeli streets.

Visitors should not feel inadequate if they know hardly anything about our street names. Neither do the natives, nor even the cab drivers. A radio quiz programme a few years ago consistently produced blank or quaintly wrong answers to questions about local street names, even such illustrious ones as Rothschild. And when the late Golda Meir was a patient in Beilinson Hospital, she was shocked to learn that the younger members of the staff knew nothing about the man after whom their institution was named, and whose little street is near Dizengoff Circle. Readers will meet him in Chapter Two of this book.

This guide is by no means comprehensive. My selections have been random, following only my curiosity and what might be called my own street-walking patterns. I thought it best not to include portraits of such famous personalities as Theodor Herzl or Chaim Weizmann, although they turn up as streets in practically every town in Israel. However, they do appear frequently in these pages as friends of other streets. On the other hand, some of our shortest and most obscure streets grew into the longest chapters, simply because I found them interesting.

I have also omitted streets named after biblical figures, because these are so well known to most Israelis. For instance, when a child tells you he lives "on the corner of Bin-Nun and Nordau," he knows perfectly well that the former is the biblical Joshua, son of Nun of the tribe of Ephraim. But Max Nordau, physician and cat-lover, whose name with good reason appears on the streets of most cities and towns here, is a mystery to nearly all their modern residents. His story opens this book.

All the stories were originally published in slightly different form in *The Jerusalem Post*. In many cases, after they appeared I received additional information from readers who had known a street or boulevard as a relative or friend; these welcome contributions are incorporated here. A few intimates of our founding fathers, who long ago became streets, are still with us, and it is a great day for the street historian when a meeting produces hitherto unpublished material. I am grateful to them and to the many, many others who helped me with this book.

H.D.

To my mother and father

1
"Death to the East African!"

Two shots rang out at the Hanukka ball. "Death to Nordau the East African!" shouted a young man with a pistol, firing at close range. He missed his target, but he did wound a bystander in the leg.

The unsuccessful terrorist was an idealistic 27-year-old Zionist student, and his attempt made front-page news. The intended victim was an international celebrity, by far the most illustrious name in the early Zionist movement. He was world-famous before anybody had heard of Theodor Herzl, and was widely recognized as Herzl's biggest catch.

At the time of this action-packed Hanukka ball, which took place in Paris in 1903, Max Nordau was a controversial and best-selling writer, whose vast output of fiction, drama and social philosophy was translated into 15 languages, including Chinese and Japanese. He himself knew 14 modern languages, as well as three classical ones. He was also a physician interested in such newly developing fields as criminology, psychiatry and women's problems having studied under the progressive Italian-Jewish professor of medicine Cesare Lombroso.

Indeed, after the attempt on his life, Nordau himself defended his attacker during the investigation, an act of remarkable generosity and tolerance.

But why would a Zionist student wish to kill this distinguished gentleman, who was Herzl's own choice to be his successor; who had drafted the Basle Programme at the First Zionist Congress and whose speech there was applauded as a brilliant analysis of Zionism; who had served as vice-president of the first six Congresses and was to be president of the next three?

And in view of this, why is his name meaningless for most people in Israel today, though there is hardly a town or village that does not have its Nordau Street, Square or Boulevard? For all but a few, it would be hardly less difficult to identify Max Nordau than Meir-Simha Südfeld, which was his original name.

The name of the unsuccessful murderer was Chaim Selig Luban, which nobody at all is expected to identify. He was found to be mentally unbalanced, but there was a reason behind his act of terrorism: ideological conflicts among early Zionists were more violent than today's when even character assassination is relatively feeble.

He fired his shots at the Hanukka ball because three months earlier, at the Sixth Zionist Congress, Max Nordau, against his better judgment and out of loyalty to Herzl, had defended the leader's doomed "Uganda Scheme." This proposal by the British Government to the World Zionist Organization for the establishment of a Jewish colony in British East Africa, on lands that are now part of Kenya, had deeply split the Congress. It has often been suggested that the fierce antagonism among delegates helped to bring about Herzl's early death the following year. The Uganda Scheme was finally rejected by the Seventh Congress.

Nordau, surviving the attempt on his life, also outlived his fame. The *Encyclopaedia Britannica* refers to his work as "pseudo-philosophy," and comments patronizingly that this once "had a great vogue." The only early Zionist whose name brought more lustre to the movement than the movement reflected on him, Nordau lived to become its forgotten man, cast aside by his and Herzl's political opponents, notably Chaim Weizmann.

It is already hard to remember, but Tel Aviv's Nordiya district was until not long ago a slum of shacks. Now it is the site of Dizengoff Centre, a concrete and chrome commercial complex which would surely have bemused the author of *Paradoxes*, who believed that "scientific ethics" would improve human life "through intelligence and compassion."

On Nordau's 90th birthday, in 1919, it was announced that a "garden city" would be established in his name. When he heard the news, the old man wrote from Spain, where he had been interned in World War I, that "the idea of seeing a garden city flourish in the Land of Israel has all the charm of an Oriental legend to me." His words come to us across the years with ghostly relevance. "While the name it bears does not matter," Nordau wrote, "it may be that, when the city has come into being, my shadow, as in a dream, will glide in silence through its groves." He dares to hope that residents "who have the gift of inner vision will be aware of the gentle rustling, of my memory."

Certainly no terrestrial city has the radiance Nordau envisioned when he heard about "his" city; and while his own "fugitive personality" was unimportant, what mattered was "that there arise a strong and happy race of men in that bright sun, in that pure air, amid the perfume of those flowers where children chase butterflies and beautiful youth will dream its dream in the shadow of tall trees..."

We for whom Nordau foresaw these "enchanting scenes," hardly merit what he wrote to these who would walk unknowingly along his streets in another age: "My blessings go out to them even now."

There are few butterflies to be chased by the children at Tel Aviv's Tel Nordau School, which perpetuates the name of another old neighbourhood, and the children there know nothing of Max. But it is well worth excavating the *tel* that is Nordau; and it is very satisfying to be able to help along that "gentle rustling of memory," though the place has nothing by way of groves for the silent gliding of dreams.

Back, now, to the turmoil of the Uganda dispute at the Sixth Zionist Congress in Basle in 1903. Most of the delegates strongly opposed Herzl's idea of a temporary asylum in Africa for the persecuted Jews of Eastern Europe. He had put it forward because the geopolitical problems of the day were placing apparently insuperable difficulties in the way of turning Palestine into a Jewish homeland, and the need for Jews to have somewhere to go had become very urgent as pogroms broke out in Tsarist Russia.

The most violent opposition to the Uganda scheme came from the Russian delegates at the Congress. They considered themselves different from, and misunderstood by, the "Western Europeans," led by Herzl and Nordau, both born in Budapest. The Russian camp, in which young Chaim Weizmann's star was rising (although he was quickly learning "Western" ways), insisted that all energies must be concentrated on the traditional homeland of the Jewish people.

Nordau, who would have been brilliant on Madison Avenue, coined the term *Nachtasy* (night shelter) for the Uganda plan. But his speech in its favour seemed to contain inner contradictions, and Weizmann noted in his autobiography that it was unconvincing, "for Nordau himself was not thoroughly convinced, and had yielded only to pressure."

Not all the issues Nordau attacked or defended are still with us. But his vituperative battle with Ahad Ha'am, with whom he actually had much in common, is not yet entirely settled. It was about the kind of society that ought to be built in the Land of Israel — a "spiritual centre" in Ahad Ha'am's ethically austere sense, or a cosmopolitan civilization in the Herzlian sense of 19th century liberal humanism.

Nordau's widow regretted the bitter personal attacks of her husband and Ahad Ha'am on each other. It was appropriate, she wrote, that they "rest side by side in the Old Cemetery of Tel Aviv. The soil of Israel has reconciled them."

Not Jerusalem or Haifa, but Tel Aviv, the city "with no past and nothing but a future," was where Nordau had wished to spend his last years. His unfulfilled dream, his daughter recounted later, was to have "a little garden and a little house within the sound of lapping waves" in Tel Aviv.

The waves at the Mediterranean end of Nordau Boulevard are today overshadowed by a concrete block called, at the moment of writing, the Grand Palace Hotel. But it has been known previously as the Holiday Inn, the Pal, and the Sheraton. It started life as the Nordau Plaza, but there was a financial scandal and it never opened under that name: a sad evolution for an apostle of progress, of "the unity of mind and love."

From the sea, Nordau's placid Tel Aviv boulevard runs, a much appreciated strip of greenery and benches down its centre, straight east to Ibn Gabirol. Nordau himself might smile wryly at the large synagogue to be found there, for religion and marriage were among what he called *The Conventional Lies of Our Civilization*, although, admittedly, he softened toward both in his later years.

The sweep of time and the march of the city have left Sderot Nordau with a solidly middle-class character. I suspect that the residents' attitudes are out of tune with the intent of Nordau's "shocking" books. *Conventional Lies*, published in 1883, was banned and confiscated in Russia and Austria as "disturbing to the public peace and inciting to hostility against religious conventions."

How Women Love and *The Right to Love* were other sure-fire Nordau titles, and his *Degeneration* denounced such men as Nietzsche, Tolstoy, Wagner, Zola and Ibsen by applying to them the theory of his teacher Lombroso, to whom the book was dedicated. Lombroso held that criminals are degenerate; Nordau extended the notion to artists, who "show the same mental characteristics as insane criminals," and "satisfy their unhealthy impulses with pen and pencil."

George Bernard Shaw wrote a whole book rebutting *Degeneration*. It was republished in New York 75 years after its first appearance and was still generating doctoral theses. No wonder, since it dealt with such evergreen topics as spiritualism, mysticism, egomania and diabolism, all energetically debunked as supernatural illusions by Nordau the rationalist.

Jerusalem's Nordau Plaza is at the entrance to town, near the Binyenei Ha'uma, the capital's big convention centre and concert hall. The location is appropriate, for Nordau was famous for thunderous speeches before large audiences. "There were over 2,000 people in the hall," he noted with satisfaction after a speech in Vienna in 1899. "I lashed out at them, rabbis, millionaires and all, and it seems they cringed and growled under my blows."

In the same vein, that same year, to an audience of 4,500 German Jews, he delivered a prophetic and wildly unpopular warning. "A day will come," Nordau thundered, "when Zionism will be as needed by you, you proud Germans, as by these wretched *Ostjuden* whom you fear and hate! A day will come when you, too, will beg our help and ask for asylum in that land which you now scorn!... I warn you of the future!"

The German Jews sneered; and even Herzl suppressed his friend's jeremiad in the report of the meeting in his own paper, *Die Welt*. Nordau described the "turbulence in the hall" that followed, the "coldness, hostility, fights between friends and enemies." Outbursts in Jerusalem, in the hall near Nordau Plaza, have never matched this level of excitement. When the meeting closed after midnight, everybody went on to a café "amid incredible scenes," Nordau finally arrived back at his hotel at 3

12

Max Nordau in the early days of Zionism.

a.m., but by 7.30 there were "streams of people pouring into my room."

The well-built houses of Haifa's Rehov Nordau were, during the Thirties, the pride of upper-middle-class immigrants from Germany. All of them, we may be sure, knew exactly who Nordau was as they discussed life at the Café Sternschuss, a popular Yekke meeting-place on Nordau. Once beautifully kept, this area near the old Technion campus has sunk to a seedy commercial level.

Haifa's Nordau is parallel to Herzl and both are one-way, in opposite directions; our old friend Nordau carries on to the east, across the square from Maccabi House, the local headquarters of the athletic organization. This site, too, is of course thought out, because Nordau's appeal at the Second Zionist Congress for "Muscle Jewry," as opposed to "Belly Jewry," inspired the formation of Jewish athletic clubs. These led to the foundation in 1903 of the *Jüdische Turnerschaft*, forerunner of the Maccabi World Union.

Ahead of his time in his concern for physical fitness, Nordau was an excellent fencer, took swimming lessons, was good at rowing, rode horseback, and did daily setting-up exercises. His height was under average, but he had broad shoulders, a powerful build, and flaming grey eyes. His prematurely white beard, combined oddly with a youthfully fresh, unwrinkled skin, gave him a magnetically prophetic appearance.

Unlike many Jewish prophets, this one loved animals. A lost dog once followed Nordau home, and he shared his meals with it although his mother hated the animal. Nordau the young cosmopolite called the dog "Garçon"; his mother did not understand and called him Gershon.

For a man who was both a practising physician and a working journalist, his literary output was vast. Starting with a volume of travel essays, *From the Kremlin to the Alhambra,* it concluded children's stories, art criticism, novels, short stories and philosophical dissertations. His last book, published posthumously 60 years after the first, was given the imposing title *The Essence of Civilization.*

Nordau inherited his tendency to be didactic, for he was the son of a teacher, Gabriel Südfeld. Gabriel was born in East Prussia and claimed descent from an ancient rabbinical line exiled from Vienna to Eastern Europe in the 14th century. He gave his son a sound Orthodox background, but also taught him Latin and Greek as well as Hebrew; and Ladino, too, since he prided himself on being descended from Abarbanel. At the time of Meir-Simha's birth, the family was living in Pest (before this town was joined with Buda). The boy turned out to be a prodigy and published his first articles in an adult newspaper at 14.

His mother kept a rigorously Orthodox home, while his father translated Schiller into Hebrew and Ecclesiastes into German. The boy went to a

Catholic and then a Calvinist high school. He worked as a journalist while studying medicine, and changed his name legally when he was 24. In 1880 he settled in Paris as a doctor, specializing in psychic disorders. That same year he wrote his first play, *The Journalists.*

It was not until he was 32, a well-known journalist and writer, and the friend of a whole set of Paris intellectuals, that he fell seriously in love for the first time. She was a young American Jewish widow with two children, beautiful, brilliant, with the same tastes in art and literature and the same aspirations as Nordau. But his mother could not accept what the woman he eventually married described as "a young woman who travelled alone and lived alone, and who simply failed to measure up to the mother's conception of a good Jewish wife for her son." There were scenes and recriminations. The poor young woman tried to kill herself. Nordau saved her life. But finally the mother's will prevailed, and the romantic lovers separated. The first real love affair of the defiant author of *Conventional Lies* ended ignominiously.

It is strange that Nordau's domineering mother did not object to his marriage, many years later, when he was 49, to a Danish Protestant widow, the mother of four children, whose husband had been a good friend of Nordau's. The marriage "was not received in all circles," Anna Nordau admitted in her biography of Nordau after his death. But "his aged mother took his wife sincerely to her heart, and racial and religious differences faded in the face of a beautiful mutual understanding."

The year after Nordau's marriage, his beloved daughter Maxa was born, and he remained fascinated for the rest of his life by his only child. He was by now supporting a household of eight; when they travelled, as they often did, "for educational reasons," the menage included Anna's four other children, Maxa, Nordau's sister and aged mother, a few sisters-in-law and nephews, two maids, and the cat.

Nordau never asked his wife to convert to Judaism: "Why? It wouldn't give you Jewish parents." And when he expressed his doubts about the marriage to Herzl, he was reassured, with a viewpoint on intermarriage hardly acceptable to many who today consider themselves Nordau's political heirs.

"I congratulate you with all my heart," Herzl wrote to Nordau. "This noble woman will give you that peace at home which will fit you better for the battle outside the home." He went on to ask, "What are we today? We are citizens of that ideal Jewish state whose realization on earth is the fairest hope of our life. If our work were accomplished, a Jewish citizen of that Jewish state would certainly not be restrained from marrying a foreigner.

"But," continued Herzl, "do you believe for a moment that I nurse any illusions about any future change in the opinion of the people? If we succeed in carrying out our enterprise, nobody will be more attacked than you and me."

Herzl and Nordau first met in 1892 when friends, worried about Herzl's mental health, urged the Viennese journalist to visit the famous doctor-writer. The result was that Herzl converted to Zionism a personality able to open for him the doors to the rich and powerful. Of course, Nordau was also deeply affected by the realities of anti-Semitism, as revealed so glaringly by the Dreyfus Affair. But from then on, though he enjoyed a long life in Europe's cosmopolitan circles, he personally probably suffered more bitterly from the wars of the Jews than from anti-Semitic attacks.

He was known as an atheist and critic of traditional nationalism, so that when he joined Herzl, many free-thinking people decided, "If a man like Nordau takes up this cause, perhaps there is something in it."

Together with David Wolfssohn, Nordau and Herzl formed a Western European triumvirate who represented "Political Zionism," as opposed to the "Practical Zionism" of the Russians. (Wolfssohn took over the presidency of the Zionist Organization after Herzl's death when Nordau refused the honour. His Tel Aviv street is in the inelegant south, near the "new" Central Bus Station, which will probably never be completed and may be considered as doomed as the Uganda scheme.)

The elegance and formality of the "Europeans" were, along with many other things, anathema to the Russian Jews. At the First Congress, where Nordau's speeches were hailed as models of brilliant rhetoric, he had intended to appear in the relative simplicity of a frock coat; but at Herzl's insistence he changed to full dress — swallow-tails and white tie.

Weizmann, in a much-criticized criticism of Nordau in his auto-biography, pronounced him not selfless like Herzl, "but artificial as well as inclined to arrogance ... a *Heldentenor,* a prima donna, a great speaker in the classical style; spadework was not his line." Weizmann writes that Nordau's talk "sparkled with epigrams; but it betrayed no depth of feeling and perception." His attitude towards the East-European Jews was "patronizing."

The most strident literary rift, however, was between Nordau and Ahad Ha'am, the Russian-born writer and proponent of "Spiritual Zionism," who also has a street in every Israeli city, whose disciples included Weizmann. This had started earlier, when the successful Nordau had given the aspiring Herzl some literary criticism. Some of Herzl's works, Nordau said, "are examples of strong, creative prose, but others are not simple enough for my taste. They are made to impress the reader, which never permits the best of writing."

Yet when Ahad Ha'am attacked Herzl's *Altneuland,* Nordau sprang violently to Herzl's defence. Here was a question not of more style, but of

16

the whole point of the Jewish state — Ahad Ha'am's "cultural" ideal Zionism versus Herzl's conception and leadership. Ahad Ha'am attacked Herzl's novel as being insufficiently "Jewish," too concerned with "tolerance" and what the gentiles would think, completely lacking in a Hebrew core, unrealistically intent on a swift solution, and bereft of a real love of the Land and the essential ethical development of the individual.

In the storm that followed, Nordau, in the opinion of some, overreacted.

"Ahad Ha'am," he wrote, "is against tolerance. The stranger is perhaps to be slaughtered, or persecuted as in Sodom and Gomorrah? The thought of tolerance disgusts him! Well, we are disgusted when such a misbegotten victim of intolerance speaks in such a manner about tolerance.

"Ahad Ha'am accuses Herzl of copying European manners — Europe's opera houses, academies and white gloves. The only things he wishes to bring with him to *Altneuland* are the promises of the Inquisition, the mores of the anti-Semites, and Russia's laws against the Jews. One would be nauseated by such a spiritual misconception, if one didn't merely have pity for it."

There was much more. Nordau launched an onslaught on Ahad Ha'am's personality and his obsession with the Hebrew language ("except that in this beautiful Hebrew he has nothing to say"), and claimed that at heart "Ahad Ha'am is no Zionist, he is the opposite of a Zionist."

These blows and counter-blows were being published in various Zionist journals in the spring of 1903, before the "Uganda Congress." Nordau later recalled that one speaker, a certain Dizengoff of the Russian camp, had noted that Zionism was concerned "not with Jews but with Judaism." Nordau countered with his much-quoted reply: "Judaism without Jews! We know you, beautiful mask! Go with this phrase and join a spiritualists' meeting."

Herzl's comment to Nordau at the height of this 1903 battle:

"I've now read your annihilation of Ahad Ha'am. It's remarkable enough that we are already forced to fight such battles. The only explanation is this: we are already in the midst of the Jewish State, though few suspect it as yet."

Then in December, the morning after the assassination attempt, Herzl wrote to Nordau that "the Ussishkins, Bernstein-Cohens and others" (today a wide range of streets) saw in the Uganda issue a way of getting rid of us." But "if there is shooting, then we stand firm. And if you are being shot at, then my bullet, too, already has my name on it." He couldn't prove it, Herzl went on, "but in my opinion, Luban's bullet was loaded in Russia."

The Russians, however, were gaining the upper hand within the Zionist movement at the expense of the "Europeans." By the time of the Tenth Congress in 1911, seven years after Herzl's death, they were firmly in control. Nordau, who had led all previous Congresses, refused to attend.

17

When World War I broke out, he was banished from France as an enemy alien.

Not long after Nordau's arrival in Madrid in November, 1914, Vladimir Jabotinsky came to consult him about the Jewish, or Zionist, Legion he was organizing to fight on England's side. Nordau sympathized, but had some reservations. He did not like the name "Zionist Legion," since there were "Zionists among all the warring nations, and they should not be made to bear the reproach of disloyalty." Besides, Nordau thought, "Zionism as such should remain above the battle. "But he approved of the principle, and convinced Jabotinsky that "Jewish Legion" was the better name.

He also discussed with him at length the danger of inciting young Palestinians to fight on England's side, for "they were Turkish subjects and Turkey had not treated them badly; in a sense, it was treason."

Weizmann, passing through Madrid on a mission to Gibraltar in 1917, also visited the Nordaus. They were "poor creatures, very sad," he wrote to his wife, "living like refugees in a small flat." Subconcious political vengeance? But, he went on, "Nordau is delighted with our work in England and is absolutely enchanted with everything."

This contrasts with Mrs. Nordau's rather cool account of the visit. In her biography of her husband, she merely notes briefly that Weizmann and Felix Frankfurter were on their way to meet Henry Morgenthau, Sr., then U.S. Ambassador in Constantinople, and the two wanted Nordau to come along "to try to convert Mr. Morgenthau to Zionism." But Nordau "thought success in that direction so unlikely as to render any effort futile."

At about this time, Nordau developed his famous — but now forgotten — "Nordau Plan." This proposed evacuating 600,000 Jews from Eastern Europe and moving them to Palestine immediately; the figure of one million was also mentioned. In this way, a majority would be established for a Jewish state, and not some vague concept such as the "national home" of the Balfour Declaration. And, as Nordau put it, "even if thousands of these Jews should fall by the wayside," they should be considered casualties of war.

Weizmann was acid in his criticism of the Nordau Plan, "if plan it can be called, which proposed the transfer of a million Jews to Palestine in one year," ignoring all practical problems and proceeding on the cruel and dangerous assumption that "if, of that million, two or three hundred thousand perished, the remaining seven or eight hundred thousand would 'somehow' be established."

But as Nordau's supporters pointed out, he was perfectly aware of the magnitude and difficulties of his proposed "evacuation" to Palestine, and rhetorically confronted his critics:

"'It isn't possible, there are no houses.' No houses? They will live in tents to begin with. Rather that than to have one's throat cut in a pogrom.

"'They will have nothing to eat.' We will feed them until the first crop. During the four years of the war, 22 million troops who neither sowed nor reaped were fed.

"'It will cost billions.' No, but many millions — and they must be found. The Jewish people will give the required money..." He took issue with defeatists who claimed that the task was "gigantic, almost superhuman." "Gigantic? Yes! Superhuman? Why?"

Jabotinsky was to adopt the plan 20 years later, in the shadow of Hitler; but Nordau's definition of the "tenets of Zionism" during the period of World War I would not go down well with today's post-Jabotinsky ideology. Though he always warned that assimilation was an illusion, for millionaires as well as for socialists, Nordau insisted that "Zionism does not pretend to lead back to the homeland of their ancestors all the Jews of the globe. The return of those who cling to the country of their birth and of their citizenship is out of the question." Its aim, he said, is free immigration to Palestine, but Zionism "has not the ambition of founding an independent Jewish state, either kingdom or republic."

By 1919 Nordau was in open conflict with Weizmann. He rejected an invitation to see Weizmann in London, accused him of being a "self-appointed representative," and attacked the Balfour Declaration as "an empty wrapper...sheer Ahad Ha'amism, in direct conflict with the .... ideas of Herzl, my guide today as truly as he was 22 years ago."

As Weizmann's star rose, Nordau's declined. He refused to accept the "minimalist" policies of Weizmann's "practical" Zionists. Subsequently, of course, Weizmann became a polished practitioner of "political" Zionism and was himself eventually shunted aside by a still younger generation; and, while the young Weizmann had been one of those Russian Jews who criticized the formal way of life of the "Europeans," he had no objection to living in grand style when his turn came.

When Nordau returned to Paris, not without difficulty, after the war, he was still regarded in some circles as the movement's Grand Old Man. Thus, he was visited by Dr. Rubinow, head of the American Medical Delegation for Palestine, and learned about Henrietta Szold and the work of Hadassah. As Mrs. Nordau put it, "he was early aware of the determination, the practical wisdom, and the perseverance of these Jewish women of America who give their all when they undertake a task worthy of accomplishment."

But, at the "Little Congress" in London in 1920, Nordau was relegated to dismal quarters and his presence was underplayed; the Zionist leadership rejected as unrealistic his plea to "open the gates and not worry about how they will be fed." A young woman journalist interviewed Nordau at the Congress; she had never read his works — his literary popularity was already past its peak — but she was aware of his reputation and was disturbed by the shoddy treatment acccorded him. "But Dr. Nordau," she said, "you are head and shoulders above everybody else here."

"I think so too," replied Nordau.

He survived the attempt on his life by 20 years and died peacefully in Paris in 1923. His beloved Siamese cat lay beside him on the bed with two kittens; his last act was to stroke her.

Death briefly revived Nordau's grandeur. In 1926 his coffin was brought to Palestine for reburial, and a special train carried it on the overland crossing from El-Arish. All of Tel Aviv seemed to turn out for the funeral procession — rabbis, officials, schoolchildren, Maccabeans, the British District Commissioner. Even "a dog joined, and it seemed more than chance," wrote Mrs. Nordau, once again stressing her husband's love of animals. "It was as if the poor beast understood how much Max Nordau loved all that was living, and wanted to mourn the loss of a friend such as he would never find again."

She and Maxa made a point of visiting Ahad Ha'am. That old adversary, who himself had only one more year to live, welcomed the women in a spirit of generosity, kindness and tolerant forgiveness.

It was the "sad but proud privilege" of Lt.-Col. Frederick Kisch, then chairman of the Palestine Zionist Executive, to deliver an oration at the cemetery. He stressed the "characteristically Jewish" nature of Nordau's "refusal to accept passing fashions or established conventions, his relentless summoning of ideas to judgment, and merciless scepticism, founded on the ardent conviction that truth must prevail."

On the centenary of Nordau's birth, in November 1949, a fullblown ceremony was held at his graveside, where an imposing monument had been set up some years earlier. All was forgiven, if also soon to be forgotten. Ministers and Knesset Members paid their respects, and Maxa spoke. She was by then a well-known painter in Paris, in the realistic-traditional style approved by her father, and the wife of a French engineer named Greenblatt, a relative of the wife of the mayor of Tel Aviv, Israel Rokah.

Her father, Maxa said, had a particular love — from afar — for Tel Aviv, and great admiration for the city's first mayor, the late Meir Dizengoff: gone were the clashes of 1903. His unfulfilled dream had been to spend his last years in the sparkling new city because, as his widow wrote, "had he not inspired his people, Tel Aviv would not exist."

2
Notes for a Musical

The Montefiore story staged as a musical is such a good idea that it has naturally been thought of, and by Israel's national theatre, Habimah, at that. The incredible adventures of Sir Moses (born in 1784, in the reign of George III; died at the age of 101, serene and still alert, during the reign of his very good friend Queen Victoria) cries out for bouncy ballads, brilliant costumes, choreography taking us to Moscow and Morocco, with a dance around the windmill in Yemin Moshe. Unfortunately, the project of setting all this to words and music has yet to get off the ground.

Such a musical would be a glorious romp through the corridors of power, with singing roles assigned to assorted emperors and sultans, tsars and pashas; with choruses of the adoring poor; affectionate dialogues with Queen Victoria about her finances; cosy evenings at home in magnificent East Cliff Lodge in Ramsgate, on England's Kentish coast; our hero's long love affair with his own wife; and, of course, his seven visits to the Holy Land.

The first, with Lady Judith, was in 1827. They went, as always, in their own carriage, through France and Italy. Then, with the help of the Royal Navy, via Malta to Alexandria and Cairo. Finally, they spent three days in Jerusalem.

The last visit was in 1875; Sir Moses, a 91-year-old widower, made the long and perilous journey once more by carriage, despite the absence of any real roads.

And a musical — a form that is cheery and neurosis-free — is most appropriate for a man who was both a kind of biblical patriarch (though he had no children) and also a British patriot; one for whom the favourite adjectives used by biographers are "luminous" and "princely"; who possessed a radiantly good character and provided a legendary example of mental and physical, not to mention financial, good health.

Since all this sounds distant, fanciful and about as relevant to our day as *Brigadoon,* here is an item with a topical echo; a message which the then Shah of Iran ordered to be sent to Sir Moses. It was written in Hebrew, Arabic, Persian and English, and dated July 5, 1873:

"His Majesty has always manifested solicitude for the welfare of his subjects... and will take care that no injustice or undue severity is shown to the Jewish community."

This came after long years of worry, on Sir Moses' part, about the Persian Jews, and appeals by them for help against "the fanaticism of the populace which had grown with the intellectual and political decline of the Moslem states," as Sir Moses' biographer, Paul Goodman, wrote in 1925. In 1865, Sir Moses, at 80, was determined to go to Persia. Only the thoughtful action of the British Foreign Office, which produced a promise from the Shah that the Jews would be well treated, persuaded him that the journey was not really necessary.

In 1871, during a famine in Persia, Sir Moses forwarded money, to be divided equally among the Jews and the local Christians and Moslems. The next year he again wanted to go; again the Foreign Office dissuaded him from the dangerous trip.

"Lord Granville of the Foreign Office was against my going at my time of life," Sir Moses wrote in his diary. "He thought I must be eighty. I was obliged to own to being in my eighty-eighth year. He was indeed most kind and friendly."

If Montefiore's name had been, say, Blumberg (the Ashkenazi equivalent for "Mountain Flower") might there have been less aristocratic solicitude? Queen Victoria, as we shall see, couldn't stand Baron von Hirsch, who so craved social acceptability. But I believe that acceptance came to Montefiore, who made it into the Athenaeum, London's most exclusive club, in 1830, not because of his mellifluous name, but because of his nobility of character: he would not have dreamed of racing horses, as Hirsch did, except to get to people needing help.

There are more than 10,000 possible ways of opening our musical, and there are many more than 10,000 pages of source materials and bibliographies. Our hero and heroine both kept extensive diaries. So did their scholarly Orientalist secretary, Louis Loewe (Eliezer Halevi). Or, to pick just one random example, those of his personal physician Dr. Thomas Hodgkin (after whom Hodgkin's Disease is named), who published a *Narrative of a Journey to Morocco.* Yes, Sir Moses made the eight-day desert crossing by camel caravan, from Gibraltar to the Atlas Mountains, aged a mere 70, to intercede with the Berber monarch on behalf of the Jews of Morocco. Dr. Hodgkin died long before his robust patient, during one of their visits here, and is buried in Jaffa.

Ruthless cutting, it is clear, will have to be demanded from any librettist working on this story. Thousands of beautiful scenes will have to go; for besides all the documents, there is no end of legends. One of these has Montefiore responsible for Victoria's becoming England's queen. According to this account, Sir Moses goes to Brussels during the "Royalty Sweepstakes" of 1819, and convinces the Duke of Kent and his pregnant wife to hurry back to England so that their child will be born there, and thus be eligible for the throne. No wonder Vicky loved "Monte."

In one possible opening scene, I see the coachman cracking his whip, the horses snorting, and the famous carriage rolling down the aisle, right through the gala first-night audience, and up a ramp to the stage. There is a collective "Ahhhh!" from the audience as a huge rear-projection film moves us past a handsome long building with beautifully arched windows and a series of decorated pillars — and smack into a string quartet.

Yes, we are in Yemin Moshe, the first Jewish settlement outside the walls of the Old City of Jerusalem, named in honour of its founder. The building called *Mishkenot Sha'ananim* — Tranquil Dwellings — built as an almshouse in 1869, is now a creative retreat for artists. At this point, a chorus of tourists, intellectuals and recording studio technicians might sing:

From alms to affluence, from poverty to art,
What a chic conclusion for such a struggling start!

It all began during the Montefiores' fourth trip to the Holy Land via Constantinople, where they received permission from the Sultan to buy land near Jerusalem. The original plan was to build a hospital for the city's Jewish residents.

"You are my friend, my brother, the apple of my eye," said the Moslem Governor of Jerusalem to Sir Moses, according to the legend. "I would not sell it to any person, but to you I give it without money..."

A good throwaway line, although in fact, after a hard day's bargaining, Sir Moses paid the Governor £1,000 for the plot. The transaction was part of the complicated administration of the estate of Judah Touro, an extremely rich Sephardi Jew from New Orleans, who had died in 1854. He had appointed Sir Moses executor of part of his will providing $50,000 for poor Jews in Jerusalem.

According to the original "Rules and Regulations of Mishkenot," the inhabitants were supposed to say prayers for their benefactor every day, and the almshouse was originally called by his name. But such was the Montefiore magic that it was usually called "Moshe." Many Americans were disturbed that Touro was in the long run forgotten. But after all, he never set foot in the Holy Land, and is said to have maintained a pew in the Episcopalian Church in New Orleans, whereas Montefiore had endured all the difficulties of his assignment and, as he wrote ironically in his diary, "Blessed be the memory of Mr. Touro. Nevertheless, his legacy has cost me £5,000."

It cost the Jerusalem Foundation, under Mayor Teddy Kollek's tirelessly enthusiastic direction, and with the generous assistance of William Levitt, of Levitown fame, much more to turn the century-old, war-ravaged, dilapidated "Touro Poor Houses" into their beautifully restored present condition, with luxurious homes, artists' studios, a music centre and an elegant restaurant, an imposing edifice with a complex of super-modern audio-visual recording equipment and facilities for music-making.

Since its opening in 1973, a heady mixture of celebrities have been guests in Mishkenot's beautifully furnished apartments. They have included such cultural superstars as Simone de Beauvoir, Saul Bellow, Artur Rubinstein, Marc Chagall, Leonard Bernstein, Alexander Calder, Yehudi Menuhin, Heinrich Böll, Isaac Stern, Friedrich Dürenmatt, Herman Wouk, Leon Uris...

To this grand group we might, with a wink, apply the comments Montefiore recorded following his visit to Jerusalem in 1866. To check on how things were going, he inspected the Touro Almshouses, and "I satisfied myself that the inmates were fully deserving of the advantage they were enjoying... Scrupulous attention is paid to the preservation of order and cleanliness, and the inmates are cheerful and happy."

The name Mishkenot Sha'ananim is taken from Isaiah (32:18): "And my people shall dwell in a peaceable habitation, and in sure dwellings, and in quiet resting places." This was far from the case for nearly the entire first century of Montefiore's project. At the start, Jews were far from anxious to move from shelter of the city's walls out to the wilderness of Mishkenot, and indeed, two residents were murdered by Arabs in the early years. During the Arab riots of 1920, Ze'ev Jabotinsky, then commander of Jerusalem's Hagana, organized the self-defence of the residents of the city, and Yemin Moshe and Mishkenot; soon after, he was arrested by the British and expelled from Palestine. And during the War of Independence, the quarter was a key position of support for the Jewish forces.

A big coloured spotlight must shine on Yemin Moshe's famous windmill, a picturesque landmark just south of the King David Hotel. It was built by an expert brought out from London because Sir Moses thought that grinding flour on the spot would lower the price for the poor of Jerusalem. Unfortunately, it broke down after a few years and became obsolete after the establishment of steam-powered mills. In 1948, it served as an observation point for Jewish fighters during the siege of Jerusalem. At one point the top was blown off, allegedly by the British; their "battle" against Monte's windmill was called "the battle of Don Quixote."

Today it is a museum, with many Montefiore mementoes on display. The most impressive is the carriage Sir Moses and Lady Judith used in many of their travels. With four seats for passengers, plus two for the drivers in front and two more at the back, it is still in working condition and was, in fact, used by Yehoram Gaon in a film about our hero.

Now, suddenly, in addition to our spotlight, we hear a loud blast of music coming, mysteriously, from beneath the rock on which the windmill stands. So we might have Sir Moses singing off-stage, in a bewildered baritone:

My windmill is making more noise than it should!
How oddly symphonic! But really, quite good!
Coachman (also offstage):
I do believe, Sir Moses,
That this very classy sound
Is from a music-room with Steinways,
Constructed underground.
Sir Moses:
How clever of my descendants!
But, oh dear me,
My windmill's gone audio-visual, with colour TV.

Yes, the Jerusalem Music Centre, inaugurated by Pablo Casals shortly before his death, has its music-room built into the rock underneath Monte's windmill, with room for 60 musicians. Across the road from Mishkenot is a hall for lectures and exhibitions; and the returning spirit of Sir Moses today would find, instead of the poor of Jerusalem, the richly creative of the world.

Having seen how grandly Jerusalem has honoured the memory of Montefiore by sprucing up and elevating his early attempts at improving the city, we now descend to Tel Aviv, where his projects have been sadly downgraded.

Our rear-projection film moves us this time through the traffic-jammed passage under the Shalom Tower and out to where it spews into the southern end of little old Montefiore Street. Here there is a striking meeting-point between the ghastly infra-structure of modern transportation and the ghost of the romantic coach. One Saturday morning I watched three boys in a cart whipping a sickly horse through the underpass. The Montefiores, I am positive, insisted on kindness to their animals; and in any case, they would never have driven them on the Sabbath.

Our overture ends with a rousing fanfare as our hero steps out of his carriage, rising to his imposing height of 1.85 metres, and sings the opening song. In tune with the times, this might be a socio-ecological lyric entitled, "What have they done with my street?"

Sir Moses (in a gorgeous baritone):
I founded Alliance Assurance, in 1824,
Together with my brother-in-law...
Lady Judith (from the carriage):
My sister Hannah's husband,
Nathan Mayer Rothschild
Bystanders, peasants, and taxi drivers:
Yes, his Rothschild brother-in-law.

Lady Judith Montefiore.

The Pagoda house at King Albert Square,
Montefiore Street, Tel Aviv.

Sir Moses Montefiore as a captain
in George III's militia.

Portrait of Montefiore from the
Hovevei Zion album.

27

He's related to Rothschilds three times more.
But it's too complicated to make clear
In the terrible traffic din here.
Sir Moses:
Never did I dream that on my little street
Forty-four insurance firms would one day meet,
Not to mention these most remarkable banks, whose number
Makes even my horses whinny in wonder:
And in that wee house, looking far from hearty,
The Tel Aviv branch of the Labour Party...

Montefiore Street was once at the centre of Tel Aviv life. The newspaper *Ha'aretz* was born here, near Allenby Road, and the Tel Aviv municipal library. The Manufacturers' Association is still hanging on, further north. The lawyers are moving away.

The Pagoda house, at King Albert Square, is a good example of the "Middle-Eastern-eclectic-romantic" style of architecture that flowered here in the early Twenties. Most of the houses of this individualistic and imaginative, if not stylistically pedigreed, school, have been destroyed by the later builders of Tel Aviv.

Built for a rich American by the architect Alexander Levy, who also dreamed up the "boat house" on Allenby, the Pagoda was the first private home to have an elevator; its wire cage still sits wistfully at the decaying entrance.

Colonnades and archways, vaulted and curved balconies with wreaths and garlands of wrought-iron and plaster, decorated façades, domes and dreaming spires, mixtures of Italianate, Gothic, Grecian, Oriental, European, and possibly even some echoes of Montefiore's own East Cliff Lodge—all of these together made Little Tel Aviv like no place else on earth. The stark, blank rectangles of the Bank Hapoalim building, just past the Pagoda, present the staring functionalism of a style that has already been rejected elsewhere. Abroad, a movement is growing, in a world of energy crises, to rescue buildings of another age by reconstructing the interiors instead of wasting the energy needed to demolish the old and replace it with the questionable attractions of the new. What an excellent project it would be to give new life to the onion dome at Yavne Street or the presently doomed Pagoda.

Further down on Montefiore, in the old days, were the Polish Consulate, the Aero Club, and such educational institutions as the Montefiore Technical School and the School for Law and Economics, later absorbed by Tel Aviv University. And how neat is fate: its classes were held at the Shevah School on Rehov Hamasger, which was once no other than the site of "Mount Hope," Clorinda Minor's Messianic colonists from Philadelphia,

28

who, as we shall see, tended Montefiore's orchard just a bit north...

Here, too, at King Albert Square, is the remarkable small restaurant run by an Orthodox benefactor known as *Jinji* ("Redhead"). He has a faithful paying clientèle who enjoy home-cooked food, but also prepares meals for the poor, without payment, and performs other acts of charity, though he doesn't call them that, "because they give me satisfaction every single day." He would be very embarrassed by the suggestion that his modest establishment is perhaps the most appropriate within many miles to the character and benevolence of the man this street commemorates.

Sir Moses would have been pleased by the way Haifa has treated him. His street is short, but beautifully sited on the top of the Carmel range. On one side of it is the Rothschild Hospital: thus two of Jewry's greatest philanthropists and benefactors have been united.

Generations ago, Montefiores settled in relatively tolerant prosperous and intellectually stimulating Italy, and the family records date back to 1630. Sir Moses' grandfather settled in England around 1784, but Monte happened to be born in Italy while his parents were on a visit to Leghorn, the family's former home. His father was already sufficiently Anglicized to love plants and gardening.

Moses had 16 uncles and aunts on his father's side alone and the family tree is luxuriant: There are Mocattas, Guedallas, Sebags, Olivettis (yes, the typewriter people, who go back six generations before Sir Moses' birth). There was Uncle Joshua, who has his own entry in the *Britannica;* he was the first Jewish officer in the British army, tried to establish a slave-free colony in Africa, wrote on law and commerce, married a Catholic second wife and raised his eight children as Protestants.

His cousin Joseph Barrow, a pioneer in Australia, helped to organize the Bank of Australia. Later on came Claude Joseph Goldsmid (of the same family as the prototype for the eponymous hero of George Eliot's *Daniel Deronda,* who opposed the Balfour Declaration, was attacked by Ahad Ha'am, and "leaned toward Christianity." In our own time, we find the Anglican Bishop Hugh William Montefiore, who started a storm by claiming that Jesus Christ was a homosexual, and who fought against the Concorde airplane on the grounds that there is no human reason to travel a billion times more rapidly (and see so infinitely less) than his collateral kinsman had done in his carriage.

Young Moses Montefiore left school early, but was tutored in Hebrew by an uncle, one of several on his mother's side. Apprenticed to a firm of grocers, he was attracted to the stock market, where a number of his relatives were doing well. When he was 23, another uncle bought him a seat on the Stock Exchange, and he became one of the "twelve Jew brokers" permitted to operate there. In 1809, he was one of the first to enlist in George III's militia, serving two years and rising to the rank of captain. He continued studying on his own, and enjoyed writing down significant facts and quotations.

In 1812, at the age of 27, he married Judith, daughter of Levi Barent Cohen, a member of a wealthy Dutch clan with a distinguished Ashkenazi family tree to match the Montefiore Sephardi branches. Sir Moses was not only "unaffected by the current prejudice against marrying German girls"; he even provided, in his will, for a fund to buy blankets and coal for the Jewish poor of London, "to be divided equally between the Sephardi and Ashkenazi communities, *but with double portions to those recipients who had married into the other section* (my italics).

> Notes for song to be sung by a chorus of the integrated poor:
> Let it rain, let it snow,
> We've got that inter-ethnic glow!
> Oh, it's ever so classy
> If you're Ashkenazi,
> And you're not at all tardy
> About marrying Sephardi...

Judith Montefiore, nine months older than her husband and slightly deformed from a childhood accident, was an inspiration to him throughout their 50 years together. He was lucky, and he knew it, because a different Lady Judith might have spent all her energies in conspicuous competition with her Rothschild in-laws. On the contrary, she encouraged him in his decision to retire from business around 1825, while still in his early forties. In this, and in almost everything else, Montefiore took his wife's advice, which was, "thank God to be content."

She loved English literature, and wrote elegantly in her voluminous diaries. She knew French and German well, Italian and Arabic somewhat, and had a better than average knowledge of Hebrew and the Bible. Apparently a paragon, she even liked to cook,and was author (or co-author) of the first Anglo-Jewish cookbook.

Judith died in 1862, leaving Sir Moses 23 years to cherish her memory and he later remarked that whatever he had accomplished was due to his "never-to-be-forgotten wife, whose enthusiasm for everything that is noble, and whose religiousness, sustained me in my career." I do not know of another such tribute to a spouse by any other of our notables.

Judith, in turn, was capable of "tears of joy" at her good fortune in her marriage. She wrote in her diary: "I do not know any circumstance more pleasing to me than to perceive that my dear Monte is religiously inclined." Characteristically for both, she added, "It is that sort of religion that in my opinion is most essential — a follow-feeling and benevolence."

The *Encyclopaedia Judaica* alleges that "contrary to accepted opinion, he was apparently somewhat lax in religious observance in earlier life." But his records and behaviour indicate great piety and observation of the letter of Jewish law, and his later travels were with his own *shohet*. He was active in London's Spanish and Portuguese Synagogue and an opponent of the Reform movement.

He saw his own prosperity as God's blessing and worked for the total equality of British Jews. He was convinced that Jews were capable of productive industrial and agricultural work, especially in Palestine. He felt human justice to be a supreme value... As a director of the Provincial Bank of Ireland and of the South Eastern Railway Company, he transacted, with Nathan Rothschild, a huge loan that enabled the British Government to carry out the Slave Emancipation Act.

Anyone wishing to be healthy, wealthy, and wise at 101 should consider Sir Moses' daily routine, described in an 1820 entry in his diary: "With God's blessing — Rise, say prayers at 7. Attend the Stock Exchange, if in London, at 10. Dinner at 5. Read, write, and learn, if possible, Hebrew and French, 6 p.m. Read Bible and say prayers, 10 p.m. Monday and Thursday evenings, attend Synagogue. Tuesday and Thursday evenings, for visiting."

Having relied until now only on documents, it is perhaps permissible at this stage to trot out a legend. A fine folk tale about Reb Moses Montefiore, with some charming historical liberties, was written by S. An-Ski (Solomon Zainwil Rapaport, who wrote *The Dybbuk* and whose Tel Aviv street is to the south). It comes conveniently ready in more or less free verse:

Far, far away, across the sea
Lived Reb Moses Montefiore...
He was the chief adviser of the British queen
And she would not take a step without consulting him.

Then comes a description of his fantastic wealth, and his "golden coach," and how,

If ever a misfortune came upon the Jew,
A libel, an expulsion, or whatsoever,
He rose up like a lion to defend his brothers...

Now, An-Ski's Queen Victoria gave a huge banquet, which all the kings attended. Monte, of course, was also there. The kings began to boast about which one of them was the greatest. Tsar Nicholas I said he was by far the greatest but had only one problem, which was too many Jews. So Montefiore agreed to go to Russia to buy them. When he got to St. Petersburg, a problem arose. The ministers convinced the Tsar that it would not be good business to let the Jews go for one rouble apiece, because each one brought in an average of 40 roubles a year... So Montefiore "became very angry and went back home, but stopped for the Sabbath in Vilna."

Now comes a big scene with Count Potocki, the Governor of Vilna, who visits Montefiore and is received with great honour. Enter a rider from Petersburg. He hands Reb Moses a sealed letter. Reb Moses examines it, puts it down on table.

Potocki (amazed): Why don't you open it? A letter from the Tsar must be opened right away.

Reb Moses: I can't unseal the letter. It's forbidden on the Sabbath. (The Count wants to open it for him, but Reb Moses stops him.) You are a great lord, and you are my guest. I cannot allow you to open my letters for me."

So the Count orders one of his servants to open the letter, which he does, and falls down dead, because the letter is poisoned.

When Reb Moses Montefiore saw what had happened,
He ordered his coach, and he rode away on the Sabbath,
And when he got home he flung himself down before the Queen,
And told her everything that he had seen.
The Queen was furious,
And declared war on Nicholas,
And that was how the Crimean War began.

Recorded history is no less interesting than the legend. Montefiore's first mission to Moscow was in 1846, after urgent appeals were received from the Jews of Poland for the famous benefactor's help in relieving their oppression. Sir Moses impressed the Tsar so much by his defence of the Jews that Nicholas is said to have commented, *"S'ils vous ressemblaient —* If only they were like you. Victoria, also impressed, made him a baronet on his return (he had been the first Jew to receive a knighthood).

A quarter of a century later, and in spite of a cholera epidemic raging there, Sir Moses returned to Moscow for a gratifying, if ultimately fruitless, visit, with Tsar Alexander II, so tolerant and cultured that he even spoke English! On the way home, he met in Kovno with Rabbi Elhanan Spektor, Russia's foremost rabbinical authority, whose little street in Tel Aviv is very close to Montefiore's.

When the pogroms began in 1881, during the reign of Alexander II's reactionary son, Alexander III, Sir Moses wrote to his nephew, "If it be thought advisable, I am quite ready to go again to St. Petersburg." Quite a message for a man of 98.

Also impressive is the personal letter to Sir Moses from the Archbishop of Canterbury, sent at the height of English popular indignation about the events in Russia. He wrote:

"My dear Sir Moses, I cannot refrain from writing to you, knowing how your heart must be torn by the distressing news from Russia. It is as if the

32

enemy of mankind was let loose to destroy the souls of so many Christians, and the bodies of your people. I cannot but hope that a united cry of indignation from England will, with God's blessing, stop this wickedness."

The response to a relief fund organized by Montefiore was a generous practical echo of the archbishop's feelings, with support coming from such men as Cardinal Manning, Matthew Arnold and Charles Darwin.

In our musical, King Louis Philippe of France would appear in a scene with Sir Moses after the "Damascus Affair" of 1840. This was when the blood libel and torture of Jews in Damascus brought Montefiore to Constantinople, together with Judith and his old friend Adolphe Crémieux, whose street will be visited. The Sultan promised Montefiore to protect the Jews, and declared them innocent of all accusations of ritual murder.

On the way home, Sir Moses handed a copy of the Sultan's decree to King Louis Philippe, "a delicate condemnation," in the words of Montefiore's biographer, "of the unworthy attitude towards the Jews adopted by the King of civilized France."

Then there is a pitch-black London scene, at one o'clock in the morning of July 11, 1860. Far away in the hills of Lebanon, the Druse have massacred Christians. Sir Moses rides through the night to the office of *The Times* to deliver a letter describing the oppression of the Christians. With his letter is a cheque for £200, initiating the formation of the British Syrian Relief Committee; the Chief Rabbi of England joins.

Now we take the road to Morocco. The year is 1863; Sir Moses has been asked to help the Jews there. In Spain, he is received by Queen Isabella; apparently he does not hold grudges about her ancestors' expulsion of his, as others less involved have done.

On the other side of the coin of tolerance, in Tangiers, he receives a deputation of Arab sheikhs, who ask him to intercede for one of their tribe, imprisoned on suspicion of having murdered two Jews.

He does so, believing that the accused should have the benefit of the doubt. The sheikhs give him their solemn pledge to be answerable for the safety of any Jews travelling "by day" in their part of the country.

Tourists today, complaining about airport inconveniences, might find it salutary to consider the conditions under which Sir Moses crossed the Sahara desert. It took eight days and nights, with 18 camels, 60 horses, and "about 100 camp followers, including soldiers... We were subject to broiling sun by day and to cold and heavy winds by night. Nevertheless, writes this indomitable 79-year-old, "we have borne our fatigues well."

The Sultan, as a result of their meeting, commanded that Jewish rights should be respected. Montefiore saw the Queen of Spain again on his return journey, and the French Emperor too. Back in England, the Under-Secretary of State for Foreign Affairs said, "When it is recollected that there are 500,000 Jews in Morocco, some idea may be formed of the great

TEL AVIV

Motzkin

Ben Yehuda

Dizengoff

Be

Hayarkon

Gordon

Ben Yehuda

Frise

Hovevei Zion

Dize

Hayarkon

Pinsker

Trumpeldot

Bograshov

Herbert Samuel

Idelson

Tchernichovsky

George

Allenby

Hess

Hamelech

Ha

Aharonson

Sheinkin

Hayarkon

Allenby

Yosef
Nasi

Eliot

Hacarmel

Kalisher

Hakovshim

Montefiore

Elhanan

Gruzenberg

Nahalat Binyamin

Herbert Samuel

Pines

Roth

Lilienblum

Hamered

Shalom Shabazi

Chelouche

Hel

Chelouche

Pines

Derech Yaf

Hamered

Levinsky

Eilat

Ha aliya

Wolfson

Eilat

Ehm

Hamered

Mibachrach

0   400   800

m

Derech

Shlomo

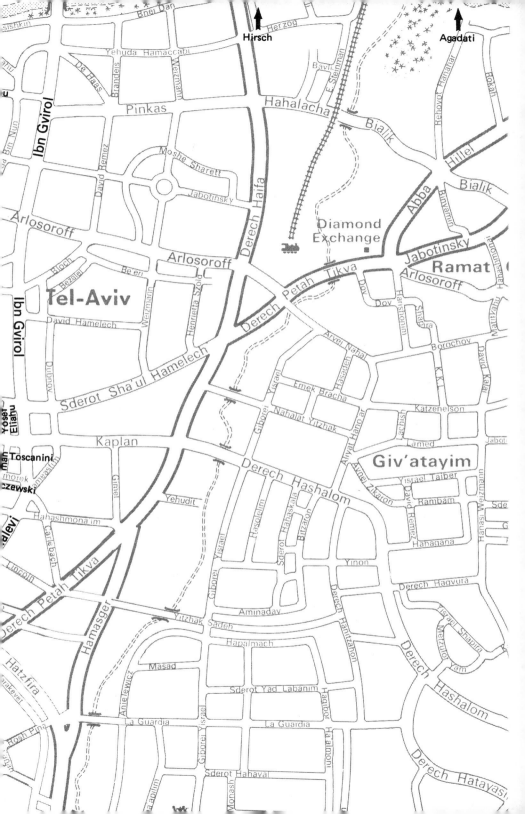

service rendered by Sir Moses Montefiore... I can bear testimony to the noble and generous spirit which actuates him, without reference to any sect or creed, which extends to the people of every nation who are suffering wrong and injustice."

Now we are in Bucharest, with a screaming mob calling for action against the Jews.

"Fire away, if you like!" cries Sir Moses, facing the crowd and refusing to run for cover. "I came here in the name of justice and humanity, to plead the cause of innocent sufferers. It is a holy cause; I trust in God, He will protect me."

This occurs in 1867, when Sir Moses is responding to appeals for help from the Jews of Rumania. He is supported by the English government and, at least formally, by the governments of Prussia, France, Austria and Italy. The Rumanian regent, Prince Charles, receives him with great cordiality (which monarch didn't?) and assures him that reports of violence against the Jews are highly exaggerated.

But perhaps we should have slotted the seven trips to Palestine into the other adventures? Here are some random notes on them:

1839: Pirates, brigands; the plague. On the last lap, for safety, Sir Moses asks Judith to stay behind in Malta. She replies, in the language of Ruth: "Whither thou goest, I will go..."

Great crowds, celebrations, everywhere — Safad, Tiberias, Nablus. Camping in tents on the Mount of Olives. In Jerusalem, Judith writes in her diary of being "lost in a sense of rapture and indescribable joy." In Jaffa, she is enchanted by the marvellous gardens, which "could compete with any English garden."

On the way back, in Cairo with Mohammed Ali, Montefiore has great plans for financing the settlement of Jews in Palestine. These are crushed soon afterwards when the Great Powers check the expansion of the Pasha of Egypt.

1855: A very busy visit. Plans made for carrying out the Touro bequest. Facilities of Sir Moses' medical mission transferred to Bikur Holim Hospital. Jerusalem rabbis persuaded to allow a girls' school to be established. Agricultural settlements set up near Safad and Tiberias.

Montefiore also bought land north of Jaffa and decided that this was to be the first Jewish venture in diversified agriculture. It was 52,120 square metres, and on it an orchard of precisely 1,406 fruit trees was planted.

Like many rich men and practically no poor men, he was exact and careful in his accounts and called for a detailed census of his trees. So we know that they included 721 orange trees, 129 sweet lemons, 60 bitter lemons, 24 etrogs, 279 pomegranates, 42 apples, 29 plums, and so on, up to a number of 1,406. Montefiore asked the Rabbi of Jaffa, Yehuda Halevi of Raguse, and Aharon Chelouche (whom we shall meet) to supervise the orchard.

Among those who, for a time, tended the fruit trees were members of an American messianic Protestant sect from Philadelphia, living nearby in the "Mount Hope" commune. Sir Moses helped their leader, a brave Philadelphia woman named Clorinda Minor who wished to assist the Jews to redeem their land through agriculture, and thus hasten the coming of the Messiah. But the American failed. The orchard always operated at a loss; and after being run for a time by the Mikve Israel Agricultural School, it was sold in 1922 to an American land-purchase company. The trees were uprooted and small housing plots were allotted to settlers, mostly Orthodox Jews from Jaffa.

A plaintive air, now, for Lady Judith, echoing the bittersweet melody of Sir Moses in our Act I opener:

Where are our dear little lemons and pears?
Where have the pomegranates gone?
Why does that sign say "Speedometer Repair?"
What is going on?

Lady Judith is standing right on her own street, Sderot Yehudit, a boulevard that has seen better days. It is the main street of the Montefiore Quarter, which is where the orchard used to be and was for many years a rather distant northern suburb of Little Tel Aviv. It has long been completely absorbed by the sprawling city, and what is left are some low-lying rows of bleak little workshops and garages to the east of the Petah Tikva Road, one of our ugliest multilane thoroughfares.

Poor Lady Judith, who was so impressed by the gardens of Jaffa so long ago, and who so hoped to make things better here, continues her sad little song:

Alas, no more trees;
But I see the tiny office of the Association for Traffic Accident
    Casualties;
Alas, no more greenery;
But I see the little office of the Association for Productivity.
And I also see the Chinese Restaurant of Mr. Wong.
Oh, Monte, what is progress? What is right and wrong?

The most recent news on Sir Moses and Lady Judith is about bringing their remains to Israel for re-interment. This has long been considered fitting; but for years the problem — would you believe it? — was lack of money.

An economic aria for Sir Moses is essential for our musical. Towards the end of his life he wrote:

"We do not want a set of indolent people, who, by poring over books, teaching the word of God, think they are performing their duties in life and wait for our support! The Jews in Jerusalem, in every part of the Holy Land, I tell you, do work; and are more industrious than many even in Europe..."

What a fine finale.

3
Everybody Knows Dizengoff

If there is one street name likely to inspire comfortable feelings of certainty as to who is being immortalized, it is certainly Dizengoff. Everyone who knows anything at all about Israel knows that Meir Dizengoff was one of Tel Aviv's founders and the city's first mayor, that he used to lead the Purim parade riding on a white horse, and that as mayor he was entitled to kiss the pretty girl selected as Queen Esther for the Purim celebrations in the good old days.

Everybody also knows his street. Starting at Ibn Gabirol, it has a brief cultural phase as it skirts the Mann Auditorium and the Rubinstein Art Pavilion. Then Dizengoff descends into Dizengoff Centre, crowded, noisy, consumer-oriented. The street has the fanciest stores, the smartest restaurants and cafés, the boutiques, the pretty girls, who are somehow always associated with the name Dizengoff. Any film about Israel must include shots of Dizengoff, the street where artists, writers, film stars, housewives and tourists congregate to stroll, shop, and sit at sidewalk cafés. Dizengoff Street is a Tel Aviv exclusive, because Mayor Meir Dizengoff was so exclusively associated with his city.

Not everybody may know, yet, that Dizengoff Street now goes under, instead of through, Dizengoff Circle. The latter has been lifted, fountain and all, atop a concrete bubble. This elevation in site, if not in charm, was made to accomodate the endless flow of traffic in Dizengoff Street, a flow which would have terrified that white horse. Saturdays, in a gesture toward civilized living, Dizengoff is closed to traffic north of the circle, and pedestrians and baby carriages take over.

People take it for granted that the circle, too, is named after the dynamic mayor. But in fact it honours his wife, and the official name on the little signs around its periphery is Kikar Tsina (pronounced Tseena, in the Russian style). Alas, her circle is rarely called by its right name, which is a pity, since so few streets are named after women.

Like his street, Dizengoff moved with the times; his action-filled life has a great deal more to it than the Purim parade. Born in a village in Bessarabia in 1861, the son of a farm manager, he became in his later years a man of affairs, dealing with municipal budgets, administrative problems and visiting dignitaries. But in his youth, Dizengoff was romantic and revolutionary. In his pre-Zionist days, he was imprisoned for anti-Tsarist socialist activities; and when he first went to Palestine in 1892, he quickly became an exceptionally close friend of the Arabs.

Dizengoff's ties with the Arabs were so strong that he was soon being urged by his Arab friends to marry one of their girls. This was long before Tel Aviv was a gleam in anybody's eye; and the most vigorous effort to promote such a match was made in Tantura, an ancient site on the beach between Caesarea and Haifa. Dizengoff had been sent there from Russia to establish a glass factory on behalf of Baron Edmond de Rothschild.

One day, riding back to Tantura from a business trip to Jaffa, Dizengoff and a companion were caught in a storm. Dizengoff did not ride a horse only in the Purim parade; he used the animal as a method of locomotion for purposes of commerce, as his successors now use executive jets.

Because of the storm, the travellers found shelter in the tents of some Beduin. Beduin hospitality included protection from the elements; food; discussions about religion, politics, the Sultan, Queen Victoria, and Rothschild; and a request that Dizengoff take the 15-year-old son of the sheikh into his household and educate him. Dizengoff did so, and later arranged a job for the boy. It is no wonder that, many social visits later, it was suggested that Dizengoff should marry an Arab girl. There was even a specific candidate, and the tragic story of what happened between her and Dizengoff could provide the theme for a romantic novel.

Fatima was the only surviving daughter of another sheikh. She was 17 years old, and very beautiful, and she was suffering from some mysterious disease. The Arabs believed that Dizengoff was a physician because they had seen so many chemicals in his laboratory. The sheikh pleaded with him to save Fatima. Dizengoff tried to explain that he was an engineer, not a doctor, and that his chemicals were used to test glass, not to treat humans. The Arabs were not convinced. Apart from seeing the laboratory, they knew that Dizengoff had indeed cured a watchman of malaria — he had administered the usual drugs given at the time for that disease.

So, reluctantly, he agreed to treat Fatima, and the treatment was successful. Everybody was delighted. The local sheikhs all agreed that the miracle worker should marry the girl he had saved. Her father was even prepared to waive the customary dowry money paid by the bridegroom.

But Dizengoff could not take up the offer, because he had to go to Alexandria to meet and marry the girl he had left behind in Russia until the factory was established. When he returned to Tantura, the heartbroken father came to him, weeping. Dizengoff has described the poor man's anguish as he cried: "God has taken my daughter from me! He sent you abroad, and Fatima fell ill again. I could not bring a strange physician to her, and so she rendered up her spirit to God. Now it is better that I should die than live life alone, without my Fatima."

Dizengoff's bride, Tsina Haya, known as Nyunya, was the daughter of Rabbi Shlomo Brenner of Zitomir, and Meir had first met her when he was a dashing officer of 21, in the Tsar's army, editing the regimental bulletin, and she was ten. After her death in 1930, he recalled her as she was in her teens:

"Forty-eight years have passed since those days, and yet the picture of that girl still shines brightly before my eyes — radiantly alive, tall, slim as a gazelle, full of charm, full of love and spiritual closeness to all human beings."

Tsina received a modern education and, was permitted to go on trips and parties with young people in socialist youth circles (prophetic word), where long arguments and Russian songs set the tone. When the arguments got too long, even for a Russian girl, Tsina-Haya-Nyunya used to say, "Oh, stop arguing and let's dance."

She was just 13 when Meir, having finished his army service, was imprisoned for anti-Tsarist and socialist agitation. She visited him regularly during his eight-month prison term. In jail, after much soul-searching, he turned from socialism to Zionism; and after his release, he met two of the most important ideologists of the Zionist movement — Pinsker and Lilienblum. The impact of both men was lasting — on Dizengoff, and on our city streets.

Dizengoff first thought of agriculture as a career, because it would be useful in Palestine. But chemical engineering was suggested by representatives of Baron Rothschild, and he went to Paris to study. When he had obtained his degree, they told him he was to set up the glass factory in Tantura.

Tsina set up housekeeping in the wilds of Tantura, and learned to ride horseback. Unfortunately, after two years the glass project was found to be a failure. The sand did not seem right, although the Romans had produced glass successfully on this same Mediterranean shore. Apart from the problem of the sand, Dizengoff's concern for his workers and his pro-labour outlook, in which Tsina supported him, irritated the Baron's representatives. He had also joined Ahad Ha'am's élite secret society, *Bnei Moshe*, whose principles of individual spiritual self-improvement ran directly counter to theirs.

In 1895, the Dizengoffs returned to Russia and Meir got a job as manager of a Belgian-owned glass factory in Odessa. His nights were spent in discussions with a circle of Zionist thinkers destined to be streets — Ahad Ha'am, Dubnow, Ben-Ami, Druyanov, Bialik. He attended the Fifth and Sixth Zionist Congresses in Basle and was a vocal member of the Russian anti-Uganda, anti-Herzl-and-Nordau camp. So was Tsina, who accompanied him: during the outburst against Herzl on the Uganda affair, she shouted tearfully in French, that he was guilty of a terrible compromise.

In 1904, Dizengoff established the *Ge'ula* company for the purchase of land in Palestine, and in 1905 the couple returned to Jaffa, where they found a severe housing shortage and rising prices. Jaffa's Jewish population was about 7,000; the new Jewish suburbs of Neve Zedek and Neve Shalom were congested.

Dizengoff was among the founders of *Ahuzat Bayit,* the home-building society set up in 1906. Its members, nearly all of them living in crowded Arab Jaffa, wanted to build a modern "garden city," along European lines, north of the port town.

A famous photograph, taken on April 11, 1909, the day on which the annals of Tel Aviv officially begin, shows a group of carefully-dressed men in suits and jackets, women in long frocks, and children in their best attire, looking strikingly surrealistic against a background of sand dunes. A natty-looking figure, wearing what appear to be white flannel trousers, a dark blazer and a white hat, stands apart from the crowd and seems to be addressing them. This was the historic moment when building plots were distributed by lot to the 60 settlers — who had paid their deposits to the Ahuzat Bayit Society. They were middle-class merchants, teachers and professionals. There was not one open shirt in the crowd.

I long assumed that the natty figure was Dizengoff, in charge of this memorable occasion. But I was wrong. The man with all the trappings of leadership was merely a Jew from Jaffa named Feingold, whose parents had converted to Christianity, and who had come to mock the group of demented dreamers and their mad project.

"What are you crazy people trying to do here? There's no water, nothing but sand, sand, sand! You are all mad!" Feingold shouted at the group.

Mad or not, they built 60 little one-storey houses that year, and paved the main streets. The residents were immeasurably proud of the cleanliness, the little gardens, the pure fresh air.

The streets were, after a few years, named Herzl, Ahad Ha'am, Judah Halevi, Lilienblum and Rothschild — though of course they did not then extend as far out as they do today.

The rule that only those who have been dead for at least two years may become streets was introduced by the Tel Aviv Municipality in 1925, and two of the greats whom the Ahuzat Bayit streets honoured were still alive at that time. Ahad Ha'am could walk his own street, pleasantly aware of his immortality, until 1927. The robust Baron Edmond de Rothschild, whose street became a tree-shaded boulevard, died in 1934, at the age of 89.

After many voluble discussions through the winter of 1909-10, the Ahuzat Bayit committee came to its decisions about the names of the streets after the new community's first tree-planting celebration on Tu Bi'shvat (Arbor Day) in 1910. It was about this time that the name Tel Aviv was chosen for the project, beating such catchy candidates as Aviva,

Ivriya and Yefefiya.

Dizengoff was elected chairman of the Ahuzat Bayit Society, and from then on, in effect, remained head of the community that became Tel Aviv until his death in 1937.

The stately home the Dizengoffs built for themselves on Rothschild Boulevard was one of Little Tel Aviv's most beautiful houses in an era when, surprising as it sounds today, the young city was graced by a large number of mansions: they have either gone to seed, or have been taken over by banks. After Tsina's death, Dizengoff bequeathed the house to the municipality to serve as Tel Aviv's museum, and it was in that building that Israel's Declaration of Independence was signed.

The years preceding World War I were, for those who had means, idyllic. Dizengoff wore a fez and was on good terms with the Turks who ran Palestine as part of the Ottoman Empire. There had been personal tragedy — the couple's only child, Shulamit, died in infancy. Tsina loved children, and she taught French at the girls' school in Jaffa. The neighbourhood children came to her for stories and songs. She also played the piano for them: Tel Aviv's strong bourgeois tradition was in the process of being formed.

Besides his civic activity, Dizengoff went into business. He established the commercial firm of M. Dizengoff & Co., still flourishing as a shipping agency connected with Zim. With his friend Yosef Eliahu Chelouche, another founder of Tel Aviv, he was granted the right to build the Gaza-Latroun highway; by employing young Jews, the two were able to protect them from conscription in the Turkish army. He organized other commercial firms to fight land speculation, which flourished even at that time.

When World War I broke out, the idyll ended. Turkey entered the war on the side of the Germans; the British invaded Palestine. As the British advanced, the Turks banished the entire population of Jaffa-Tel Aviv, and the beautiful new garden city became a ghost town.

Dizengoff rose to the challenge, took responsibility for "his" citizens, and worked ceaselessly — in Haifa, Damascus, Petah Tikva and Tiberias — to help the dispersed Tel Avivians. There were cases of death from starvation. There was no medical care; some people lived in the open. Though he himself had Turkish citizenship and could have remained in Tel Aviv, it did not occur to him to do so.

As chairman of the Committee of Tel Aviv, Dizengoff, together with Yosef Eliahu Chelouche, dealt with the Turkish authorities, scrounged funds, kept up morale. Here is his description of his last walk in the already deserted city, in 1917, before going into banishment with his people:

"The streets were silent. Nobody walked in them. No mothers pushed their carriages. No laughter of playing children... Only the day before, the

43

Tsina Haya, Dizengoff's
bride-to-be.

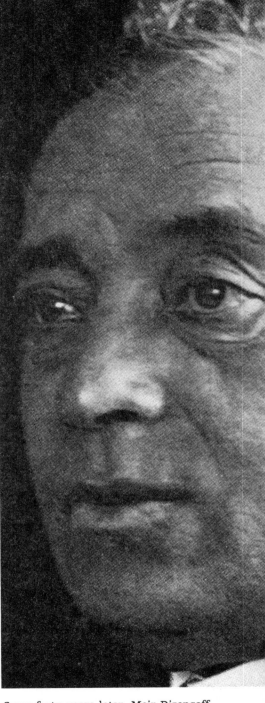

Dizengoff as a soldier in the
Tzar's army.

Some forty years later, Meir Dizengoff
as first mayor of Tel Aviv.

streets were bustling with people... Now, where were we? How did the city become so solitary? Could it be that I was in Pompeii? For everything is in its place — here is the Committee building, the table is covered with its green cloth. Paper and pencils are ready, just as if the Committee members would soon enter for a meeting. Yet what a dreadful silence all around!''

When the Turks retreated, in the autumn of 1918, Dizengoff returned to Tel Aviv with the rest of the exiles. Tsina "wept tears of joy" as Tel Avivians thronged to the Dizengoff's house to greet them. He was re-elected head of the Tel Aviv Committee. On November 22, 1918, he received the victorious British general, and presided at the ceremony at which Allenby Road was named for the liberator of Palestine. It was then a sandy stretch frequented by camels, with very few houses. Allenby is said to have remarked, in injured tones, when he saw it, *"This is* what they are going to name after me?''

Dizengoff presided over years of such ceremonies with charm and poise. His long public life is documented in great detail: there are photographs of him with Albert Einstein when the great scientist received an honorary citizenship of Tel Aviv in 1923; with Baron Edmond de Rothschild when the Baron was similarly honoured in 1924; and with Lord Balfour, when the British statesman became an honorary Tel Avivian, in 1925.

Balfour's street was named on that occasion. The ceremony was followed by a gymnastics display at the Herzliya High School. It was very efficiently organized by Dizengoff, and it impressed Balfour greatly. Weizmann, who was present, describes how his party commented "with one voice" (hard though this is to accept literally) that "these boys might have come from Harrow" and that "Mr. Dizengoff might easily be the mayor of Liverpool or of Manchester!'' Weizmann hastens to add that both remarks were meant, and taken, "as the highest compliments.''

In 1923, Dizengoff went to America for a familiar purpose: to raise a loan of $25,000 for his city's development. For three years, starting in 1925, he resigned his office each year for a familiar reason: budgetary disagreements with the city council. By 1928 he was again mayor. He enjoyed the company of artists, and beat Teddy Kollek by several decades to a meeting with Marc Chagall in Paris, on behalf of the Tel Aviv Museum, to which he devoted his last years.

For his 70th birthday, the city decided to establish a municipal garden in his name, *Gan Meir,* off King George Street, on property donated by his friend Chelouche; we shall visit it in another chapter, and reconstruct a once famous murder which took place there. For the city's own 25th birthday, in 1934, in a justifiable bending of the rule about naming streets for the dead, an unpaved strip going bravely north, with practically no houses along it, was named for him.

45

Here we come, for a moment, to the shady side of Dizengoff — the man, not the street; and hesitantly, I mention a rumour that circulated in Tel Aviv in the old days. Dizengoff was said to have an Arab mistress by whom he had an illegitimate son; he saw to it that the boy was given a job at a municipal installation.

Late in life, Dizengoff continued to ride horseback along the beach every morning, and even organized a group of gentlemen — and ladies — to join him in an invigorating daily canter. He was a member of the Zionist Executive and played a role in the World Zionist Organization.

Into this constructive and pleasant existence crashed the tragedy of the Arab riots of 1936. It has been suggested that they contributed to Dizengoff's death in September, for to him they constituted a double tragedy. First, the British authorities handled the Arab rioters with unwarranted leniency, and Dizengoff had always admired the qualities of fairness and justice in the British. Second, because, as has frequently been said, Dizengoff was one of the best friends the Arabs ever had. Unlike other Zionist leaders, he was never condescending to them; he admired Arab culture, and aspired towards peace between Arab and Jew.

The Mandatory authority continued to take no action, and Dizengoff's last act was to send a sharp memorandum of protest in the style of *J'Accuse* denouncing British indifference in the face of murder.

When Dizengoff died, Arthur Ruppin wrote in his diary:

"Four years ago... Dizengoff told me that he would like to live until Tel Aviv had 100,000 inhabitants. Today it has 150,000. Who among us, when he dies, finds his wishes surpassed by 50 per cent? He was a good man; upright, not a careerist, easily aroused to enthusiasms, always searching for a way of improving his Tel Aviv."

Having loitered so educationally along Dizengoff and around Tsina, it would be a shame not to meet, at least briefly, the other street personalities converging at the Circle. First, at about seven o'clock, if we think of the Circle as a watch-face numbered for the hours, is Pinsker Street. And Pinsker, we may remember, was one of the Zionist thinkers whom Dizengoff met in Odessa, and who impressed him so much in his post-socialist, post-prison youth.

Dr. Leon (or Judah Leib) Pinsker was born in Tomaszow, Russia, in 1821 and died in Odessa in 1891. Like many other Zionist personalities who became streets, he was both a physician and a writer. His epoch-making pamphlet *Auto-Emancipation* appeared in 1881-82. In it, Pinsker analysed the psychological and social roots of anti-Semitism and called for the establishment of a Jewish national centre. It led to the formation of *Hibbat Zion,* whose members were called *Hovevei Zion.* (Hovevei Zion, the street, is off to our left.)

Of *Auto-Emancipation,* Herzl is said to have remarked that, had he known of the brochure before starting his *Judenstaat*, he would never have written his own book. "The Jewish people have no fatherland," Pinsker wrote, "though they claim many motherlands. They have no government... They are to be found everywhere, but are nowhere at home."

Pinsker Street today features a shop or two with Puma T-shirts and Adidas shoes, the Tel Aviv Cinema, and rows of the traditional Tel Aviv three-storey blocks of flats. There is also a do-it-yourself shop, a form of auto-emancipation. But what really comes to mind, auto-emancipation-wise, is that Pinsker Street's recent tunnel, like the others that go under the Circle, is an attempt to emancipate us from the automobile.

On the way to Dizengoff, Pinsker runs into Golda's old friend Beilinson, which curves along the Circle, and which in turn runs into Ben-Ami Street, at about ten o'clock.

Mordechai Ben-Ami, as we have said, was another of the influences on Dizengoff in the Odessa circle, immortalized here as elements surrounding Dizengoff Circle; but some of the landmarks on this short street, such as a popular bridge club, are far from the stark realities of the man's life.

He was born Mordechai Rabinowicz in Russia in 1854, and died in Tel Aviv in 1932. The son of a very poor Hassid, he was orphaned at the age of four, brought up in orphanages, and shunted from relative to relative. With great difficulty he put himself through school, teaching others while still in high school, and helping his brother's family. Always a believer in religion, he criticized the Jewish intelligentsia who renounced Jewish values. He became a friend of Ahad Ha'am and Herzl, who he revered. Ben-Ami (the Hebrew name he chose means "son of my people") left Russia in 1905, lived in Switzerland for 18 years, and came to Palestine in 1923.

On the other side of the Circle, opposite Ben-Ami, at about three o'clock, is the father of Esperanto, the Polish Ludwig Lazar Zamenhof (1859-1917). The sign on his street very sweetly gives us a taste of Esperanto, explaining that he was the *Kreinto de la Internacia Lingvo*. It adds in Hebrew that he was a member of *Hovevei Zion* "in his youth," implying that he left the cause later on. Other sources report that in a pamphlet, he presented Judaism as the "philosophy of humanism."

Zamenhof, was, by profession, an eye doctor, his interest in philology came from his father, a language teacher. He finished drafting the fundamentals of his new language — which contains only 900 root words and 16 rules of grammar — in 1887, three years before Eliezer Ben Yehuda arrived in Jerusalem to start his long struggle for the revival of Hebrew.

Esperanto had its day earlier in this century, when its supporters believed that an international language would help bring about understanding and peace among nations. Israel's Esperanto Association is alive and well. Its members, who enjoy meeting their colleagues abroad, insist that it is a tremendous help in communication between those who otherwise speak non-universal tongues, such as Japanese, or Swedish — or Hebrew.

Zamenhof's street has a Persian restaurant whose menu features, among other specialities, *Gondi Nochochi,* which is translated as "houmus and meat," all of which would be simpler in Esperanto.

At exactly one o'clock, east of Dizengoff and taking traffic north from under the Circle, is Reines Street.

"Reines Girls," in Dizengoff Street parlance, are girls you wouldn't want to be seen with on Dizengoff proper, however willing you might be to entertain them on this less luminous street. Reines the man could not have been further from this kind of secular whimsy. The founder of the Mizrachi movement, he was a religious leader largely responsible for bringing the organization of Orthodox Jewry into the Zionist camp.

Isaac Jacob Reines, who was born in Vilna in 1839 and died in 1915 was a rabbi who, in the words of his biographer, "knew no language but Hebrew and had no general education," but was "a Talmudic sage, a genius, a preacher of the rarest type." It was Reines who steered a clear path within the Orthodox camp, which was split by factionalism, and stood apart from the early Zionist Congresses on the thorny question of the relation between political and national Zionism on the one hand, and Judaism as a religion on the other.

Reines was also an educational innovator. He founded yeshivot into which he introduced secular studies, in the face of extreme Orthodox opposition. Fate has dealt harshly with his views. There is not only a French hairdresser on Reines Street but a Chinese restaurant; and his street is open to traffic on the Sabbath, whereas secular Dizengoff enjoys at least part of one day of careless relaxation.

4
Mary Ann and Gracia

Mrs. John Walter Cross was 61 years old, ill and depressed. She had married just a few months earlier, for the first time. This, one might think, would have cheered her up. But no; despite her marriage, Mrs. Cross was still mourning her late lover, George Lewes. He had died two years earlier, after 23 exceptionally happy years of life together in what was than called "sin." After Mr. Lewes' death, an old friend, Mr. Cross, urged her to let him take care of her, and so she had agreed to marry him.

Sitting at her desk in their new London home, she faced the manuscript of George's unfinished final work, which she was preparing for publication. *The Problems of Life and Mind,* he had called it, rather sweepingly. It dealt with biological, psychological and religious matters, as well as all those philosophical and ethical issues that had absorbed the two of them. She and George, a philosopher and critic, were both profoundly serious about life and supremely moral in outlook. They considered themselves married in every way, although no clergyman had blessed their union. There was a non-philosophical reason for their failure to marry: the trouble was, as so often happens, that his wife objected.

Mrs. Cross's thoughts drifted away from George's manuscript and turned back to the last of her literary children. (Other than their books, she and George had had no children together, though she had been like a mother to his wife's sons).

The name of this final child of hers was Daniel.

"But I think I should not have picked that English officer as the model for my Daniel," she now said to herself. "That one — Albert Edward Williamson Goldsmid — isn't showing the slightest sign of going to Palestine. Which was the whole point of my novel. Well," she sighed, "one ought not to expect life to imitate art, just because one causes art to imitate life.

"Ah, why did I not, instead, take that interesting young man of the 16th century, Joseph Something? Better yet, his Aunt Gracia...Gracia Nasi. And Nasi means 'prince,' as I know from my Hebrew studies..."

I have taken the liberty of inventing this scene and soliloquy because in Tel Aviv, Rehov George Eliot, tucked away in an elderly neighbourhood, runs right to Rehov Yosef Nasi. In fact, when you turn in from Lord Melchett to George Eliot you *must* go to Yosef Nasi. There is no alternative.

At this inevitable street meeting, it soon becomes clear that this is no simple matter of George and Yossi. There are women behind these streets, and several changes of names.

Our characters, in brief, are:

Mrs. J.W. Cross, 1819-1880. Mary Ann (or Marian) Evans, daughter of a strict Church of England father. While she considered herself married to George Lewes, died as Mrs. Cross, the name she wrote under and made famous was George Eliot. Her street is here by virtue of her "Zionist" novel, *Daniel Deronda*.

Albert Edward Williamson Goldsmid, 1846-1904. English soldier of a distinguished assimilated Sephardi family. Thought to have been George Eliot's model for Daniel Deronda.

Yosef (Joseph) Nasi, c. 1524-1579. Portuguese Marrano statesman, known originally by the Christian name Joao Micas; also known by his title Duke of Naxos. In 1561, he obtained from the Sultan a grant to rebuild Tiberias — to establish industries, build homes, attract and settle Jews from Europe, and set up a Galilee mini-state — "the only practical attempt to establish some sort of Jewish political centre in Palestine between the fourth and 19th centuries."

Gracia Nasi, c. 1510-1569, Marrano stateswoman (the *Encyclopaedia Judaica's* description — and how many of these have we?), originally known by the Christian name Beatrice de Luna. Joseph's aunt; also his mother-in-law — he married her only child, Reyna.

Gracia has been called "perhaps the outstanding Jewish woman of the entire period between the fall of the Jewish state and the present." According to Cecil Roth, the historian of the Marranos, "she was perhaps the most noteworthy Jewish woman in all history, and the possibility that she arrived in Palestine must not be ruled out. What her nephew did during her lifetime was almost entirely due to her tutelage. She was his model, his constant inspiration, and it was only after her death that his own personality developed to the full..."

Considering all these shifts in names, it is in a way fitting, though unfortunate, that George Eliot's street sign on the wall of the building on the corner of Melchett has been painted over. I assume that many Israelis know that behind that obliterated masculine name there is a remarkable woman. As for Dona Gracia, while I don't for a moment begrudge her nephew his street, it seems too bad that the power behind him is commemorated only in a Tiberias street and café, without a mention of her in any of the three main cities.

I imagine that the group that knows about George Eliot rarely coincides with the group that knows about the Nasis. Yet the whimsical finger of fate neatly links our two little streets, for on Yosef Nasi is a publishing firm called Ahiassaf (which was once directed by Ahad Ha'am), and that is the very name of the Warsaw firm that published a Hebrew edition of *Daniel Deronda* long ago. The streets join so fortuitously, there between Sheinkin and Balfour, that I cannot help imagining what might have happened if...

...If only portions of a hitherto lost George Eliot manuscript were to turn up, suitable for a television series! We would have a family business that not only deals in spices and banking, with a veritable pre-Rothschild network of European agents, but also runs an escape underground for Portuguese Marranos. The head of the family would be the marvellous Dona Gracia, who organizes an economic boycott of the Italian city of Ancona in reprisal for atrocities against Marranos there, only to be politically bested by Joshua Soncino, Rabbi of Constantinople. Rabbi Joshua, though he fought a bitter political battle against Dona Gracia, nevertheless called her "the chaplet of grace of the Hosts of Israel..."

What costumes! What intrigues! The court at Constantinople, the Nasi's palace at Belvedere. Decadent Turks and upright Jews, piracy and scholarship. George Eliot would have been delighted with the research; she wrote reams of it in Florence, for *Romola,* her novel about Savonarola. What a battlefield of good and evil, virtue and sin in true George Eliot tradition!

It is only in Tel Aviv that Rehov George Eliot leads so unerringly to Rehov Yosef Nasi. In Jerusalem, her little street has quite different connections, but they too can be instructive.

Geoge Eliot Street in Jerusalem is a narrow defile, bounded at one end by the walls of the American Consulate: behind these walls is a beautiful old building set in beautiful grounds. On the other side are the high and mysterious walls of a convent belonging to the Soeurs du Rosarie. The street begins in one of Jerusalem's main arteries, Rehov Gershon Agron, named after the founder and first editor of *The Palestine Post,* now *The Jerusalem Post,* Israel's English daily newspaper. Agron later became mayor of Jerusalem, so he is a fit companion to the dreamer of Zion restored.

If Agron's street is a traffic artery, George Eliot's is a capillary. Beyond the walls of the consulate and the convent, there is a section cut from rocks, then come the equally formidable walls of the Solomon and Mary Litt Building, the headquarters of the Jewish Welfare Board (Israel).

At the other end, George Eliot leads, appropriately, to Moshe Hess, whose *Rome and Jerusalem,* published in 1862, is an early classic of Zionist literature. George Eliot's George Lewes is reported to have known Hess, a socialist and social philosopher. Hess and George Eliot appear together (with Disraeli) in an entry in Herzl's diary for May 1897, as "representative exponents of the Zionist idea."

Jerusalem, too, has a Yosef Nasi Street, but it is nowhere near George Eliot's. In the Mekor Baruch quarter, in a district whose streets are named after Maccabean heroes, Yosef Nasi is a narrow one-way road, just one block long, hardly worthy of its name. But it does connect such famous people as Bar Giora and Rashi. The people living in the houses lining it are mostly of Ashkenazi origin, which is rather a pity, as Yosef Nasi is such a Sephardi hero.

The city of Tiberias, where Dona Gracia may or may not have spent her last years, has both a short Don Yosef Street and a short but picturesque Dona Gracia Street, near the old citadel.

George Eliot Street in Haifa is one of the shortest in the city, which has many short streets — there are altogether only six buildings in it. At one end it goes into Elhanan Street, at the other end it comes to a stop. This may explain why, although it is on the central Carmel, only a few yards away from the busiest shopping area in the region, George Eliot gives an impression of quiet, serenity, greenery, a gentle oasis in a humming modern world. Very close to her Haifa street is Wedgwood Avenue, honouring another English gentile and supporter of Zionism.

George Eliot met Lewes when she was 32. He was part of a circle of acquaintances that included Thomas Carlyle and Herbert Spencer. Hebrew was one of several languages she had chosen to learn, and her closest friends included a scholar of Talmud. Lord Morley said she was "Bishop-like," and though "outwardly serene, cried buckets." She was tormented by headaches, poor health, nervous troubles, and doubts about religion and about her work. Yet three years after he met her, Lewes left his wife to live with her.

Encouraged by Lewes ("ugly, lively, genial, amusing, warm-hearted, a brilliant editor and an excellent journalist"), she began to write fiction at 37. Needing a masculine pen-name, she borrowed the George from him, and took Eliot because "it was a good, mouth-filling, easily pronounced name."

It is George Eliot's fate often to be confused with Georges Sand, the pen-name of another 19th-century woman novelist, Aurore Dupin. But where Aurore, a rebel by temperament, had eccentric manners and several glamorous lovers, Mary Ann always dressed as a Victorian matron: "...dreamy and immobile, her massive features, somewhat grim...were incongruously bordered by a hat...," wrote Sir Edmund Gosse.

Earnestly ethical, she stressed the "profoundly serious nature of my relation to Mr. Lewes... Light and easily broken ties are what I neither desire theoretically nor could live for practically." She believed not in liberation but in virtue.

Daniel Deronda, a call for a return to Zion, was published in 1876, 21 years before the first Zionist Congress, and it exerted a strong influence on such early Zionists as Y.L. Gordon, Lilienblum, Ben-Yehuda and Smolenskin.

George Eliot, novelist and author of "Zionist" novel *Daniel Deronda*.

Opinions vary about the novel's literary qualities. Students in my day were reluctantly reading not *Daniel Deronda,* but *Silas Marner.*

The story is about a young Englishman, raised as a Christian, who discovers that he was born a Jew and decides to go to Palestine to help "revive the organic centre" of his people's existence. It is also about Gwendolen, one of George Eliot's many tragic heroines who fail to find personal happiness. She is "high-spirited and self-confident and marries Henleigh Grandcourt, an arrogant, selfish man." Things go badly and melodramatically; Daniel "is drawn to Mordechai, a noble Jew," and though he becomes Gwendolen's "only hope, he decides to marry Mirah, Mordechai's gentle sister."

The real-life model for Daniel Deronda, A.E.W. Goldsmid, "returned to Judaism in maturity" (he was 32 when the book was published). He was a founder of the Maccabeans and the Jewish Lads' Brigade, and active in the English Hovevei Zion.

"I am Daniel Deronda." With this ringing phrase, Captain Goldsmid, then commanding a Welsh regiment, introduced himself to Herzl when the latter first visited England in 1898.

I assume that he dined out often on this distinction; and it was as well that George Eliot was by now long in her grave, for, unlike Deronda, Captain — later Colonel — Goldsmid did not intend to move to Palestine, although he did come for a visit. However, he proudly told Herzl that his daughters, Rachel and Carmel, were learning Hebrew, and that he planned to devote his life to the liberation of the Jews.

The next year, though, he wrote to Rothschild, warning him against Herzl. Goldsmid was active on behalf of Baron Hirsch's ICA settlement projects, and agreed to supervise the experiment in Argentina. His first appearance there was unsuitably dramatic; he arrived in dress uniform in a carriage drawn by white horses, and announced that he was "Michael, of the people of Israel, called Lieutenant-Colonel Albert Edward Williamson Goldsmid."

On the other hand, he saw Argentina as a "nursery" for Palestine. Indeed, he wrote to Herzl that he was "an unwavering believer in the Idea that the Salvation of Israel can only be worked out by the realization of the National Idea," and that he was "firmly convinced that the only possible locale for a permanent State of Israel is in Eretz Israel."

But unlike Daniel Deronda, Goldsmid felt no personal conflict; and he is said to have been fond of putting it, "Israel is my father and Britain is my mother." Ahad Ha'am, never one to conceal his own feelings of intellectual superiority, wrote after meeting Goldsmid and his cousin d'Avigdor. "They are both good Hovevei Zion and have much goodwill, but it seems to me that their ability is much smaller than their will."

And who can blame his attachment to England? The Goldsmid family, had its own dramatic saga. Two ancestors, financiers in England during the French Revolution, committed suicide; others included the first Jew to receive a hereditary title, and the first Jewish barrister.

During Herzl's second trip to England, which was much less successful than the first, Goldsmid had to be off inspecting his troops. A Maccabean dinner turned out badly, and Herzl from then on referred to them condescendingly as "the Pickwickians." Exit George Eliot's lofty moral drama, enter Dickensian comedy.

The scenery on George Eliot's little street in Tel Aviv includes the Israeli Purchasing Managers' Association, the usual sprinkling of insurance companies and accountants infiltrating all our residential neighbourhoods, the derelict emblem of what seems to have been the Ecuadorian Embassy, and even a detective agency.

And before we know it we are at Yosef Hanasi, with its own quota of lawyers and insurance firms. Also a dentist, a little printing press, a laundry and, brightly announced with hearts and spades, a bridge school.

At No. 11, a weathered ruin provides a model for our scenario. It is an odd echo of a palace built nearly 400 years ago for Yosef's aunt on the shores of Lake Kinneret, near the Hot Springs.

And so, for this week's instalment of our spectacular series. We open with Gracia's triumphal entry into Constantinople: four huge coaches — "triumphal chariots," the excited populace call them — and her escort of 40 armed men for protection during the dangerous journey from Italy through the Balkans. A gala occasion for the Ottoman capital! Thousands of ducats are distributed to the poor on that spring day in 1553 when the richly-dressed Gracia — "La Senora" and "Hageveret" she was called — accompanied by her ladies, passes that way.

But first, for those who missed any of the previous instalments of our TV serial, here is a summary of a little of what has gone before.

Nephew and aunt have been closely associated for years. The family is "rich beyond the dreams of normal avarice," probably descended from the ancient Spanish Jewish family of Nasi, and, according to some sources, probably known as Benvenisti in Christian circles.

The interrelations are intricate. Sets of brothers married sets of sisters, cousin-nephews married cousin-nieces, and the family tree looks rather like a street map, with historians tending not to agree about the dotted lines.

Joseph's father, a professor of medicine and royal physician, was Gracia's brother, her first husband had a brother who married her sister, Reyna — a wicked, jealous sister who twice denounced her.

Widowed at 27, with one daughter, also named Reyna, Gracia left Portugal with her 13-year-old nephew, going first to England, then to the Netherlands, then on to France and Italy, where occasionally parts of the family fortune were seized by the authorities. As rich and well-connected Marranos, they travelled widely; what is unusual is that, having got so far west, they did not remain in those hospitable lands. Instead, while rising in aristocratic circles, Gracia (still as Beatrice) helped her brother-in-law to aid less fortunate Marranos — they organized an escape route from the lands of the Inquisition and even used influence to counter its terrors. Joao-Joseph studied at a Belgian university, entered his uncle's banking firm in Antwerp, moved in the royal circle of the Hapsburg Emperor, Charles V, and is said to have been the "jousting partner of the future Emperor Maximilian."

In Venice, Gracia was imprisoned when her jealous sister Reyna denounced her as Jewish. Joseph the Sultan's representative secured her release by saying that the wealthy woman was planning to bring her fortune to Turkey; so the Turkish ambassador arranged for Gracia to be given her freedom. Some sources say this led indirectly to a renewal of Turkey's war with Venice.

The reason for Reyna's treachery is not clear to me, and this is a very long story for such a short street, but melodrama is melodrama. In fact, it was not entirely clear to the French ambassador on the spot, who commenting on the sisters' "great hatred" for each other (though they later appeared to be reconciled), observed that "all these things are so obscure to me that I cannot find out the truth" — thus providing a perfect licence of freedom for our series.

Sub-plot: The Sultan's physician, Moses Hamon, also helps to arrange the release, because he hopes for a good match for his son — Gracia's daughter Reyna, the greatest Jewish heiress of the age. But to no avail, for Reyna is in love with her handsome cousin Joa.

In Ferrara (shades of the Finzi-Continis) Gracia runs her network of business agents spread throughout Europe, and continues to organize an escape underground for Marranos. The first translation of the Bible into Spanish is dedicated to her, for she has "the intrinsic piety of Miriam, the great prudence of Deborah, the infinite virtues and sanctity of Esther," and she brings her oppressed brothers "to safe land and does not cease to guide them..."

Omitting many adventures and the repeated confiscation of parts of the family fortune (which, however, still left plenty available) we come to Gracia's arrival in Constantinople in 1553. Jaoa arrives the following year, assumes the name Joseph, and undergoes circumcision. We have a fabulous wedding scene with Reyna. From now on, "he is closely associated with his aunt in her commercial and political activities" — such as, the following year, the Nasis' attempted blockade of Ancona in retaliation for the burning of 26 Marranos.

1558: Gracia pays the Sultan 1,000 ducats and receives "a grant for the ruined city of Tiberias" and seven nearby villages. Joseph extends the grant three years later, sends a circular letter to Jewish communities in Italy inviting them to settle in his mini-state, and provides ships for transportation. One entire Jewish community of one town is said to have been prepared to come, but there is no evidence that it did so.

The perils of early immigration: a ship from Venice with 102 would-be settlers is captured by Maltese pirates and all the passengers are sold into slavery.

A mansion is built for Dona Gracia near the Hot Springs. Great excitement! News of plans for development and (heavily subsidized) industry travel far, but, as usual, few immigrants actually arrive and most newcomers to the town have travelled no further than from Safad. Nevertheless, Joseph sends overseers and workers to Tiberias, and by 1565 they have rebuilt the city walls, constructed new houses and a synagogue (near the sea, possibly on the site of the present museum of antiquities). They plant mulberry trees to be the basis of a silk industry, and import cloth from Venice to start, yes, a fashion industry.

Meanwhile, Joseph is deep in politics and its handmaiden, commerce. Prominent in peace negotiations between Poland and Turkey in 1562, he later encourages the Netherlands to revolt against Spain, promising Turkish support. Then, in turn, there is his monopoly on wine imports through the Bosphorus, which brings an estimated 15,000 ducats annually (incalculable in terms of the current Israeli shekel), plus trading privileges in Poland.

Colourful doings at the Sublime Porte: Sultan Suleiman the Magnificent's family troubles involve two surviving sons, Selim, who is a friend of our hero, and Bayazid. The Sultan orders the execution of Bayazid in Persia; earlier he had ordered another son to be strangled. This leaves Selim, who succeeds as ruler in 1566.

1567: Selim makes Joseph Duke of Naxos as a reward for financial aid against Bayazid. Three years later, Joseph persuades his friend the Sultan to declare war on Venice after the latter has refused to cede to him Cyprus, which some think the Duke may have intended as another refuge for Jews.

With all these goings-on, it is no wonder Joseph is diverted from the Tiberias project. And Dona Gracia, her health failing, is growing weary. Her fleet of ships continues the import-export business; her kitchens feed 80 of the poor every day. She manages a spectacular feat, arranging, it is reported, to have her husband's remains brought from his grave in Lisbon for reburial in the Holy Land. She continues to be praised, not least for establishing a yeshiva in Tiberias. "Many daughters have done virtuously, but she hath excelled them all," said Rabbi Moses Trani of Safad, the son-in-law and successor of Joseph Caro.

The development town project grinds to a halt because of intrigues between the native Moslems and Christians, and general indifference on the part of the Jews. Still, the local population eagerly awaits Gracia's promised arrival at her empty home near the Hot Springs.

Did she ever come? Or did she die in Constantinople around 1569? We shall never know — not unless one of those long-lost manuscripts turns up.

And even better than George Eliot's notes for a novel would be, of course, something like a diary left by Gracia's daughter, the Duchess of Naxos. Reyna was much given to the written word; and after her husband's death, 10 years after Gracia died, she maintained his library and even set up a printing press in her own palace.

Joseph's power declined after his aunt's death; he and Reyna had no children. And so, until some misty memoirs are unearthed, we have at least a few minor streets leading back to these women's histories.

But, as George Eliot wrote in *The Mill on the Floss*, "The happiest women, like the happiest nations, have no history."

5
Outside the Establishment

An optimistic hymn to love, trust friendship and peace often opens the Independence Day celebrations in Jerusalem. The words are from Shaul Tchernichowsky's poem *Ani Ma'amin* ("I Believe"), popularly known from its opening words as *Sachki, Sachki*. This, to clear up linguistic details from the start, is the feminine singular imperative of the Hebrew verb, "to laugh derisively."

The poem begins:
Laugh at all my dreams, my dearest;
Laugh, and I repeat anew
That I still believe in man —
As I still believe in you.
In that day shall my own people
Rooted in its soil arise,
Shake the yoke from off its shoulders
And the darkness from its eyes...

The dramatic recitation at the ceremony, the lighting of torches, the staccato military commands and the religious undertones do not seem entirely in tune with the poem, long a favourite of romantic secular youth. But in any event, the final stanza is eerily reminiscent of Max Nordau's call from the grave to the generations to come:
Then a new song shall be lifted
To the young, the free, the brave,
And the wreath to crown the singer
Shall be gathered from my grave.

Tchernichowsky's grave is in the old cemetery in Tel Aviv, and the monument over it was erected by the municipality because the poet left no assets to cover such an expenditure. But I hope his spirit hovers over the Jerusalem night at the Independence celebrations to enjoy the impressive production of his work: he would have relished the spectacle of being taken so grandly to the bosom of an establishment of which he was never really a part.

He was a man of the world, and of world literature, in contrast to his contemporary, Chaim Nahman Bialik, a product of East European Jewry with a deep background in Jewish culture. Tchernichowsky was a master of European languages, modern and classical. The range of his translations is quite incredible — Plato, Homer, Goethe, Shakespeare, Molière; Babylonian and Finnish and Russian epics; Longfellow and Francis Thompson. Bialik, in this pantheon, would be unthinkable, just as he would be cuddling a lamb. Tchernichowsky, who loved animals, flowers, and nature in general, is seen doing just that in a famous photograph, and is often pictured with a dog at his feet.

A quick cliché for criticizing Tchernichowsky alleges that he had an "insufficiently Jewish" viewpoint, and attributes to him "Hellenism, paganism, and love of physical beauty."

One of the poems which best expresses this, and is best remembered by Israeli high-school students, is his famous "Before the Statue of Apollo." In Maurice Samuel's translation, it begins:

To thee I come, O long-abandoned god
Of early moons and unremembered days.
To thee whose reign was in a greener world
Among a race of men divine with youth...

Enough, surely, to irritate large numbers of even the most free-thinking early Zionists. Tchernichowsky continues:

I am the Jew. Dost thou remember me?
Between us there is enmity forever
...and a dark abyss between us yawning.

This might reassure some; but worse is yet to come. The poet cries that "my people and its God have aged together," and continues to address Apollo:

My blood is clamorous with desire of life...
And here before thy pedestal I kneel...
I kneel to all the passionate desires
Which they, the dead-in-life, the bloodless ones,
The sick, have stifled in the living God.
The God of wonders of the wilderness,
The God of gods, Who took Canaan with storm
Before they bound Him in phylacteries.

I have read some nervous attempts to deal with this, such as "The thesis of his Hellenic character has never been satisfactorily proven; it was popularized by some critics who exaggerated the significance of a few poems glorifying Greek beauty and harmony..."

It is probably safest to retreat to the notion that he encompassed an enormous range of conflicting attitudes. For there is also Tchernichowsky the sentimental depicter of the idylls of village life. A sabra friend admits that she still cries whenever she reads the story about Velvele, the little boy in the snowbound village in Eastern Europe who decides to follow the *shaliah*, the emissary from Israel, and to find warmth and sunshine. Instead, he dies of fever.

Literary critics also mention his "critical attitude toward Diaspora

Jewish culture and the yoke of exile," his "marginal socialism," and, toward the end of his life, during the period of Arab riots and the Holocaust, "support of the Jewish maximalist-nationalist position."

The sixth verse of *Ani Ma'amin* is certainly a rousing formulation of Zionist nationalism, in which Tchernichowsky fervently believed, and the whole poem is, of course, wonderfully optimistic. But at other times Tchernichowsky expressed deep pessimism and was imbued with what literary critics call "tragic introspection." The Hebrew verb form makes it clear that the poet is addressing a woman and not any male comrade in any maximalist movement; but then, so many of Tchernichowsky's poems were written to women.

Bialik and Tchernichowsky, so often bracketed as the two giants of modern Hebrew poetry, are, as personalities, still well within living memory. Tchernichowsky died in 1943, at the age of 68; Bialik died in 1934, aged 61.

Tchernichowsky is recalled as warm, lively, approachable, and impractical — in this last respect, the exact opposite of Bialik, an excellent businessman who knew the value of money very well. Tchernichowsky, although famous, rarely had money in his pocket. In Tel Aviv, he rented a tiny single room from a family living on the corner of Ahad Ha'am and Hahashmona'im, and the local grocer grumbled about giving him credit.

Yet he was not only a prolific and widely published poet; he was also a practising physician, holding down, at least for a few years, a half-time job within the Tel Aviv school system.

"He made a tremendous impression on all of us children," a friend of mine told me. "He was always smiling, and he looked marvellous — that big moustache, and all that curly hair."

Indeed, on some photographs Tchernichowsky bears an uncanny resemblance to Mark Twain. He was proud of his romantic looks, and very gallant towards women, many of whom found him irresistible. These are failings — if failings they are — of which Bialik has never been accused. From what I have managed to learn about Tchernichowsky, he must have been one of the most attractive, complex, unusual and impressive personalities ever to have walked our streets and to have left his name in our telephone directories and poetry books.

In a very small and unscientific Tchernichowsky-Bialik survey I carried out once, I noticed that in most cases, the interviewee's eyes lit up, at the mention of Tchernichowsky, while response tended to be cooler for Bialik, who always officially gets the really top spot.

The poet Anda Amir, whose house on Ahad Ha'am was just down the street from Tchernichowsky's room, told me that she thinks he will still be read 200 years from now, precisely because his appeal is universal. Bialik, by contrast, she says, requires a deep Jewish background, which we are in the process of losing.

The two share one date: 1921, the year they both left their native Russia. Both moved to Berlin, where Bialik continued to do well in publishing, while Tchernichowsky earned a meagre living from his writing and scientific editing. Bialik arrived in Tel Aviv in 1924, a wealthy man able to build a beautiful house on the street now bearing his name; he was the leader of the literary establishment here, and founded two publishing houses. Tchernichowsky did not manage to settle here until 1931.

In Tel Aviv, the city with which the two poets were most closely connected, their streets start together at Allenby, diverging with a very acute angle between them. Then they run roughly parallel for the length of Bialik, which is shorter and ends at the old City Hall, now the Tel Aviv Historical Museum.

Bialik's house, in which he and his wife presided over Tel Aviv's intellectual and literary life, is now a library and a museum dedicated to his memory Perhaps to compensate for the shortness of this street, he also has a boulevard running north from the Mann Auditorium, called *Chen,* which in Hebrew stands for neither charm nor the acronym for the Women's Army Corps, but for Chaim Nachman. There is also a little lane far south, off Herzl, called *Aluf Batslut* — General Onion — after one of his children's stories.

Tchernichowsky never lived on the street bearing his name, which skirts the west side of Gan Meir and ends at Bograshov, at what used to be a pleasant little tree-shaded circle. This was recently scraped down and lacerated with roadways to accommodate the belching traffic; a municipal official said at the time that "the Circle was never any good." A WIZO nursery is situated here, and I feel sorry for the children breathing the exhaust fumes all day. Tchernichowsky the children's doctor would have been in despair.

The vista from this end of Tchernichowsky ascends up a cement ramp leading to Dizengoff Centre, which looks for all the world like Israel's magnificent preparation for the international bobsled championship.

Naturally, there are Tchernichowsky streets in Jerusalem and Haifa as well. In Jerusalem, it is an important thoroughfare, starting at the lower end of Gaza Road, near the Valley of the Cross. Tchernichowsky curves right and then left (appropriate, for a poet of so many moods) and on both sides of the street are handsome stone apartment houses, typical of Jerusalem as its modern best, whose balconies often have well-tended flower boxes. This is also appropriate, considering Tchernichowsky's love of growing things. One of his last acts in Tel Aviv, before coming to Jerusalem for the final days of his fatal illness, was to bring his neighbour, Anda Amir, his favourite cactus plant, "to take care of, meanwhile."

But his street comes to a sad end: a dead end. Just after the crossing where Tchernichowsky pauses to pass the time of day with another poet, his contemporary David Shimoni, there is a descent in elegance in the houses. Then the unsuspecting driver will suddenly arrive at a gravel turn-around, and there the street stops. If you need to go further south, you must take a left turn and continue along Katznelson, leaving Tchernichowsky Street to its dead end.

Haifa has treated Tchernichowsky with a repect somewhat surprising for a city which is, politically, a Labour stronghold: despite Tchernichowsky's attitude to the Zionist socialist movement, the politicians in City Hall have given him one of the most handsome thoroughfares at their disposal. It is a continuation of what was once named United Nations Boulevard. When that body passed its notorious resolution identifying Zionism with racism, the name was changed to Zionist Boulevard, a defiant gesture which no doubt caused dismay and shame in the glass building beside the East River.

The street runs, wide and stately, through the French Carmel, one of the most beautiful suburbs in Haifa. From all points there are magnificent views of the pines and other trees on the Carmel stretching down to the blue Mediterranean.

At the beginning of Tchernichowsky there is a fortress-like wall: this is the convent of Saint Theresa. But it is the only forbidding building on this long street, which passes luxurious old houses, luxurious new houses, wooded areas, small parks, and a new shopping centre.

Shaul Tchernichowsky was born in the village of Mikhailovka, in the Crimea, in 1875. His parents were "pious, but open to the influences of the Haskala, and *Hibbat Zion*" — that is to say, the Enlightenment and love of Zion movements.

His mother came from a home unusual for that time and place: her father knew French and Italian, and translated Ukrainian poetry into Hebrew. It was from his mother that he is said to have inherited a love of poetry. Her sister was so emancipated as to have been one of the first Russian women students exiled to Siberia for socialist activity.

From this aunt Shaul learned Russian when he was five, after which his father taught him Hebrew. When he was eight, a Hebrew tutor of the "new, modern method" taught him first the language and then the Bible, a revolutionary trend at that time. When he was 10, he composed his first Hebrew poem.

At 14 he was sent to a commercial high school in Odessa, but this kind of education did not seem to do him much good: although his father was said to have been an excellent businessman, Shaul was always a poor one. Nevertheless, he graduated with distinction in 1896. Instead of applying his knowledge to making money, he read poetry widely — Heine, Byron,

Burns, Pushkin, Lermontov — and was especially interested in languages — German, French, English, Greek and Latin. During this period he met young Zionists in Odessa, including Josef Klausner.

He had started to publish verses in magazines in 1892; but despite his literary interests he now decided to study medicine. In his entrance examination for a Russian university, he passed in Greek and Latin, but failed in — of all things — Russian. His examiners in this language condemned his style as being "too poetic."

From the Russian university, he went to Germany in 1898, the year his first volume of verse appeared, and studied medicine at Heidelberg for four years, going to Switzerland for specialization at Lausanne. In 1907, he was a full-fledged surgeon and pediatrician. All this time he was also producing a stream of poetry and managed, as well, to be enbroiled in "a constant series of love affairs with Christian girls."

Returning to Russia, he had difficulty finding a job as a doctor because he had no Russian degree. He was arrested as a political agitator. He wandered from place to place until his degree was finally recognized, and then obtained a post as a regional physician — and translated Longfellow's *Hiawatha* into Hebrew. At another post, he worked on a Hebrew-Russian encyclopaedia, and translated the Finnish epic, *Kalevala* into Hebrew. (The least the rest of us ought to know is that this ancient saga influenced Longfellow, who employed the same alliterative metric form of trochaic dimeter in *Hiawatha*.)

During World War I, Tchernichowsky served in the Russian army as a doctor; after the Revolution he experienced the hardships of the famine in many parts of Russia. During these years, he translated Homer's *Odyssey* into Russian and wrote more poetry, including sonnets and long narrative works.

Finally, in 1921, he was able to leave Russia, as part of a group headed by Bialik. When his efforts to get a job in Palestine failed, he settled in Germany. He visited Palestine for the first time in 1925, was warmly welcomed, but again could not find a medical job: "His fame as a poet interfered." In 1931 he came to settle with his wife and daughter, living first in Jerusalem.

Tchernichowsky had many good personal friends in this country, but he remained, by and large, an outsider. The literary reason for his exclusion was that embarrassing "Hellenism," an aspect of his cosmopolitan, culturally international outlook and way of life (shared by Nordau, not to mention Jabotinsky) in the face of the local atmosphere, during the Mandate, which was infinitely more provincial than it is today.

The personal reason was his marriage to a wife who was not only gentile, but a demonstratively observant member of the Russian Orthodox Church: so much so, in fact, that she chose to dress in the long, flowing garb of a nun and to wear a large cross on her bosom. The two lived apart during most of Tchernichowsky's life here — she in Jerusalem in a small flat owned by the Russian Church, he in Tel Aviv in that little room on Ahad Ha'am Street.

It was something of a scandal here that when he died, penniless and embittered, his death occurred on property owned by the Russian Church. A garbled version has him dying in a Russian monastery. In fact, it was in his wife's little flat. During his fatal illness, our second greatest poet had nowhere else to go.

The reasons for the marriage of this ill-assorted couple are by now long past understanding; but he was always loyal to her in his fashion. Their only child, a daughter who arrived here bearing the difficult name Isolde, married a Haifa engineer named Wilensky and made this country her home, which is more than can be said for the children of some of our most illustrious and properly pedigreed Zionists.

Tchernichowsky loved children in general, and, in particular, his grandson, Alexander, also now a Haifa engineer. Among his prodigious literary output are children's stories, some illustrated by Nahum Guttman. Bialik, who had no children, is of course also known for his children's stories.

A diversion here may be in order, on the subject of why so many of our leading figures had so few children. This question, so the story goes, was once asked of Joseph Klausner, the historian and early admirer of Tchernichowsky. "Ah yes," replied Klausner, who is said to have had no sense of humour. "Well, we do nothing whatsoever which would prevent our having children. On the other hand, we do nothing which would lead to our having children."

Tchernichowsky's first job on settling in this country was the editing in three languages — Hebrew, Latin and English — of a medical dictionary, *The Book of Medical and Scientific Terms*, compiled by Dr. A. M. Masie.

Once he had completed this immense task — the work contains no less than 600,000 entries — he moved from Jerusalem to Tel Aviv. There he was appointed a part-time physician within the city's school system, at a monthly salary of LP6.50.

He was also under contract to the Schocken publishing firm and continued writing poetry. In terms of literary criticism, in this last period "tragic retrospection gives way to direct and optimistic identification with contemporary life."

There was a measure of recognition. The Finnish government awarded him the Order of the White Rose, in honour of his translation of *Kalevala*; he was three times elected to represent the Hebrew branch of the P.E.N. Club; and in 1935, on the occasion of his 60th birthday, he was made an honorary citizen of Tel Aviv. His poems were translated into Russian, Ger-

Cosmopolitan man of letters, Shaul Tchernichowsky.

man, Italian and English.

Other sources disclose much bitterness during his final years. For some reason, never made officially clear, he was removed from his post as school doctor, though he maintained a private practice. As one biographical summary puts it, "the children loved him no less than he loved them"; remembered gossip has it that he was overly fond of the girl students.

His financial situation was very bad: although his books were selling very well, he considered himself poorly paid by his publisher, though perhaps his expansive Russian temperament made him incapable of handling money sensibly.

"You've stopped writing," a friend once observed in amazement at a café gathering during that last dark period.

"Give me a table to write on, and I'll write," replied Tchernichowsky, with what has been described as "his usual gaiety."

"Do you seriously mean that you haven't got a table to write on?" asked another member of the party.

"Not to write on, and not to eat on," was the answer.

In a literary mini-scandal in the Seventies, Tchernichowsky's Hebrew prose was criticized as needing correction, and he has been charged with being "less than careful" in his translations. But considering his incredible output, plus the fact that he also found time to be a practising physician, and also to sit around in cafés talking with his friends, and to earn a reputation as a lady's man, his accuracy is astonishing.

Poor Tchernichowsky managed to be turned down by very important people. Lilienblum rejected one of his poems which had him hearing "the Word of God," observing tartly that he did not believe God spoke to Tchernichowsky. Ahad Ha'am, on the other hand, rejected another Tchernichowsky lyric as being too full of passionate embraces.

In politics — if not in love — Tchernichowsky was on the side of Ahad Ha'am in the great controversy of 1903, when Herzl's *Altneuland* was attacked by Ahad Ha'am who was in turn attacked by Nordau, and the teams lined up in the Hebrew press for an ideological football match.

In July 1944, a year after his death, a long and strongly-worded article by Ben-Zion Katz, a journalist and close friend who had published his works, appeared in *Ha'zman* under the title, "The Last Days of Tchernichowsky." Katz takes the whole Yishuv establishment to task — publishers, doctors, and the hospital that treated him during his final illness "and presented enormous bills."

Katz condemns old friends who neglected the poet when he most needed them and observes that Tchernichowsky, as a doctor, knew exactly the fatal nature of his illness, cancer, and faced it bravely.

As one might expect, today a three-storey building in Tel Aviv bearing his name houses the Israeli Writers' Association on Rehov Kaplan just off

Ibn Gabirol. It is a shade smaller than its neighbour, Beit Sokolow, home of the Journalists' Association, but compared with Tchernichowsky's straitened living quarters, it is a palace. In the basement are archives of writings by and about every Hebrew writer worth mentioning; upstairs are the offices of *Mozna'im,* the writers' periodical which has since published many a learned treatise on our poet. There is also a bibliographical card index, and the cards pertaining to Tchernichowsky himself run to a thickness, it seems to me, of about two metres.

One room in the house, kept under lock and key, is dedicated to Tchernichowsky's memory. Here are his table (so yes, he did have one after all, but it was a very plain wooden one), his writing pad and blotter; photos of his daughter and wife; books in Russian and a Tel Aviv Municipality yearbook; his horoscope; his cane and his Finnish medal. His pen, bequeathed to his grandson, has rather sadly found its way back to this silent room.

Faded photographs show Tchernichowsky in Russia; in Berlin; on a visit to Cleveland, Ohio, in 1929; at Beit Shean in 1940. With a lamb, with a fox terrier. With Bialik on a visit to a factory in Ramat Gan.

Preserved for our speculation are some of his doodles. The most frequent themes are horses, crowns, skulls, pyramids, trumpets, a coat of arms. In the doctor's medicine cabinet are some preparations time has passed by: a little box of Dermo-Plastel; Zinc-Protamin. Something called *Sexo-Tonikum — Yohimbe Effekt.*

The clock stands at 11.42 and the page on the calendar pad, from a medical supply company, is open at September 24, 1942. It is sad in this room because it is so quiet; at least, it was when I visited it alone. At other times, of course, there must be groups of visitors. But it makes an eerie connection between the man whose room is duplicated here, and the streets named after him, which were, after all, what led me to it.

For our purposes, a little essay Tchernichowsky wrote the year before his death, on the changing nature of Tel Aviv, evokes the connection even more strongly. Written in a chatty style, it begins with the subject of the city's trees.

Tchernichowsky mentions the "eight sycamores on King George" — now down to a dusty five — and mourns the passing of "that other Tel Aviv, which is every day diminishing and disappearing" — Little Tel Aviv, "the city of tiny streets and small houses, each house in its own ugly style, or in its own original lack of style," but rich in dreams and neighbourly love.

When a house is built by and for the man who will live in it, it will have beauty, Tchernichowsky wrote nearly 40 years ago; but when contractors build blocks for profit, the dream is gone.

In that forgotten essay on premature nostalgia, Tchernichowsky also wrote that, in spite of the ravages of progress, "it is nevertheless impossible not to love crowded Tel Aviv, because this is after all the only spot on earth where a Jew can be simply a human being called a Jew...without any feeling that he is a Jew, and without even being aware of it."

6
Huberman Meets Toscanini

Huberman meets Toscanini right opposite the box-office of the Mann Auditorium. Their permanent encounter at this Tel Aviv corner is planned and absolutely appropriate. For these two streets were named in 1957, when the Mann Auditorium, home of the Israel Philharmonic Orchestra, was completed. The Palestine Symphony Orchestra, as it was originally called, was founded, as I suppose everybody knows, by the Polish violin virtuoso, Bronislaw Huberman, and its festive first concert in December 1936 was conducted by Arturo Toscanini — not, of course, in the Mann Auditorium, which was still a tree-covered hill, but in a rebuilt hall at Tel Aviv's old Levant Fair grounds.

When the world's most famous conductor accepted the invitation of his good friend Huberman to come to Palestine it was a politically demonstrative act by a committed anti-Fascist: Toscanini had been physically attacked in Italy five years earlier for refusing to play the Italian Fascist anthem. "It is everyone's duty to fight and help in this cause according to one's means," the Maestro said to Huberman, and his statement appeared on the opening page of the first concert's programme.

By the autumn of 1936 — the year Hitler invaded the Rhineland, the Rome-Berlin-Tokyo Axis was formed, the Spanish Civil War started, and the Stalin purge trials began — Huberman was, as usual, on a European concert tour. At the same time he was sending off impassioned but also analytical letters to friends throughout Europe and in Palestine (to Ben-Gurion, to Col. Kisch, treasurer of the Palestine Orchestra Trust, and to Judah Magnes) about his determination to create an orchestra here. His plan, "great, simple, and practical" as the music critic David Rosolio wrote, was "to unite the desire of the country for an orchestra with the desire of the Jewish musicians for a country." And, from the start, it was to be "not just another orchestra, but one of the best in the world."

Not long before, Huberman had described himself as "more European than Jewish in feeling, and if anything, rather anti-Zionist." He deplored what he called "Jewish chauvinism" and never stopped pursuing the ever-receding goal of humanism and international brotherhood. Yet what he accomplished, single-mindedly, and at first singlehanded, puts to shame many a project, and many a failure, of the most vociferous nationalists.

Though his battles with the Tel Aviv Municipality and the Jewish Agency make marvellous reading today, fortunately he found many supporters among the most prominent citizens of Jerusalem.

Even after the infant orchestra acquired trustees and a management — all the result of Huberman's initiative — he still insisted on directing every administrative, artistic and policy detail, often autocratically, as he himself admitted. In effect, he was the orchestra's executive director, public relations officer, musical director, fundraiser, immigration officer, insurance consultant, personnel director, housing planner, acoustics consultant, travel agent, purchasing specialist and ideologist.

At the same time, he continued to perform the world over, often in benefit concerts for his Palestinian baby, producing the pure and famous "Huberman tone" which was said to induce fainting in the audience. But he was also known as an uneven performer. Sometimes his level was celestial, sometimes it was as poor as a student's. This was hardly surprising, considering all the non-musical problems with which his mind was preoccupied.

Huberman spent most of his life travelling, accompanied by a devoted secretary, Ida Ibbeken. He and his wife were divorced; their child lived with her. Huberman was moody, complex, unapproachable. He suffered from headaches and a nervous squint. He was terribly sensitive to noise. How unhappy he would have been if he had lived, as I so long did, in his street.

By December 1936, the magic of Toscanini's impending arrival in Palestine, postponed from October because of the security situation had the whole country feverish with excitement. Probably only those who experienced it can grasp the national tumult that high-grade cultural event caused. "The hoopla of the Eurovision concert in Jerusalem can't compare in any way at all," said a friend of mine who was here during the Toscanini fever.

Sceptical as always, local residents had been certain that Toscanini would never come. He was nearly 70, the Arab-Jewish conflict was intensifying, world events were grim. Matching the public scepticism, the members of the new orchestra were sure that, if he did come, he would leave the next day, immediately after hearing them. They had been practising since October under Hans Steinberg, previously director of the Frankfurt Opera, who had come from Switzerland to prepare the orchestra for the Maestro. But they had been "blown together" from many countries; they lacked cohesion, tradition, even a common language. The closest they came to a *lingua franca* was to use German: this remained the language of most Israeli musicians for many years, even when they had learned Hebrew.

Of the 71 musicians listed in the first concert programme, all but nine were brand-new immigrants. The "locals" included seven who had come as children from Russia, and two, a brother and a sister, who had actually been born in Jaffa, although they were hired for the orchestra in France. The son of the brother has gone rather far afield as pop singer Ariel Silber. *Pace* Huberman.

Suddenly, as so often happens in Israel, everything changed. The same public, which earlier had been reluctant to buy tickets for a concert it was sure would not take place, became hysterical to get them as soon as Toscanini announced that he was actually on the way. People stooped to blackmail and theft; the box-office was stormed and the police had to be called in to "protect" the orchestra staff from ticket-hungry crowds. The coming of Toscanini became the topic of conversation of all Palestine. In pioneering, open-necked Tel Aviv, submerged but luxuriant bourgeois yearnings came to the fore and the wives of ticket-holders began frantic dressmaking sessions. That was the decade of the backless sheath, and the vision of pioneer music-lovers in deep decolleté astonished those who had never seen such a spectacle.

Captain Orde Wingate, the legendary British officer who trained the Jewish defence forces told Vera Weizmann that he would like to attend the opening concert. But since not a ticket was to be had, not even by Vera, Chaim Weizmann gave up his to Wingate and missed the event. A chair was made available in the hall for Wingate's beautiful wife Lorna. After the concert, something happened of which old Tel Avivians are still proud, and which could not happen today: a fleet of public-transport buses was waiting outside the Levant Fair hall, and no concert-goer was left stranded in the far north. Such, such were the days of glamour without traffic jams.

In eight days, in public rehearsals and concerts in Jerusalem (at the Edison Cinema) and Haifa (at the Armon Hall) 15,000 people heard Toscanini conduct the orchestra. Four more concerts by the orchestra, under Toscanini, in Cairo and Alexandria, in January 1937, also sold out as soon as announced. "The Near East, from Haifa to Alexandria, had been won for the orchestra," Dr. Elsa Thalheimer wrote in a short history of the orchestra's first five years — printed in 1942, in Cairo, and dedicated to Bronislaw Huberman. He himself did not appear as soloist during that first triumphal season, in order to prevent even the faintest suspicion that he had created the orchestra as background for himself.

When it was over, Toscanini said, "How it pains me to leave this orchestra, Huberman! I am coming back next year." Political conditions postponed his second tour with the Palestine Symphony until April 1938.

Pre-Huberman Palestine was certainly not a musical desert. Over the decades there had been various musical societies and performing groups; after earlier attempts, there had even been a "Palestine Philharmonic Symphony Union," which in 1934 formed a 50-strong orchestra under Friedlaender, Jacobsohn and Michael Taube, to name only three of the many names that should appear here. Among the earliest music schools

72

Huberman and Erica Morini after a joint recital.

Bronislaw Huberman and Arturo Toscanini.

was *Beit Sefer Shulamit*, founded by Arthur Ruppin's first wife Selma in 1910 and directed by M. Hopenko. But the standards demanded by Huberman were, by and large, well beyond what was previously available here. Ruppin himself wrote in his diary, on the last night of the year 1936: "Yesterday Jerusalem had the most important musical experience in its history — the concert of the newly formed Philharmonic."

I must confess that my knowledge of Huberman's role was vague until I started digging into the street, although Huberman and Toscanini were among the very few Israeli street names that were familiar to me when I first arrived in the country. My parents are both musicians, and so the names heard in my home when I was a child were those of musicians. There was never a whisper about Ahad Ha'am or Bialik, or even Jabotinsky or Weizmann.

Among the five conductors whom Huberman was most interested in engaging for the new orchestra were Issay Dobrowen and Pierre Monteux. They happened to be, in turn, the conductors of the San Francisco Orchestra, and my father played in the violin section of that orchestra under both.

So whichever minor muse is in charge of deciding who is to live on whose street certainly arranged things neatly by setting me down on Huberman's street, and having me read there, years later, one particular letter of his, written by Huberman in January 1936, from Athens, to Salo B. Lewertoff, general secretary of the newly formed Palestine Orchestra Association in Tel Aviv. After reading through Huberman on wardrobe rooms, practice rooms, facilities for cars, "at least 400 lightly upholstered chairs," a buffet, outdoor concerts, the percentage for a restaurant, schedules for workers' and students' concerts, and transportation problems to the kibbutzim, I finally came to his list of suggested soloists.

Here Huberman mentions Adolf Busch, the great German non-Jewish violinist who was the orchestra's first soloist, and two other violinists and two cellists he would like to engage. Morini or Heifetz, "Casals or Feuermann."

The reason I was so happy to come across this is because the violinist he mentions, Erica Morini, is my aunt. She was a close friend of Huberman's, and played the Bach Double Concerto with him in Vienna long, long ago. My mother, a pianist, accompanied her sister Erica throughout Europe. She tells me that Erica Morini and Huberman shared a tendency to insomnia and used to take long walks together at night.

In 1957, ten years after his death, Erica Morini was selected by Ida Ibbeken to be soloist with the I.P.O. in a special memorial concert. Interviewed on that occasion by *The Jerusalem Post*, she recalled that Huberman, who had been present at her first concert as a child prodigy in Vienna, declared her to be "a future genius," and out of sheer excitement immediately dedicated to her a Chopin waltz he was adapting for the violin.

Huberman's street is a geometric impossibility: it has just one side, with nothing but even numbers to its row of apartment blocks. Across the street is the parking-lot of the Habimah Theatre and the Mann Auditorium, the modern home of the orchestra that Huberman created. Before 1957, the street was known as Rehov Tarsat Bet; a Rehov Tarsat (formerly Aleph, and having only odd numbers) still exists on the opposite side of the square. In my ignorance, I used to assume that Tarsat was an acronym, or possibly Aramaic, for some version of *Tismoret*, the Hebrew for orchestra. Not at all: as the street sign explains, it stands for the year 1909, when Tel Aviv was founded.

Before it was surpassed in glory by newer buildings further north, Huberman was considered one of Tel Aviv's finest streets; plenty of long, sleek cars still glisten alongside, and sometimes on its sidewalks. At concert times it is a festival for cars. Huberman Street used to be called *Schokoladestrasse*, in honour of the coffee-and-candy company whose family owned several of the plots on it.

Toscanini and Huberman streets are at the heart of the city's culture — the Habimah, the Auditorium, and the Rubinstein Art Pavilion. Gan Yaakov, a charming little park, helps a little to soften the parking-lot-culture ambience, and the police band used to give mini-concerts here, in the spirit of the flowers and shrubs.

There are no fewer than nine streets converging on the square — Huberman, Toscanini, Dizengoff, Tarsat, Chissin, Ben-Zion, Kikar Habimah, Rothschild and Marmorek. Long before culture and parking-lots, the square was a farm, with chickens clucking where audiences now do; and then it became the Municipality's tree nursery. Then came Habimah, first in its modest form; then the other houses of culture, and the apartment houses of Huberman, with their uniform square fronts. The balconies are hardly ever used now because of the noise (made by the cars, not by the orchestra). My Huberman neighbours remember when the sound-effects used to be the sound of the jackals, and one could ride a horse to the back doors of Huberman.

At the time of the orchestra's first concert at the Levant Fair hall the Huberman-Toscanini area of today was outside Tel Aviv's municipal boundary, and the orchards bloom clearly on a map in the Steimatzky Palestine Guide Book for 1935. And while that season's fruit was in blossom, Huberman was under the spell of Palestine after a tour of the country.

"Nowhere else can such ideals, such enthusiasm, be found," he wrote from London in March, 1934. "True, there are individual idealists everywhere. But mass idealism, collective idealism as it exists in Palestine, cannot be found in any country in the world. That is one of the reasons why I no longer see any incompatibility between my Pan-Europeanism and Palestine."

While he feared that prosperity would have a bad moral effect on Palestine and pleaded with the low paid musicians to do without "foreign subsidies," he himself was practical about money. He was one of those musicians who "count the house" during the opening bars, and was not above telling his assistant to "sell so-and-so many shares of such-and-such a stock" just before going on stage. In this respect, he would feel at home among us today.

Like Toscanini, he was at once a liberal, an internationalist, and a patriot. It pained him that the Jews of his native Poland were making such a poor showing in contributing to orchestra funds. In October 1936 he wrote from Italy to his friend Jakob Surowicz in Warsaw (later a violinist with the orchestra and its inspector): "This is the only land, my fatherland, which till now hasn't produced a penny for the cause."

Huberman continued to play on the three strings of human unity, patriotism, and Zionism. To Dobrowen in San Francisco he wrote, from Yugoslavia, a glowing letter about pioneering in Palestine, where he had just given 12 sold-out concerts in 18 days. It opened with the rather stark query, "How do you stand on Zionism?"

Then, in a revealing paragraph toward the end of the letter, he explains that "naturally, in the present phase of national rebirth, considerable emphasis is put on the fact that the leader of the orchestra should not be a converted Jew. But I would ask you not to view this as generally characteristic of the entire viewpoint of the Jews there. On the contrary, there are many impulses toward human brotherhood, and among many of the Zionist pioneers, the hope exists that from there a solution to humanity's problems will emerge..."

But Polish patriotism dies hard. At the time of the Toscanini concerts, Huberman had a short meeting with a distant cousin named Gershon Huberman, who had immigrated that year from Danzig to study farming at Mikveh Israel. He told the youth:

"You have done the wrong thing in coming here. A great war is coming. You are a Pole, and your duty was to stay in Poland and fight the Nazi enemy." In fact, when the time came, Gershon joined the British Army and spent five years in uniform.

Bronislaw Huberman was born in 1882 in Czestochowa, the son of a cultured but not very rich lawyer. He was recognized as a prodigy by the famous teacher Joachim. After a tremendously successful debut, the little boy received a gift of money, and a violin, from no less a patron than the Emperor Franz Joseph.

At 13, in Vienna, he played the Brahms Concerto in the presence of the composer. According to legend, Brahms was moved to tears and after the performance, embraced the boy, who responded, "Too bad the applause started during the melody after the cadenza."

Brahms: "You should not have played the cadenza so beautifully."

Glory and honours followed, and gifts from the rich and mighty. Sultan Abdul Hamid, for instance, gave Huberman a silver-framed mirror. It rests today in a case, together with Huberman's bow and a medley of medals and much else, in the Tel Aviv Music Library as part of the Huberman Archives. His voluminous correspondence, in Polish, German, French, English and Italian, with such people as Einstein, Queen Elizabeth of Rumania, Jan Masaryk, King Albert of Belgium, and every musician worth knowing, was catalogued by the composer Zvi Avni and Ida Ibbe who, though not Jewish, spent her last years here.

The archives include the famous silhouette showing little Bronislaw playing for bearded Brahms. It somehow matches the 1866 caricature of *Il bambino Toscanini*, a babyish 19-year-old conducting in Brazil, taking over the baton in an emergency and thus starting his sensational career.

Huberman's first concert tour in Palestine was in 1929. He was still deeply involved in the Pan-Europe movement, to which he contributed a great deal of money, and for which he wrote a book, *Vaterland Europa*. He came for a second tour in 1931, but told an interviewer for a Viennese newspaper: "Even to me, it is not clear why I have come a second time to Palestine." However, he felt that everyone had the duty to contribute what he could to the "realization of the great work" going on in Palestine. Until now, he said, he had always thought that only Europe held a real future for Jews. But that was before he saw what was happening in Palestine.

In October 1937, during a world tour, Huberman was seriously injured in a plane crash in Java. Even before this accident, he was exhausted, worrying about plans for a musicians' housing scheme in Tel Aviv, concern about the Arab-Jewish conflict, choosing musicians, and the incredible clerical burden of carrying on the whole enterprise while on tour. Then, crashing in the jungle, he suffered injuries to his entire body. The worst catastrophe was that his left arm and right hand were damaged; the local doctors believed he would never play again. A fractured rib led to nearly fatal pneumonia. He was hospitalized in a tiny hospital of the Shell Petroleum Company for five weeks, and in another hospital for two more before he was able to sail to Europe. From Sumatra, his cable to the orchestra in Tel Aviv expressed only his sorrow at not being able to be with them in Palestine that season, and his hope to work with them again soon.

His miraculous eventual recovery was due, according to one report, to the fact that, as the plane crashed — and they crashed more slowly in those days — Huberman instinctively lifted his precious violin, thus lessening the impact on his hands. That, plus an indomitable will, and a course of treatment and exercise in Switzerland.

The next year, after an Egyptian tour in November 1938, he came to Palestine, and finally appeared in triumph as soloist in the Beethoven Concerto. He returned again in 1940, and was given a tumultuous reception; that was his last appearance with the orchestra.

Several new immigrant musicians from Europe had arrived by 1938.

One of them, Heinz Berger, is an old friend of mine, who for years played in the oboe and English horn section and is now working in the orchestra's archives. In 1938, he was a very young oboist in the Berlin *Jüdischer Kulturbund*, an organization created by the Nazis themselves as a framework for the Jewish population. The situation in Germany was unbelievable, but real: Jews were in concentration camps, but also in Nazi-initiated orchestras and other cultural projects.

"There is no doubt that Huberman saved my life, and the lives of many other musicians," Berger told me. At first he did not really want to go to Palestine, because he was convinced that he was "not yet ready to play with Toscanini." (And of course he never did: no further visits by Toscanini to Palestine materialized.)

"But friends of mine from Germany were already in Palestine with the orchestra. They told me there was an opening for an oboe and they urged me to apply, so I did. I was auditioned in Berlin by Steinberg and Taube, and accepted. In October 1938, I went straight from my last performance of *Rigoletto* with the *Jüdischer Kulturbund* on to a train, with my oboe. And a few days later I was rehearsing in Tel Aviv..."

The members of the orchestra were in complete awe of Huberman, Berger told me. "He was very intelligent, very reserved. And after all, he could decide our fate. Our contracts were for only one year."

Huberman, meanwhile, though they did not know it, was battling for higher wages, for more subsidy from the Municipality, contributing his own money from his own benefit performances, and working out the orchestra's relationship to the Palestine Broadcasting Service.

Huberman gave much thought to the question of "Jews in the highest spheres of creative power." The reason why there had not been "a Jewish Bach or Mozart or Beethoven," in his view, was because the great flowering of composition in Europe preceded the emancipation of the Jews. In an essay printed in the programme notes for the Palestine Symphony's opening concert, he points out that throughout history art has flourished only for brief periods, preceded and followed by darkness. The Bach to Beethoven period was "a conjuncture of unique events that occur every thousand years or so." But during that period, the Jews were still in the ghetto, and "when finally the barriers of the ghetto were overcome, the art of music had passed its zenith — for Jews no less than for non-Jews."

78

"Modern functionalism," Huberman suggests, that idea "which musical circles, even more than others, were so proud to have achieved," many "first have to be overcome" before great music will again be written. In rejecting what is called "contemporary" music, Huberman and Toscanini were in perfect agreement.

In his credo, Huberman lists certain Jewish composers, among them Meyerbeer (whose Tel Aviv street is in Kiryat Shalom), Offenbach, Anton Rubinstein, Max Bruch, Mahler, Schönberg, Bloch, Milhaud — and Ravel, though a journalist soon pointed out that Ravel is "as Basque as Basque can be."

It is easy to jog the length of Huberman in under three minutes. The house numbers go up to 24, but remember, there are only even numbers, which means only 12 buildings. The first, at the southern or Marmorek end, is an elderly synagogue which has for years been planning to move, but it continues to protrude into the road, which agitates some of the residents. I am all for this protrusion, on the theory that it helps decrease the speed of vehicles turning into Huberman. I had hopes for a much-needed traffic light here when Menachem Begin, our neighbour to the north, was elevated to the status of prime minister. But either he did not worry as much as I did about risking his life crossing the street, or his influence was inadequate.

On Marmorek, just opposite the synagogue, is the Scala Café, another triumph for the minor muse of street sitings, for Toscanini was associated with La Scala, Milan's famous opera house, for 30 years.

His own street is a two-minute trot to the north, and just past it is another tribute to the conductor and yet another triumph for our muse. Because the last house on Huberman is the Italian Embassy, which is certainly fitting for an Italian patriot who fought under Garibaldi. (Huberman has the embassies of Italy and Japan. Toscanini is very heavy with lawyers, accountants and architects. The symbolism here evades me.)

Arturo Toscanini (born in Parma in 1867, died in New York in 1957) was fond of telling friends that he believed himself to be of Jewish origin. The Nazis, who understandably hated the world's most famous conductor, produced propaganda calling him Tosenstein. Toscanini would laugh, and say that Jews in Italy traditionally took the names of cities and provinces, and that his own name undoubtedly had started out as Toscano or Toscani.

I don't wish to make too much of Toscanini and the Jewish problem. But here, on the other side of the coin, is the place to recall that Toscanini insisted on playing Wagner during his 1938 tour here, maintaining that "nothing should interfere with music." And he kept playing Wagner after the war began, because "Wagner belonged to the world, and the world must not let the Nazis take exclusive possession of his music."

A few Toscanini stories, out of a vast corpus of anecdotes.

When Toscanini decided to boycott the Wagner Festival at Bayreuth as a political slap against the Nazis and take up the Salzburg Festival in pre-Nazi Austria instead, he told Huberman and then asked, "Well, what do you think of me now."

Huberman: "As a demonstration against Nazism, very good. But what about a positive demonstration in favour of the Jewish victims of Nazism?" When Toscanini asked what he had in mind, Huberman came right out and said, "Come to Palestine and conduct the orchestra I am forming there." And, in this version, Toscanini said, simply, "Right."

Then there is the famous story about the birds during the first rehearsal at the Levant Fair hall. In those days and for many pleasant days thereafter before air-conditioning put its icy grip on our summers, buildings such as post offices, the Lydda airport and factories used to be full of songbirds skimming in and out the windows. The presence of the birds in the presence of Toscanini at the rehearsal had everybody petrified, since tales of Toscanini's tantrums, threats and insults would fill many volumes. Toscanini began the rehearsal, the orchestra played, and the birds began enthusiastically to sing along. All present expected a terrible outburst. Instead, Toscanini suddenly brought down his baton and said to the musicians, "Please, why can't you sing like these birds?"

In another apocryphal story about that first rehearsal, this time without birds, Toscanini mounts the podium to raise his baton for the first time. The tension is terrific. In his husky voice, he calls for the Brahms Symphony, second movement. The orchestra plays. There is an ominous silence. The players tremble. Then Toscanini says: "Not bad. Not bad at all."

But life with Toscanini was never all hearts and flowers. Old-timers have for years exchanged views on whether or not Toscanini actually broke a baton in wrath at some orchestra mishap. Yes, he did, and he did it *with his teeth.* This firmly documented incident I have from the best of witnesses, Yaakov Ajolo, the orchestra's stage manager for 30 years, starting with the first concert. Toscanini bit the baton in two because somebody in the viola section played a wrong note. Perhaps fortunately, the culprit was a woman, so she was able to burst into tears and nothing really fatal followed.

Then there was the mishap with the trumpet in Haifa, when... But Toscanini stories, even during his short stay here, are endless.

The one about his orange grove began during Toscanini's first visit, when Moshe Chelouche presented him with the deed to a grove at Ramot Hashavim in a little ceremony complete with a chorus of children and gifts of oranges and honey. When he returned in 1938 and was brought oranges picked from his own grove, "he held them in his hands and wept," according to his biographer Howard Taubman, of *The New York Times.*

Taubman also tells how Toscanini, who accepted no fee for any of his appearances with the Palestine Orchestra, arrived at a hall here and found nobody waiting outside. It was only half an hour to the concert. Would nobody come? Then he entered the hall and found it was jammed: the audience was something incredible. "As he raised his baton, he felt like weeping."

Toscanini never lost his interest in Palestine. In 1945 he signed a petition to King Farouk requesting leniency for the two Palestinian Jews sentenced to death for the assassination of Lord Moyne.

I am afraid we did not always deserve that intense concern and affection. Early in 1946, Huberman wrote a brave but sad letter from New York to his beloved orchestra. Recovering from a heart attack, he first outlines his plan to come again, as soloist, for the sole purpose of raising funds for the orchestra. Then he adds that Toscanini had recently inquired about his plot at the Ramot Hashavim orchard and about his Freedom of the City of Tel Aviv. "As you remember, we both have received this distinction, but nobody in the City Council ever thought of sending us the official certificate... Maestro Toscanini is most eager to get it. Please see immediately that something is done about it. And also that he gets some news about his oranges."

A certificate of Freedom of the City could still be arranged, but alas, the beautiful orange grove was covered with a housing development.

Just at the time the orchestra's management was facing the embarrassing task of explaining what had happened, it was also celebrating the conclusion of its 22nd tour to Egypt. Between 1937 and early 1946, more than 16 per cent of the orchestra's 1,358 concerts had taken place in Egypt, either for troops during the war or as "culturally normal" events.

The orchestra's remarkable Egyptian connection was first initiated on the shores of the Dead Sea early in 1934, when Huberman outlined details of his plan to Mayor Dizengoff.

"On the basis of my familiarity with the musical situation in Egypt," Huberman wrote, "an idea has occurred to me whose realization could lead to the musical enrichment of both countries, and to closer mutual contacts. Cairo has a particular love of opera. But the economic crises of the last few years has made the support of the traditional opera season very difficult. So..."

Toscanini conducted the orchestra's first Egyptian appearances at the Alhambra Theatre in Alexandria in January 1937. The message in that concert's programme notes in French, reads: "The first foreign trip of the Palestine Orchestra is to Egypt — a symbol of the new spirit in the Orient, and of the fraternity among races and nations."

Cairo's guest soloists from Europe that year included Rubinstein,

Heifetz, Erica Morini and Huberman — still dutifully refraining from appearing with the Palestine Orchestra.

For real togetherness, it is hard to beat the "Anglo-Russian Music Festival" featured in a special Cairo concert in 1943, which brought together in the Gizeh University hall the Palestine Symphony Orchestra, the Cairo Symphony Orchestra, the Cairo Military Band, and Trumpeters from the RAF, playing Russian music under the Union Jack entwined with the Hammer and Sickle. "Get Your Lunch at Groppi's," suggested the programme advertisements.

Pnina Salzman appeared with the orchestra in Egypt that year. Other concerts across the Canal featured the Jerusalem Quartet, whose members included, at various times and among others, Margaret Bentwich and her sister Thelma Yellin, Boris Schatz and Emil Hauser.

In Egypt, the Palestine Symphony gave 15 charity concerts for the benefits of such causes as the Red Cross, the Fund for Malaria Victims of Upper Egypt, Jewish benevolent societies and British war charities, and — I mention this with glad surprise — the Egyptian Royal Society for the Protection of Animals.

There were youth concerts too. In Heliopolis, the soloist with the Palestine Orchestra was a 12-year-old Armenian boy from Cairo who played the Mendelssohn Violin Concerto. His name was Jerard Kantarjian. Where may he be today?

When World War II ended, and before Israel's War of Independence began, the orchestra was flourishing, and its founder was mortally ill. Thinking he had been cured, he wrote this letter from Italy to a friend in Holland:

"I am more than happy to send you the news that I am fully recovered and plan to start my concert activities again this summer... Perhaps this terrible experience has that one great advantage: that life, art, concerts, and successes, which otherwise would have continued to be for me a matter of fact, now appear as a divine gift."

Four months later, in June 1947, Huberman died in Switzerland.

7

The Swedish Steps

Just before lunch, on a bright March day at the height of the 1900 tourist season, the American Consul in Jerusalem knocked on the door of a guest at the Grand New Hotel, the best in the Old City — and launched into an agitated warning.

"The American Colony is not a house for ladies to visit. It is a wicked place. You are deceived in what you see there. They pretend to be saintly, but you do not know what goes on at night. It ought not to bear the name of America. And Mrs. Spafford is the worst of all. She is a notorious free lover..."

The tourist toward whom these intriguing accusations were directed was the Swedish novelist, Selma Lagerlöf, who was to become the first woman to win the Nobel Prize for Literature She was visiting the Holy Land with a Jewish friend, Sophie Elkan, who was also a writer.

"They break up the marriage relation between men and their wives," the Consul, whose own wife was portly and comfortable, sputtered on. "They have group meetings, and afterwards men and women go together into dark rooms and have love affairs." It was quite a performance, considering that the ladies had never been properly introduced to the American Consul.

His name was Selah Merrill and he came from Andover, Massachusetts. He had a degree in theology, had taught Hebrew at Andover Academy and was a writer and an archaeologist. For nearly 20 years, during three tours of duty in Jerusalem, he had spent tremendous amounts of time and energy, and so also much of the American taxpayer's money, attacking the "American Colony," although, as he was always careful to make clear, he had never "degraded himself" by setting foot in the place.

The Colony was a strange messianic group that had come to Jerusalem in 1881. Their leader, Horatio Spafford, a Chicago lawyer, died in 1886, and his widow Anna, a mystical woman of great charm, intensified the peculiar way of life of the commune. Jerusalem's missionary establishment bitterly opposed the group, which practised a form of early Christian communism which nobody on the outside understood. To the American Consul and others, it seemed thrillingly likely that if property was held in common, so too were the women.

In 1896, the original American settlers were joined by two groups of Swedes, one from Chicago, the other from a village in Sweden. They had learned about the American Colony through a widely-reported Chicago lawsuit over an inheritance, in which a central issue was the suitability of the Colony as a place for bringing up the two young heirs. The Colony emerged with its reputation vindicated and an increased following.

"They throw young girls in the way of men," Dr. Merrill went on. Then he made his big mistake. "Mrs. Spafford will not let you see the Swedes alone," he said. "She keeps them hypnotized."

Selma Lagerlöf knew that Swedish farmers were living at the Colony. That was why the place had interested her from the time she first heard about it. In Sweden, she had learned about the wave of apocalyptic, messianic belief that swept entire villages. And now the American Consul was telling her that her countrymen were being held in bondage in a bizarre and depraved community!

Miss Lagerlöf and Miss Elkan ate their lunch and decided to investigate the Colony as soon as possible.

They visited the Colony several times during their three-week stay in Jerusalem to gather material for their books — instant journalism is not such a new invention as some people think — and they were completely charmed by Anna Spafford and her daughter Bertha. Two years later, Selma Lagerlöf's best-seller, *Jerusalem*, was published, and translated into many languages. It is a melodrama which makes the Colony into a model for the conflict between the individual and the group, between fanaticism and benevolence, between human love and love of God. But, in fact as well as fiction, the Colony can be seen as a model of the conflict between America's official presence in Jerusalem and an unofficial idealistic transplant.

Selma Lagerlöf received her Nobel Prize for "the noble idealism, the richness of imagination, the generosity and beauty of form which characterise her work." *Jerusalem* is not one of her best known works; even in Sweden, the second volume is barely read today, and is considered by critics to be weaker than the first. Far better known are her novels *Gosta Berling* and *The Ring of the Lowenskolds*, not to mention her children's classic, *The Wonderful Adventures of Nils*.

Born in 1858 in a Swedish province rich in tradition and folklore, Selma Lagerlöf was trained as a teacher. She won first prize in a literary competition in a weekly paper with the first chapters of *Gosta Berling* and soon after was able to devote herself to writing. She travelled to Sicily, also with Sophie Elkan, to do research on her novel, *The Miracles of Antichrist*, in which the atmosphere of the apocalypse is palpable. ("We do not fear him. When the Antichrist comes... we shall meet him, and we shall lead him to Christ. We shall make peace between earth and heaven.")

In her acceptance speech at the Nobel Prize ceremony in 1909, Miss Lagerlöf said that, during her train trip to Stockholm, she dreamed that she "had been carried in thought to heaven, there to tell her father that she had won the prize." Like the other women who dominate this story, she lived to a ripe old age, dying in 1940 at 82.

Seventy-five years after her visit to Jerusalem, on a clear autumn day in 1975, the Municipality named a thoroughfare in her honour, a series of landscaped steps joining two streets in the Rassco neighbourhood, with shrubbery and benches and sandboxes.

Admittedly, the Selma Lagerlöf Steps are somewhat obscure, and are a very short and simple passageway along which to convey a long and complicated story. There is little room for choice or complications; after all, the steps lead either down from Tchernichowsky Street, or up from Shimoni Street.

Threading our way through the story is another matter. There is a century of history, by now almost as obscure as the steps, although once front-page news and a delicate problem for the State Department. There are three books, all written by women and all contradictory. And there are the consular records, stored away in Washington on reels of microfilm.

The story of the Colony, celebrated by Selma Lagerlöf and embodied by the American Colony Hotel is now beginning to attract the interest of Ph.D. doctoral candidates in Jerusalem. But I think that I was the first to read all of the different categories of material which the Colony's turbulent history produced; I did so simply because I found it such a fascinatingly unusual, if marginal, slice of Jerusalem's history. Besides, where else but in the Holy City could a commune based on Christian brotherhood develop into a corporation managing a luxury hotel?

Much of the action in the Lagerlöf novel took place far to the east of the steps, at the "pasha's palace" on Nablus Road; there, at what is now the American Colony Hotel, probably not one in a thousand of the guests who have enjoyed breakfast or a drink at dusk in its flower-bordered courtyard, with its little fountain and tile-topped tables or who have attended receptions in the big room upstairs under its blue-and-gold Damascene ceiling, has any notion of the conflicts that once raged here.

And while many Jerusalemites know Horatio Vester and his sister, Anna Grace Lind, both of whom have been managers of the hotel, not many know that their grandmother, the Chicago matron who came to Jerusalem to await the coming of the Messiah, was the object of obsessive hatred at the American Consulate.

I am probably the only recent guest at the hotel who has gone back to the Chicago newspapers' coverage of that sensational trial nearly a century ago, when the American Colony defended its principles, and Anna Spafford took the stand to describe her views, which were actually a form of Zionism.

"I had suffered great loss and affliction," said Anna Spafford to the

JERUSALEM

Sderot Weizmann

Panim Meirot
Zichron Meiron
Zichron Ya'akov
Petah
Obal

Star of David

Rome
Yafo
N
Sc

Kelav Sofer
Givat Shaul
Onkelos
Ben Uziel
Aman Gaon
Naina
Kotler
Bet
Shlomo
Ben Zion
Beines
Maimon
Sderot Sha
(Yehuda Hale

Kanfei Nesharim
Yemin Avot
Ben Dor
Ha'aliya

Kiryat Moshe

Hirsch
Hamon
Ha'aliya

Kiryat Moshe
Sderot Herzl
Rahel Imenu
Epstein

Wolffsohn

Ha

Beit Hakerem
Bityamin

Kaelon
Ruppin

Ha'shazim
Beit Hakerem
Hechalutz

Wise

Yefeh Nof
Bialik
Hchalutz
Gianot

Birhei Hen
Hamevasrim
Brachyahu
Hchalutz
Habanai

Hebrew
University

Yad Vashem
Brachyahu
Hasatat

Sderot Herzl

Hazikaron

Hanassa
Sharei Bayit

Ein Kerem
Levin
Haktav
Harav Uziel
Shalian

Olsvanger
Shma'aahu
Tura Ya'avor
Bayit Vegan

Brazil
Hantke
Gordon
Frank

Hevron
Burocho
Wardrug
Mithlin

Motzkin
Zarikwill
Rabinoviz

Szold Tahon
Chile
Yanush
Skorczak
Assael

Uruguay
Mexico

Ringelblum
Stern

Hakarkom
Hanard

Costa Rica
Hanurit

Costa Rica

Derech Manahat

Selma Lagerlöf St

Herzog
Heller
Sarna
Gold
Shahal

Shimoni

Shmuel

Eliyahu Golomb

Kadoshei Struma
Sharett

Paff
Yehuda Hana

Dov Hos
Hashomer
Saber

Yitzhak
Maria
Bar Yohai

0   400   800
m

jury, "and wanted to draw very near to God." The group had chosen Jerusalem "because we wished to be there when God brought the Jews back. The changes in Jerusalem are wonderful. God is fulfilling his work. Ten years ago there were only 4,000 Jews in Jerusalem. Now there are 40,000, and colonies of them are building outside the city wall..."

Mrs. Spafford's statistics owed more to her messianic hopes than to facts. While there had been over 10,000 Jews in Jerusalem in 1875, twenty years before the lawsuit, at the time she gave her evidence the total population of the city was not very much more than 40,000, of whom Jews numbered some 28,000.

At the time of the step-naming ceremony, I had been engrossed by the consular reports and had read all three of the books, written by three women in which the Colony is the central subject, I felt, therefore, entitled to a certain flow of superiority over the others present, who included such VIPs as the Swedish Ambassador, the Mayor of Jerusalem, the niece and nephew of Selma Lagerlöf, who had come from Sweden for the event, and the grandchildren of Anna Spafford.

Very soon after Consul Merrill's warning that day in 1900, in a long-vanished hotel in the Old City, Miss Lagerlöf and her friend arrived by carriage at the imposing house on Nablus Road to which the growing Colony had by now moved from the Old City and which is today the American Colony Hotel. They were met by Bertha Spafford, aged 22, radiantly beautiful — as she still would be five decades later — and in love. But marriage, as we shall see, was not permitted at the Colony.

Bertha took the guests to the big room upstairs, and under that glamorous blue-and-gold ceiling they first met Anna Spafford. She was 58, plump and white-haired, with a very soft voice, and a good decade's experience at telling her exotic story. Born in Norway, she had been taken to America as a young girl during the great Scandinavian migration to the U.S.

Anna immediately began a friendly conversation. "Ah, so you are from Sweden? You have many compatriots here then, and they will be delighted to see you."

Miss Lagerlöf at first sat nervously on the edge of her chair, "as though she were afraid of contamination," as Bertha later described it. Merrill's warnings were thrillingly distinct in her mind. Nothing here, she had been told, was as it seemed by daylight.

But then Bertha went off to call the Swedish members and to see about tea and cake, and Anna began to tell the story.

"Mrs. Spafford, you are the best-looking woman I have ever seen to be so wicked," said Miss Lagerlöf with a smile, during their discussion of the American Consul's accusations. The ice broke, and then the Swedes began to troop in — nearly 70 of them, farmers with names like Lars and Katrin,

Olof and Eric...

The Swedes told their part of the story, and Anna Spafford told hers. What Selma Lagerlöf heard that day, and in the visits to come, is related in our second source, *Our Jerusalem*, the memoirs of Anna's daughter, Bertha Spafford Vester. Her book is no literary masterpiece, but it gives a fascinating slice of Jerusalem history as seen through acclimatized yet obstinately American eyes. First published in America in 1950 with an introduction by Lowell Thomas, and the following year in England with an introduction by Sir Ronald Storrs, it was reprinted in Lebanon at some later unspecified date. Careful readers may notice that in the later edition, vitriolic anti-Israel insertions have been made by an unacknowledged hand. Mrs. Vester's book dismisses the whole Swedish connection, to which Selma Lagerlöf devoted two volumes, in a very few pages.

Our Jerusalem describes the childhood of both Horatio and Anna — his, a comfortable background in Upstate New York, hers stark poverty in Scandinavia. The event which set in motion their pilgrimage to Jerusalem was the Great Chicago Fire of 1871, in which 250 people died and which plunged the city into chaos, crime, and an atmosphere of apocalypse.

The Spaffords were a normal and prosperous young couple, up until the fire. So Selma Lagerlöf learned from Anna, and so did Bertha; and so, too, did the third woman who wrote about the Colony: the events appear, as fiction and as fact, in three books. Perhaps Horatio was more devout than many American lawyers, but they lived well in a pleasant Chicago suburb with their four little girls. Horatio was active in business and civic activities. The fire started a chain of events which changed all that.

To recover from caring for the city's refugees and from the difficult birth of her fourth daughter, Anna Spafford sailed with the children for Europe on the French luxury liner "Ville du Havre," Horatio, delayed by business, planned to follow later. At about 2 a.m. on November 22, 1873 the liner was rammed by an English ship and sank in 16 minutes. The four little girls and their governess were among the 230 passengers drowned; their mother was one of the 57 saved.

In her novel, Selma Lagerlöf calls Mrs. Spafford "Mrs. Gordon"; to the doomed ship she gives the name "L'Univers." The name is, of course, symbolic, for the author was a pacifist deeply troubled by human discord and, in all her work, she was concerned with the fate of mankind. But while she raised the story she heard to a metaphysical level, she reduced the details: Mrs. Gordon loses two little boys in the shipwreck. Apparently the novelist felt that the factual death of four children might simply not seem credible to the reader. Mrs. Gordon hears the same divine words that Anna Spafford heard: "Death is easy. To live is difficult."

Bereft and back in Chicago (we are now in Bertha's account), Anna gave birth to a little boy in 1876, and a girl, Bertha, in 1878. The boy died of scarlet fever when he was three. According to the theology of the day, the Spaffords' afflictions were God's punishment for sin. But it was becoming harder and harder for them to accept this doctrine. In an era of hell-fire-and-brimstone theology, the Spaffords became early disciples of a God-is-love belief; for this premature liberalism, Horatio was expelled from the Presbyterian church in Chicago he had helped found.

Early in 1881, a year after the death of their son and soon after the birth of another girl, Grace, the Spaffords decided to make the long voyage to Jerusalem. They travelled with the two surviving babies of their seven children, and with a few friends who shared their nonconformist views. The press picked up the story and called them "Overcomers" and wrote that they "expect to receive a new and direct revelation from the Lord." Horatio wrote to a friend that in Jerusalem he hoped "to find peace," to try to "see things plainly and more in perspective," and "to learn how to live, suffer, and especially to conquer."

They did not come as missionaries, although they did convert to Christianity several Arabs and Jews — the result, they insisted of the example of real Christian living rather than moralizing. They helped the poor of the Old City with instruction in hygiene and education.

The timing of their arrival fits in with a wave of interest in the Holy Land that was felt in widely separated parts of the world. The year 1882 marks the start of the Bilu "return to Israel" movement of Jews in Eastern Europe; messianic sectarianism was alive and well in America; in Sweden, the stage was set for apocalyptic religious fervour: and in Yemen, in the inaccessible desert of Saudi Arabia, a group of Jews decided the time had come to return to the homeland. One of these Yemenite groups — whom the Jews of Jerusalem considered Arabs — the Colony supported for decades.

From the start, the Spaffords were more intrigued by the "biblical" look of the Arab-speaking Sephardi and Yemenite Jews than by the Yiddish-speaking Ashkenazim from Eastern Europe. The Colony children grew up speaking Arabic, and the Colony's ties tended increasingly to be with the Arab population. Decades later, the sympathies of the Colony were undoubtedly on the Arab side of the Jewish-Arab conflict.

The contemporary outgrowth of the Christian example is the Anna Spafford Child Care Centre in the Old City, directed by Anna's granddaughter, Anna Grace. In another form, under Jordanian rule it was the only children's hospital in Jordan. The Centre is in the house the group originally occupied in 1881. The hotel did not develop into anything like its present form till more than half a century later. The original idea for a hotel incidentally, came from an old friend who lived in Jaffa, none other than the grandfather of the actor Peter Ustinov.

In the early days nobody did any real work, a point which especially irritated the hardworking consuls. The expectation was that "God would provide," which He usually did. Horatio taught English at a Jewish school, but he did it without pay. His colleague and friend there was Eliezer Ben-Yehuda, the father of modern Hebrew. In 1888 Horatio died; Anna took over, and the enmity of the consuls came into the open.

Bertha married Frederick Vester, the Jerusalem-born son of German-Swiss missionaries, and they had six children, all born in Jerusalem. Bertha was as pragmatic as her mother was mystical, and she and Frederick ran the Colony with efficiency and sound business sense. She reigned in a certain segment of Jerusalem society as an uncrowned queen, and during the Mandatory period infinitely preferred the polished manners of British officers to the noisy endeavours of the Jews.

The third of the source books about the Colony is *Dalarna Folk in the Holy Land*, by Edith Larsson, a Swedish member of the Colony, who became Bertha Vester's competitor for leadership and, to put it bluntly, her enemy. Edith was the model for the daughter of Selma Lagerlöf's fictional character Helgum, the simple Swedish sailor and religious leader who led his countrymen to join Anna Spafford's group in Jerusalem. Edith was born in Chicago; in 1896 she was brought to Jerusalem as a three-year-old child, exactly as Bertha had been 15 years earlier.

Her book of memoirs is a rebuttal of both Selma Lagerlöf and Bertha Vester. In an introduction, a Swedish professor observes that Lagerlöf's novel is overly romanticized. The emotional motivation and inner lives of the peasants, he suggests, "was probably foreign" to Selma Lagerlöf, who, after all, came from the middle classes "and did not have the right contact with those who did experience this religious awakening." (The Swedish edition, published in 1957, is a translation from Mrs. Larsson's English manuscript: by the time she got around to writing her memoirs, she had forgotten her Swedish.)

Edith describes how her father came to regret his decision to bring his flock into the Colony, and how his position of leadership was usurped by the Americans — first by Anna (who appears in this book as "Mrs. Gates," and whom Edith respected as an idealistic, if imperious leader) and later by Bertha (who appears as "Mrs. F.," in a most uncomplimentary guise).

In addition to these three books, there are those thousands of pages of consular reports from Jerusalem. There are the protocols of not one but two court cases heard in America. There is a top secret but mysteriously missing Inspector General's report filed in Constantinople in 1908, judging the Colony; and, in our day, there is many a paperback Near-Eastern thriller for which the American Colony Hotel provides the glamorous setting.

The action of the first volume of *Jerusalem*, set in the Swedish village of Nos in Dalarna, has been dramatized and has been presented there every summer since 1959 as *The Ingmar Play*, after its hero. The second volume, in which the action moves to the Holy City, has yet to be produced as a sound-and-light spectacle in the American Colony Hotel's charming courtyard.

No current blockbuster can beat Lagerlöf's melodrama. Here is a taste of a bit of Volume One: Ingmar, the hero, goes with his sweetheart, Gertrude, and his widowed sister Karin to a village dance in a hut on a hill. Suddenly the lights go out, a strange howling is heard. An unknown preacher, Helgum, appears and thunders about sin and the end of the world. Karin is paralysed by the thunderstorm and the preacher's doom-laden words, but Helgum cures her by a miracle. The villlagers are caught in a revivalist fever. Helgum goes to America, meets a group of Americans with similar messianic religious convictions. He writes back to the villagers ordering them to sell their farms and emigrate to Jerusalem, to experience the Apocalypse in the Holy City. Ingmar, in despair at the thought of selling the family farm, agrees to marry Gunhild, the daughter of a rich man. Gertrude, drifting into madness, takes this as a sign that she must go to Jerusalem. Ingmar discovers that his wife is under a curse. Her male children are doomed to be blind and idiots, and their first child dies...

Things are just as tragic in Part Two, when the Swedes join the Colony in Jerusalem, but there are also charming chapters with a legend-like quality. One of them tells how the Americans acquired the big new house which the new contingents moved into as soon as they arrived — 77 Swedes from Chicago and 38 from Nos, both under Helgum's leadership. The village group turned up on a sweltering day in August 1896, in their peasant costumes, and unpacked their looms, and carpentry and farming tools in the palace built around a courtyard. The Colony now numbered 120, with the Swedes the majority.

The new house, according to Spafford family history, was a palace which had been standing empty since the death of its owner, a Turkish official, Rabbah Effendi, who had lived there with his three wives. The hotel's plan still dimly reflects its harem origin. Each wife had her summer room on the ground floor, opening out on the courtyard, and her winter room upstairs, along a corridor with arched windows also overlooking the courtyard. This upstairs corridor led to the large room with the blue ceiling, under whose gold stars the effendi dispensed justice.

But not one of his three wives produced a male heir and the pasha had therefore married a young fourth wife. He was especially fond of her, and so she got not just one room downstairs and one upstairs, but two on each floor — today suites at the hotel.

The effendi's new marital happiness had fatal results. Soon after his fourth marriage he died, leaving 140 heirs and an empty house. The Colony bought out half of them in 1895 and took possession, but it was years before the rest were tracked down. So much for the facts.

In Selma Lagerlöf's account of how the house was acquired, the owner was not a typical effendi with four wives, but a grieving widower and, for a Moslem, unusually monogamous. Baram Pasha, as she calls him, built his beautiful house for his (one) wife, "whom he loved above everything in this world." Things went wrong as soon as this atypical pasha moved in. The first week a daughter (not a son) died. The second week another daughter (not a son) followed, and the third week, his wife died. He had the mansion shut up and swore never to set foot in it again.

Now the novelist deals for the first time with the antagonism to the Colony. In a chapter entitled "The Jerusalem that Kills," the "Catholic speaks evil of Protestant, the Methodist of the Quaker, the Lutheran of the Reformist, the Russian of the Armenian." The Jews are absent from this attractive list of residents in a city where there is no tolerance but only envy, and where "in the name of God, everyone hates everyone else."

By now, in Selma Lagerlöf's novel, the Colonists — Americans and new Swedish arrivals — have moved into the palace rented to them by grieving Baram Pasha. The Colonists began to notice "a marked change in the attitude toward them" — first "minor rudeness, then real insults." It would pass, they thought, as it had before. But instead, things grew worse. Finally, a friendly German explained to Mrs. Gordon (Anna Spafford): "It is the missionaries who are vilifying you. They cannot bear the thought of your having gained so many converts." They accused the Colonists of immorality, of not allowing marriage "as God has commanded," and "the Americans, from the Consul down," were the loudest critics.

Some of these Americans went to see Baram Pasha and told him "vile things" about his tenants. How could he allow "such disreputable people" to live in the house he had built out of love for his wife? The old pasha decided to see for himself. In a detailed chapter, he goes expecting to see "dancing women and evil-doers, drinking and throwing dice," whom he will drive from his house. Instead, of course, and hard though it is for him to believe his eyes, he sees only beautifully-behaved children and an absolute idyll of communal activity — a kind of Brook Farm in the Levant.

A "Miss Young" — (Bertha, barely disguised) — who speaks fluent Arabic, takes him on a guided tour of the laundry, bakery, carpentry shop, kitchen and sewing room. All is "strict orderliness and simplicity." Miss Young quite bowls over the pasha with her pure beauty. As for Anna, "her face expressed rare intelligence and authority, and although she was simply dressed in a plain black gown, one could see that she was accustomed to rule over many people." The forces of sweetness and light finally win the pasha over completely. He deeply regrets his earlier suspicions, and sends his beautiful white donkey to the Colony as a gift, to take the little children to school from his house to the old house on the wall.

This fictional landlord was, of course, based on Anna's tales to Miss Lagerlöf. Six years later, in 1906, she was to run through her standard repertoire again to an American journalist, with wide-ranging results. In the article the journalist published in *Appleton's Magazine*, the Consul — Edwin Wallace by then, who succeeded Merrill and continued the battle against the Colony — went to the effendi and "offered to use his office" to evict the Colony. As reported by Anna, the effendi replied: "I have known the Americans for many years and trust them. I do not know you at all. God has given me the Americans for my friends. It is His will that I do not betray them." Wallace sued *Appleton's* for $50,000 for libel, and lost.

A very different story in a very different style is told by Wallace himself in the record he sent to Washington nine years earlier of his interrogation of two defectors from the Colony. One of them, J.B. Adamson, of Harvey, Illinois was interrogated at the Consulate one morning. in April 1897, and the event was witnessed by a visiting Presbyterian Minister from South Wales, who must have been all ears. The verbatim transcript, elegantly handwritten runs thus:

How long have you known the Spafford Community?
Eighteen months.
When did you come to Jerusalem?
On April 7, 1896.
Have you lived in the Spafford House during this time?
Yes, without interruption.
Are you living there now?
No, we left on Saturday.
Why did you leave?
Because we were thoroughly out of harmony with the conditions of existence.
To which conditions did you object?
To the religious and social conditions.
What were the religious conditions to which you objected?
The answer to this is involved in the name they assume, i.e., "The Over-comers."
What do the Spaffords mean by the name "Overcomers"?
That they conquer all natural affections and desires is their meaning.
What is their method of conquering?
By exposing themselves to all sorts of temptations, particularly sexual.
Is immorality — as that word is generally understood — openly indulged in?
Not openly.
Do you have reason to believe that immorality is secretly practised?
Reasons sufficient to convince any reasonable person that immorality must result.

What are those reasons that convinced you?

The general atmosphere of the Spafford house... Mrs. Spafford has proclaimed that the marriage relation is wrong, and has given permission to married men to mingle freely with the young women and has exhorted the latter not to be afraid of the men but to put themselves freely in the way of the "brothers," as the men are termed.

What was the result of this advice from Mrs. Spafford?

It was freely and openly acted upon. Married men were seen by us on various occasions suspiciously intimate with certain female members of the household. As late as one o'clock in the morning, men have been with women in dark parts of the house, and afterwards, in public meetings at which children were present, these night wanderers professed that they were "seeking the flesh and not the spirit." At these public meetings, confessions were frequently made that could not but cause a blush of shame to any right-thinking person.

What did Mrs. Spafford say in reply to these confessions?

"Now you are clean," or "Now you are white, having made this confession."

Did you ever express disapproval of these practices while you were members?

Yes.

How was your disapproval met?

By such language and treatment as really terrified us into silence.

You were not, then, free agents while residing in that house?

No.

Why, then, did you not leave?

Because they had taken all our means. The community has all things in common, in the hands of a treasurer. No money is ever given to the members, not even enough to buy a postage stamp.

How then have you the means to live now?

Friends in America have sent us 100 dollars. With that we are starting in the hope of reaching America.

Are there any other disaffected Americans who would leave if they could?

There are; but they are in the same condition we were, with no one to assist them. Such a spirit of espionage is kept over them and such spiritual terror exercised that they are not allowed to converse freely with outsiders or with each other.

Why do they not complain to the Consul?

They cannot. They are terrified by a spiritual power which they cannot resist. Their wills are powerless.

In his covering memorandum, which is so detailed as to make any present-day diplomat blush with shame (he ran the Consulate almost

95

Swedish novelist, Selma Lagerlöf.

First edition of *Jerusalem*.

Courtyard of American Colony hotel.

Anna Grace Vester Lind.

singlehanded), Wallace summarizes the situation:

"The Community is composed of religious fanatics whose fanaticism leads them to the commission of acts illegal and at variance with the usages of decent society. In any other place the community would be broken up by the police, for it outrages society.

"The leader of the Community is a Mrs. Spafford, formerly of Chicago, a woman remarkable in many respects. She is an absolute autocrat over the household which bears her name and never dares oppose her. By falshehood, she induces the ignorant and unsuspecting to sell all they have in America and come here... Then they cannot leave...

"The household at present consists of 140 souls, most of whom have come from the U.S. The last accession numbered 70... I am satisfied the majority would leave if they could. Their condition is most deplorable. Still, I do not feel justified in interfering officially as no direct complaint has ever been laid before me by anyone now residing among them."

The last two sentences have been marked in Washington by a cautious bureaucratic hand. Wallace continues with the statement that the Community has done "untold, but well known injury to many persons," and that "Mrs. Spafford claims to be beyond the reach of law and boldly tells her dupes that her sovereignty transcends any earthly authority."

At the time of Selma Lagerlöf's visit, Consul Merrill had returned to Jerusalem as Wallace's successor a matter of shifts in Democratic and Republican regimes — and was once again preparing one of his periodic outpourings about the Colony, heavy with irony, for the benefit of the State Department:

"Passions and appetites can become spiritualized," which ends all such concepts as "law, human or divine." This done, "there is no Bible, no Christ, no sin, no sacraments, no marriage, no offspring, for these all belong to the flesh, which is vile." Once one rises above all that, "then two 'pure affinities' can sleep together in one bed, there is no sin in it whatever... Provided they do not happen to have a baby. That undoes the whole business."

The Colony also prohibited traditional medical treatment; this, it was charged, resulted in several needless deaths. Doctors' visits were not permitted — until, as Edith Larsson bitterly observed, Anna's daughter Bertha became pregnant with the first of her five babies.

It was not true, Merrill claimed, that all worldly goods were shared equally at the Colony, as early Christian communism required. In the dining room, Mrs. Spafford's special table was served delicious meals, while the others got "only the poorest food" — rice with stones in it, stale bread, the worst coffee. Bertha "dresses in silks" while the others wear "the meanest, coarsest clothes." Bertha alone was "allowed to take music lessons, paid for by the community," and there was "always a donkey ready for Mrs. Spafford while the old, feeble sisters must always walk."

Mrs. Spafford had a simple explanation for this, according to a disgruntled member who had left the Colony and come to Merrill with juicy information. Arrangements were as they were because "she herself, Bertha (and one other member) have overcome all desire for these things and therefore were entitled to the good things of this world."

One of the Colonists' problems was that they were never permitted to see the actual charges against them. In her book, Mrs. Vester, writing 50 years after Consul Wallace's venemous memoranda — which she never saw — decided to come to grips with the celibacy issue (by then long forgotten) in her own way.

"I think it best that we be perfectly frank," she wrote, about "the trouble that was distorted by evil minds into charges of moral laxity... The actual animus was over the theological questions which in a day of fanatical dogmatism aroused the intensest passions against any who were in any way different." That was why so much of the Colony's life at this time was taken up with "persecution" by which "enemies of our Group sought to discredit it." Here is her background to the conflict:

"Some time after my parents came to Jerusalem, Father told Mother in private that he wanted to live Matthew 19:12, 'and there are eunuchs which have made themselves eunuchs for the kingdom of heaven's sake.' Nothing about this resolution was mentioned at the time to any of the other members of the Group." Anna finally spoke of this to another couple in the group, and found "they had made much the same choice.

"It was a solemn undertaking, a personal dedication which did not concern any except those who chose to live it. Celibacy was never meant to become a governing canon of the Group. Somehow this had leaked out. It was misinterpreted and degraded by our opponents."

After her father's death in 1888, "Dr. Merrill became less cautious in his attacks and accused us of forbidding marriage," and apparently briefed Wallace well in this interesting area. Besides, Mrs. Vester adds in her explanation, "there were no young people in the Colony at the time to get married, so we had no means of disputing this new charge."

But — which time? By 1897 the Colony was fairly bursting with nubile young Swedes; and for some, the prohibition of marriage — which does seem to have been the clear law — meant personal tragedy. Dutiful young daughters accompanied their families from Dalarna to Jerusalem, leaving behind boys they wanted to marry. They died spinsters decades later, to lie alone under gravestones in the Colony's cemetery on the Mount of Olives.

Edith Larsson, in her book makes clear the Swedes' resentment that Mrs. Spafford maintained her law until the time her own daughter, Bertha, wanted to marry in 1904. Until then, she notes, only Swedes had wished to do so.

Devotedly pro-Spaffordite though she was, Selma Lagerlöf also makes this clear, in an idyllic chapter of flower-picking one spring morning. Gertrude is walking with a young Swede who has fallen in love with her; Gertrude has tried hard to give up all "earthly love," as required. So, too, has this new young man, whose name is Bo. But first, the novelist explains the facts of Colony life. Among the flower-pickers were:

"the beautiful Miss Young and an English youth who had been in the Colony about two years. Bo knew, as everyone did, that the Englishman was in love with Miss Young and had come among them in the hope of marrying her. There was no doubt that the girl was fond of him; but of course the Gordonites could not relax their stringent rules in her case any more than for the others, and thus the two had gone on living at the Colony, hoping against hope. They walked side by side, and spoke only to each other..."

Bo makes a valiant attempt to convince himself that all is well with him on this basis of enforced inner serenity. He says to himself,

"I'm quite satisfied with things as they are. Much as I think of Gertrude, I no longer desire to marry her. All that agonizing and love-sickness that kept me in a state of torment in the past has gone now..."

Everybody picks flowers and enjoys the beauties of nature and talks about universal love and brotherhood. But finally Bo realizes he has been lying to himself. Back at the Colony at sunset, he and Gertrude sit and talk under an old sycamore tree outside the gate. Bo suddenly puts his head in his hands and, "overcome by love," groans,

"No, Lord, I am not as a little child; I cannot enter Thy Kingdom. Perhaps the others can, but I cannot put out the fire in my soul and deaden the life in my body..."

Selma Lagerlöf's account of the Colony stops, of course, at the year 1900. We turn to Edith Larsson's version of the theological thunderbolt that struck four years later, when Bertha finally persuaded her mother to reverse her dogma that "marriage is a licence to sin." Suddenly, after seven years of what had seemed a hopeless romance, Anna announced that 23-year-old Bertha, and Frederick Vester, twelve years her senior, would be permitted to marry.

What had for so long been denounced as lust and carnal evil in a regime that had led to so many tragedies was now to be celebrated in a festival of cake-baking and floral decorations. Anna had explained the change at a remarkable meeting in the big room upstairs:

"The time has now come when marriage can be taken the right way, and we can render to Caesar the things belonging to Caesar." Till now, she went on in her low voice, the Colonists had been put to the test in their life in Jerusalem. Slowly, they had advanced spiritually — and financially — because of their selfless service.

Other weddings followed this milestone, though never without Anna's approval. Every young man always consulted her before daring to propose to a girl "to be one with him," as engagements were called. In 1909 the same German pastor officiated at the marriage of Anna's younger daughter Grace, about whom very little is heard in Bertha's memoirs, to John Whiting.

Three years later, Edith Larsson was permitted to marry. Her husband, who was the Swedish Consul in Jerusalem, happened to be named Lars Larsson; though he was known later as Lewis Larsson.

Edith was often accused of "being too much like her father" and of "wanting to lead." But at 18, she was tense and nervous before her wedding, and very confused when Anna informed her that marriage was "a union of the spirit," and that "all earthly desires must be subjected to the great ideal of the Kingdom of God."

Until her death in 1923, Anna remained the spiritual arbiter of the Colony. But she was never interested in practical matters, and Bertha and her husband took increasing charge of daily life and, most important, business. Bertha had, as a child, suffered from the stigma of belonging to a peculiar group. She was determined to make the Colony socially acceptable, and this was achieved with intelligence, charm and energy.

Until World War I, life at the Colony was an idyll in an oasis of American hygiene and culture, surrounded by Ottoman inefficiency and primitive ways. Some of the younger Swedish members began to consider themselves exploited. But even Edith Larsson, who later led the "Swedish revolt" against the Americans, describes the complicated and delightful picnics, the campfires, the evening entertainments of musical chairs and charades, and the robust American patriotism of the little outpost.

At the Christmas season, there were special performances — one evening was set aside for the Moslem ladies — and the children recited such popular numbers as "Over the Hill to the Poorhouse." On Good Friday, the Colonists walked *en masse* to the Garden of Gethsemane with lanterns and hymn books, to raise their voices under Jerusalem's stars in "Man of Sorrows" and "It was alone the Saviour Prayed."

The most enthusiastic celebration, because it was the most American, was the 4th of July. Up went a series of tents in the garden, and preparations and rehearsals went on for days. There were prizes for the best "tableaux." In one memorable one, Edith Larsson was the Statue of Liberty, in white muslin and a silvery headdress, holding a horn of plenty. During the dress rehearsal, Anna nervously watched Edith posing without moving for 20 minutes, and thoughtfully suggested an invisible prop under the drapery, to help hold Edith's right hand aloft.

100

Under the Middle Eastern sky, there were egg races and sack races and needle-threading races, and the Colony choir and orchestra, and by now also the Colony brass band, played the "Star Spangled Banner." There were sandwiches and tea, buttered scones, cakes, ice-cream and lemonade. And everybody gave three cheers for America: Hip, hip, hurrah.

The old communal austerity was fading. Every day still began and ended with a hymn, but the Colony's business branches — photography, baking, a gift shop, and eventually tourism — expanded every year. "They came to do good," a British judge observed some years later, "and stayed to do well."

In this golden age of tourism, visitors from America and Europe arrived each Easter season, and each year told their friends that a visit to the Colony was a "must." "We were welcomed although perfect strangers, and invited to partake of refreshments," a visiting journalist wrote in a post-Lagerlöf, pre-World War I year. As always, they heard from Anna about the romantic past, the good deeds of the Colony, the nature of Christian socialism, the Kingdom of God to come, and the thrilling difficulties with the consuls.

For the tourist seasons before World War I, the Colonists moved out of their rooms in the big house to make room for paying guests. A real hotel as such did not start till well into the British Mandate period, and then only on a small scale; the biggest impetus and expansion came only after the Six Day War, when Jerusalem was reunited.

The Colony's story during this century, or since Selma Lagerlöf's visit, is, of course, outside the framework of her steps and novel. But we might summarize very briefly some of the things that happened to some of her characters and prototypes.

Because of all the "unpleasantness," Consul Merrill was reassigned by the State Department to a new and ghastly post — Georgetown, British Guiana, at an annual salary of $3,500. He tried unsuccessfully to appeal, for by now he was suffering from cancer of the throat and unable to speak normally. ("The judgment of God," it was rumoured in Jerusalem.) With a glass tube in his throat, the hapless Consul wrote of "swamps, alligators, mosquitoes, fevers, blacks, and 120 inches of rain a year," pleading for a better post. But times were changing and Washington was heartless. In 1908, after nearly 30 years in the Foreign Service, Selah Merrill resigned. The victory of the Colonists — Selma Lagerlöf's team — was complete. Poor old Dr. Merrill returned to Jerusalem as a private citizen, and his portly, peace-loving wife actually saw to it that he and the Spafford family were present at the same Jerusalem party one evening in 1910.

The Colony was by now socially acceptable. Its romantic and beleaguered past came to a complete end with World War I, which changed all of Jerusalem, and the entire Middle East, beyond recognition.

During the fighting, the Colony played a valiant role, running a hospital and caring for Turkish and Allied soldiers alike, although the Americans were fervently pro-Allied and the Swedes were pacifistically neutral.

Greetings from Selma Lagerlöf were brought from Sweden during the war by the famous explorer, Sven Hedin, whose book about Jerusalem (dedicated to the defeat of England and the victory of Germany) was illustrated by photographs made by Lewis Larsson. The famous photograph of the surrender of Jerusalem to Allenby's soldiers is also a Colony photograph — and the white flag, according to Vester family tradition, was a bedsheet from the Colony's hospital.

During the British Mandate, the Colony was the elegant "in" place for British officers, with tennis, good talk, and tea and cakes in the courtyard; the lovely Vester girls at parties in the big upstairs room were admiringly said to be "as beautiful as flowers." It was all far, far different from the mystical and embattled beginnings.

Selma Lagerlöf had not forgotten the old saga. In 1925, at a Christian conference in Stockholm, she delivered an impassioned speech based on the story of the American Colony. Once again she described the dramatic scene of the sinking ship when Anna, facing death, heard "a mighty voice" telling her that "it is easy to die, what is difficult is to live." She recapitulated the early Christian aims of the Colony, "to search out the sick in the narrow lanes of the Holy City, to feed the hungry and help the orphaned, and to live a simple communal life." She recalled the arrival of the Swedes, and the unique blending of "Anglo-Saxon energy with oriental mysticism and northern sincerity." And she resurrected the attacks on the Colonists by the Christian missionaries, who "accused them of leading despicable lives." Anna Spafford, said Selma Lagerlöf, dreamed of "unity — unity with one's fellow men as they now are — selfish, self-righteous, false, dissipated, sinful."

The final blow to Anna's visionary dream of unity came a few years later when the Swedes, led by Edith and Lewis Larsson, broke away from the Colony and moved out into their own homes in the expanding city. The Colony ended as it began, with the Americans, plus a few very old and still very devout Swedes. It became a corporation, and property was divided in a hearing under an impartial arbitrator who came from Cairo for the purpose. A friend of mine who attended that hearing told me the arbitrator had difficulty keeping his mind on the issues because he couldn't help staring at Bertha Vester (then in her late fifties) "because she was such a handsome woman." She died in 1970, aged 87, active nearly to the end, an American citizen who served Jerusalem under four regimes — the Turks, the British, the Jordanians and the Israelis. Two of her children continued to do so — Anna Grace Spafford at the children's centre, Horatio at the hotel. As an old-time Jerusalemite observed of the two,

"Now it is Horatio and Anna again, just as it once was."

Anna Grace's beliefs are, in fact, close to those of her grandmother, for she devoutly believes that the return of the Jews to their homeland must precede the coming of the Messianic Age, and that all events are part of a divine plan, no matter how strewn with difficulties the working out of that plan may be. Like Anna, Anna Grace accepts all human beings as God's children. Without her faith, she could not have given decades of her life to what amounts to social work for slum children in the Old City, living alone in a house on the wall full of memories.

Bertha, Anna Grace's mother, was on the best of terms with King Hussein of Jordan, and received a medal of honour from him. Anna Grace was awarded the city of Jerusalem's highest honour by Mayor Teddy Kollek for her work on behalf of Arab children at the Anna Spafford Children's Centre.

Anna Grace managed the American Colony Hotel for several years. Later, her brother gave up his practise as a London barrister and returned to Jerusalem to do so.

If Horatio has modelled the hotel on anything except itself, he has sought the effect of a good British hotel. But the atmosphere, and the cuisine, are a unique blend of Middle East, Colonial British, and 19th-century America — the recipe for the American Colony's famous chocolate cake came from Chicago nearly a century ago.

Right after the Six Day War, when the hotel once again became accessible to Israelis, there were those who arrived in droves to enjoy the unusual charm — both the youngsters, who did not know it existed, and the old-timers, who remembered. Others have always looked at the place with suspicion, or at least discomfort. Hardly one of the guests — foreign correspondents, diplomats, spies — is aware of all the conflicts that have raged in that tranquil courtyard.

Bertha's old adversary Edith Larsson, like Bertha herself, did not take kindly to noisy Jewish democracy after the genteel pleasures of bygone days; one of her sons had been arrested by the Hagana during the War of Independence. After the Six Day War, a very elderly widow, she moved to an old-age home in Sweden, mourning the warm, exotic city she had known all her life. The high point in this sad ending was her appearance in a Swedish television documentary which, once again, told the Colony story, with emphasis on the Swedish connection.

Selma Lagerlöf, I am sure, would have relished what happened during the party at the hotel the evening of her step-naming day, for as the guests were gathering, all the lights went out exactly as they did in her dramatic scene in the novel, when the young people are dancing and suddenly a terrifying realization of evil and doom sweeps down on them, and the hut is plunged into darkness. Except that, then, the candles were put out by an old fiddler who understands elves; and in our case, the candles were quickly lit by the efficient hotel staff when we were plunged into darkness by electrical power failure.

We were given, not a feeling of doom, but wonderful hors d'oeuvres; and guests were, of course, entirely unruffled, unlike poor Ingmar and Gertrude in the doom-filled dark. I talked to the daughter of Eliezer Ben-Yehuda who, as a baby, had been pulled through a case of typhoid fever by the American Colony nurses, the first child in Jerusalem to survive the disease; and I chatted with the wife of the Finnish general in command of the UN Peacekeeping Force.

By candlelight, Selma Lagerlöf's niece showed me a postcard her aunt had sent to Sweden from Jerusalem 75 years earlier. The message, which she translated for me, said that the writer was very happy to be in the Holy Land, the cradle of Christianity; that the roads were bad, and everything very expensive.

Below the blue-and-gold ceiling, invisible this night because the impromptu candles were too weak, the chatter continued affably over the drinks. Nobody, of course, mentioned the Apocalypse, or the battle between good and evil, or the sinful ways of mankind, which once constituted the urgent and solemn subjects here. Selma Lagerlöf has Mrs. Gordon cry out one night, "Oh Lord, why have you ordered me to preach unity? Strife and conflict are the only realities since the beginning of the world." I thought of Merrill, whose ghost, in the end, deserves some kind of congratulation at this unquestioned triumph of conventional small-talk over mysterious nonconformism.

Suddenly the lights came on, and the ceiling sprang back to its usual splendour. Just then a friend arrived, who knew of my American Colony readings. We had often sat in the courtyard, and I had kept him up to date on the Consul's accusations and Anna Spafford's faith in her vision of the wonderful world to come, after Armageddon. My friend's comment was, "This is the way the world ends. Not with a bang, but a luxury hotel."

8
The Mighty Baron's Mini-Streets

I should have driven north to the Baron's street in a slow, straw-laden, horse-drawn wagon. For that is what he wanted for us — the simple, unambitious life of the land. At the same time, as befits a luxury-loving multi-millionaire with an unusual social conscience, he supported us with more grand generosity than any single man before or since.

Instead, I went by taxi. This is also appropriate, if you are going to see the street of one of the world's richest men, and are whimsically trying to match the visit to the vibrations of his street's neighbourhood.

"Do you know about Baron de Hirsch?" I asked the cab driver as we set out for Ramat Aviv.

"I've heard, but I've forgotten," he answered judiciously. And soon after, in the manner of conversations with Tel Aviv cab drivers, we were off on a discussion of the school problems of his younger son. So I barely had time to launch into the briefest sketch of Baron Maurice de Hirsch auf Gereaut — probably richer than any one Rothschild, he was the biggest single contributor to East European Jews, the bosom buddy of the Prince of Wales, and the owner of some tremendous race-horses — when we were already turning left on Reading the Marquess and into the quiet, leafy dead-end called Baron Hirsch.

His street is as tiny as Reading's is impressive, but in a way it is surprising that it exists here at all, because Baron Hirsch's name was not well thought of in Zionist circles. He turned down Herzl (but then again Herzl didn't have a much easier time with the Rothschilds), and his activities on behalf of the Jews extended practically everywhere except the Holy Land.

Not that he opposed settlement in this area on principle. But Baron Hirsch, who astounded sceptics by managing to build the railroad from Europe through the Balkans to Constantinople, where he lived for a long time, was much more familiar with Ottoman realities than any of the earliest Zionists; and he died at a dramatic point, as we shall see, just as Herzl was about to turn to him again.

This was in 1896, over a year before the first Zionist Congress, and at about the time that Herzl was complaining that "the House of Rothschild is a national misfortune for the Jews." Hirsch was non-religious, though less "socially assimilated" than the Rothschilds. He probably had more in common with Herzl than did the supremely paternalistic Baron Edmond; he came to regard mass emigration from Eastern Europe as an imperative, and he saw the need for a normalized Jewish existence, which he perceived as agricultural. So it doesn't seem fair for practically every town in Israel to have its Rothschild Street while Tel Aviv has just this little dead-end arrangement, curiously shaped in the form of an "F". For Finance, perhaps; or else, as we shall see, for Fun.

The Baron's street has much greenery, which would have made him happy even though it is purely decorative; some small, one-storey houses; and rows of two-storey *shikunim*. I suppose you would call it middle class, as defined about 20 years ago; certainly the look is much less grand than a great deal of North Tel Aviv.

There is a spot of recent glamour, though, for Golda Meir lived on Baron Hirsch Street. Her house is a long, low-slung, two-storey building — two houses joined, actually, and when she lived there, a sentry was always on guard in the sentry-box at the front. Another former prime minister, Yitzhak Rabin, lives not far from here, though in a much newer neighbourhood, and at penthouse level.

I explained to the driver that I wanted no particular address, that I wished only to inhale the atmosphere of the man who gave away so many millions but believed in more than philanthropy. The cab drove off, leaving me on a peaceful, deserted, sunny corner, to inspect the street and to contemplate its implications.

On the side of a house near Golda's former residence I found a blue street-sign that gives Hirsch's dates (1831-1896) and describes him as "One of the biggest benefactors, and founder of the Jewish Colonization Association."

The Baron founded ICA, as it was known, in 1891 to help improve farming methods in Russia and Poland. He later added many millions to his original £2 million, largely in order to help establish agricultural colonies, mainly in Argentina and mainly unsuccessful. Edmond de Rothschild's PICA took over from ICA to found and assist settlements in Palestine. As such, it existed till 1957, when its property was transferred to the State of Israel.

Of course, all these details are not on the street sign, and I naturally realize that, as with Wordsworth's Lucy, few passers-by would know or care when PICA ceased to be; besides, the sign was half hidden by a bush. I have done quite a bit of scrambling through the underbrush to peer up at educational street signs, and, often, as well, into the astonished eyes of some citizen at the window in his underwear.

But I assume that Hirsch was rarely called "Moshe," as the sign wistfully adds after the Hebrew for Maurice. His grandfather, the first Jewish landowner in Bavaria, was ennobled in 1818. His father, banker to the King of Bavaria, was made a baron in 1869. His mother's family was connected with most important banking families in Europe; an ancestor had been both banker of Emperor Charles VI and Chief Rabbi of Hungary. She married his father in 1855; the dowry was about $4 million. She had received a liberal education, spoke four languages, had been her father's private secretary, knew about his philanthropic work, and is said to have guided her husband toward Jewish philanthropy.

She gave her son the best Hebrew and religious education, but he was never religious; he once allegedly stated that "the contrast between precept and practice on the part of one of his early teachers alienated him from religion, and he never entered a house of worship."

Young Maurice went into the family business at 17, but when he was 24 he moved to another banking house, Bishoffsheim & Goldschmidt, of Brussels, London and Paris, and married Clara Bischoffsheim, the boss's daughter.

Clara's father's firm was active in railway bonds; the family was involved in the biggest foreign loan to Egypt, and owned banks in Cairo, London, and San Francisco. From this excellent springboard, Hirsch speculated in sugar and copper, and obtained the railway concessions in Austria, the Balkans and Turkey. His philanthropic donations have been estimated at an incredible £18 million; his wife's own philanthropy came to a mere £8 million. When he died, Hirsch's assets could not be estimated closely: the guesses were between £14 million and £30 million. A relative described him as having "that rare financial genius that succeeds rather through diplomatic skill than economic reasoning. Under different conditions, he might have been a famous statesman."

Hirsch was tall and slim, and had an excellent posture. He liked to go for walks; he liked to go to parties; and he had a tremendous capacity for work. Coming home late at night, he was perfectly capable of keeping his secretaries busy with dictation till morning.

Like many rich men, he was thrifty — very critical of expenditures by his agents and always suspicious of being exploited. He was frugal about his own food, but fed his guests lavishly. He did his buying in Vienna because prices were lower there than in Paris; he avoided sending telegrams when letters would do. He hired cabs from a stand around the corner where they were slightly cheaper, and he didn't eat at the Grand Hotel in Paris because "he couldn't afford it."

Once he stood in the pouring rain haggling with a cabman about sixpence on the fare. A friend, also a baron, watched the encounter. "Why not pay him and come in out of the wet?" he asked. "You'll catch a cold and be laid up for weeks."

"That's all very well, but I have my principles," replied Hirsch.

The two sides to Hirsch's character become clear through his connections with two very different men. One was Edward VII when he was still the Prince of Wales, during the last decade of Hirsch's life, and this was a glorious romp at the top of the jet set. The other, in the last year of his life, was Theodor Herzl. These two men represent the Baron's two dominant passions — what has been called his "morbid social ambition" on the one hand, and on the other, his determination to solve the Jewish problem on a meaningful scale and with a new viewpoint.

The real name-dropping and the truly glorious social calendar starts in 1886, when Austria's tragically dissolute Archduke Rudolph (better known as Charles Boyer in *Mayerling*) arranged an introduction for Hirsch to the Prince of Wales "in consideration of a loan of 190,000 gulden."

That same year, Hirsch's dinner partner at a very high-class evening was a beautiful and witty English girl named Margot Tennant, who spilled champagne down her dress. Hirsch, all aplomb, ignored the crisis and instead had a long conversation with Margot, who he decided would make an excellent wife for his only son, Lucien.

"I want you to marry Lucien," said Hirsch forthrightly, and went on to explain why. "He is quite unlike me, he is very respectable and hates money. He likes books and collects manuscripts and is highly educated. He would make you an excellent husband. He does not like society or racing, or any of the things I care for."

Margot declined, and went on to marry the Earl of Asquith, later Prime Minister of England. Lucien died the following year at the age of 31, leaving an illegitimate daughter, Lucienne. This penchant for siring illegitimate children, not uncommon in the Victorian age, ran in the family, as we shall see. The Hirsch offspring all did well for themselves: Lucienne married a banker who became the first Jew to be granted a Belgian barony.

After Lucien's death, Hirsch announced that, from now on, "humanity will be my heir." This was not entirely accurate; but his philanthropy was vast, as was his social conscience — even though it went with a high-grade life style. Worried about the Jews of Eastern Europe, although rejecting their outward traditions and sharing none of their natural hardships, Hirsch first thought they could be retrained for productive work within the Russian Empire, but later decided that they must be transferred elsewhere.

In 1888, to celebrate the 40th anniversary of Franz Joseph's accession as Emperor of Austria and Hungary, Hirsch donated £500,000 to schools in Galicia and Bukovina. At the same time, he was busy building up his string of race-horses, as fine as, if not finer than, the Rothschilds. He got into the Marlborough Club but not into the Jockey Club, though the Rothschilds did, which must have rankled.

Hirsch had offered the Russian government £2 million for a system of secular schools in the Jewish pale. The Russians were ready to accept the money, but refused to allow any foreigner to administer the fund. Hirsch

Baron Hirsch ''one of the biggest benefactors.''

decided that mass emigration was the only solution for East European Jews, and that they must be taught to lead normal, productive and healthy lives. This he saw as tied to simple agricultural work: the Jews, he was sure — at a time when no one else envisaged it — could make good farmers.

But heaven forbid that they should try to rise too high, as he himself had; or as Léon Blum was soon to do (the little unpaved street of Léon Blum, France's Socialist leader and first Jewish prime minister, runs into the top rung of the "F" of Rehov Hirsch). Or as Mordechai Emanual Noah had already done in the first half of the 19th century. A successful American politican who also served as consul to Tunis, Noah had tried to establish a Jewish colony in New York State; and *his* little street is the extension of the vertical stroke of Hirsch's "F."

In 1889, there were rumours that the Prince of Wales, who adored gambling, food and women, owed large sums of money to "unsuitable persons." It was thought that he obtained essential funds from the French Rothschilds. But the British ambassador to Paris wrote to the British prime minister that "it was probably Hirsch and not Rothschild who advanced the money."

1890: on April 1, Hirsch and the Prince of Wales had tea at the Hotel Bristol in Paris. The next day the Prince lunched at Hirsch's home, which was a palace on the Rue d'Elysée. Hirsch now became the Prince's unofficial financial adviser and confidant. Throughout "the season" the Baron was constantly in the company of the Prince and a frequent guest at the houses of the Prince's friends. The Prince was known to be "amused" by the idea of annoying the Continental nobility who had long snubbed Hirsch; he actually seemed to like Jews, and not just for their money. Socially, his circle included the Rothschilds and the Sassons — not a dull crowd.

June 14, 1890: Queen Victoria refuses to invite Hirsch to a state concert at Buckingham Palace, in the face of her son's express request. The Prince is "dreadfully annoyed," his secretary wrote, "as he looks on him as a personal friend; whether he is a good one or not is another question; and looks upon the step which the Queen has taken as a personal slight."

Three weeks later, Lady Randolph Churchill gives a dinner party. The guests included the Gladstones, the Roseberys, the Russian ambassador, the Hirsches. The Prince of Wales, having his little revenge, describes it as "delightfully mixed."

October 1890: The Prince goes to Hungary to visit Hirsch's estate, where the house-party indulges in a massacre of partridges, with hundreds of men beating the birds out of the bushes.

1891: Hirsch establishes a trust fund to help Jewish immigrants in America.

110

And so it goes, high living hand-in-hand with an emerging philosophy of constructive philanthropy. Hirsch was heavily subsidizing the Alliance Israélite chain of schools, and the sums he gave to ICA eventually totalled some £18m.

In 1894 (to descend to smaller figures), the Prince of Wales lost £600 on Hirsch's horse, the favourite in the Paris Grand Prix.

A June house-party at the Prince's country estate included both Hirsch and the Tsarevitch Nicholas II, who married Prince Edward's niece. The Tsarevitch wrote to his mother, the Empress, that it was all "rather strange" because the company "included a Baron Hirsch (not that the Tsars did not have their own Jewish bankers, such as the Barons Guenzberg); but he "tried to keep away as much as possible and not to talk."

Almost exactly a year after that house-party, Hirsch met Herzl in Paris. The meeting was initiated by Herzl, in a letter he sat on for two weeks before dispatching.

Under the spell of Wagner's *Tannhäuser*, in a mood switching from euphoria to gloom in a Paris hotel, Herzl wrote to ask the Baron, "When may I have the honour of visiting you? I want to discuss the Jewish problem with you." It was not a matter of a journalistic interview nor even a simple request for money, but a political discussion "that perhaps will work itself out at a time when neither you nor I will be here."

The journalist went on to lecture the tycoon in stern terms. He was certain that everything the Baron had accomplished so far was "as generous as it was misconceived, as costly as it was pointless." He would like to see Baron Hirsch if possible on a Sunday, for an undisturbed two hours.

Hirsch replied that he would be coming to Paris on such-and-such a Sunday, and would receive Herzl at his home. Herzl immediately began, in a storm of inspiration, to jot down notes and outline the case he wished to make. They ran to 22 pages, and were in effect the first formulation of his theory of the Jewish state.

Promptly at 10.30 in the morning on June 2, 1895, carefully dressed but not too carefully (he was after "discreet care," and made a point of using, just once beforehand, a new pair of gloves, because "one ought not show rich people too much respect") Herzl arrived at the baronial palace.

"You will find what I have to say too simple, and also too fantastic," Herzl began, launching into the original example of political Zionist *hasbara*. Philanthropy, he said, was wrong; Hirsch's Argentinian colonies were failures because charity destroys the will to work. It was wrong to "export" a few Jews, because whatever each one cost, "he wasn't worth it." No, a political central force was essential; and with it, a plan to let Jews achieve "moral beauty... great achievements — in short, greatness." Yes, insisted Herzl in great excitement, this would lead to an "elevation of

111

the moral level" of the Jews...

Here Baron Hirsch, who had been trying for some time to get in a word, interrupted: "No, no, no! I don't want to raise the moral level! All the trouble comes from the fact that the Jews want to rise too high. We have too many intellectuals. My whole purpose is to restrain the Jews from their striving. They shouldn't make such progress: this is the source of all the hatred."

Poor, rich, social-climbing, generous, discriminated-against Baron. Good that he missed knowing that Albert Einstein, a wide thoroughfare to the north, runs straight to Tel Aviv University to the east, where throngs of students, whose subsidies would keep many barons busy, drive their private cars to their lectures. Poor Herzl, too, who had told the benefactor: "You are creating *schnorrers!*"

Hirsch countered, "Emigration is the only solution. There are plenty of countries that can be bought..."

At which Herzl shouted, "And who says that I'm against emigration? Here, it's all written down..." And he pointed to his plans for political action, conversations with the Kaiser...

Hirsch: "And where will you get the money? Rothschild will give you 500 pounds..."

Herzl, laughing perversely: "The money? I'll raise a loan of 10 million marks."

Hirsch, also laughing: "Fantasy! The rich Jews won't give you a thing, they're not interested in the suffering of the poor."

But at the close of the conversation, Hirsch said it was not their last meeting. The two felt a rapport, a common intelligence, although their viewpoints were so different.

Next day, Herzl sent off a long and explicit letter to the Baron further developing his ideas. His conversation with Hirsch had, in fact, clarified his own thinking, and he spent the next three weeks in a state of tremendous emotional tension, writing a long memorandum which grew into *Der Judenstaat*. In this second letter to Hirsch, which induced that intense emotional effort ("During these weeks I was more than once afraid that I was going out of my mind," he noted in his diary), Herzl wrote Hirsch that he was launching a national, not a philanthropic, movement; and that it would have a flag, and "with a flag people are led — perhaps even to the Promised Land."

Herzl had already decided to write a novel "which would include everything that he regretted having told Hirsch, which Hirsch perhaps laughingly has showed around to his friends." But Hirsch answered Herzl's letter politely, saying he would be glad to see him again when he returned to Paris in a few months.

Herzl replied promptly: "I will still try to do something *for* the Jews. But not *with* the Jews. And if I had dared to think that anybody would understand my thoughts, you were the one. From other Jews I can expect even less..."

The following April, after intermittent bouts of euphoria and gloom, ups and downs regarding meetings with the Kaiser, Herzl drafted an explicit letter to our friend Max Nordau saying that he wished to meet Hirsch once again. Swallowing the earlier defeat, he wanted to try to get "a few millions," which could do wonders.

He sent off the letter the next day. An hour later, he learned that Hirsch had died at his estate in Hungary during the night.

"What an incredible coincidence," Herzl wrote in his diary. "My brochure, *Der Judenstaat,* has been finished for months. I showed it to everybody except Hirsch. At the moment I decided to do that, he dies. His cooperation would have helped our cause tremendously. In any event, his death is a loss for the Jewish cause. Among rich Jews, he was the only one who wanted to do something great for the poor. Perhaps I didn't know how to handle him properly. Perhaps I should have written the letter to Nordau two weeks ago. Our cause has today lost a great deal. For I always had it in mind to win Hirsch for our plan."

The Jews, he observed, "have lost Hirsch, but they have me; and after me will come others."

That same day, a long-awaited audience with the Archduke Frederick of Baden, uncle of the Kaiser, was finally granted, and Herzl's literary soul perceived the date of Hirsch's death as marking "the end of philanthropy and the beginning of 'Jewish politics.'"

Herzl meets Hirsch again in Jerusalem, where Herzl is a mighty boulevard leading up to Har Herzl and Yad Vashem, while "The Baron Hirsch Street" — not a mere baron, but *The* Baron, on the street sign — is a short road ending two corners from Herzl Boulevard by twisting and becoming Eliezer Halevi Street. This area, in Kiryat Moshe, is an imposing collection of private homes with balcony gardens, and almost all the residents are Orthodox.

In Haifa, Baron Hirsch has only a very short street, difficult to find, especially as it is wrongly inscribed on all the usual maps of Haifa. In suitably aristocratic company, it is a sort of continuation of Baron Rothschild Boulevard, with Lord Allenby Avenue crossing between them, although another interloper also gets a mention at the corner. Altogether, there are only a dozen buildings on Hirsch, which very quickly is transformed into Stella Maris Road.

But Baron Hirsch's line did not expire with these short streets. He also had two illegitimate sons. His widow, the remarkably understanding and generous Clara, adopted both boys, probably after Hirsch's death.

Raymond lived only to the age of 32, but Arnold, a year older, was 89 when he died at Biarritz in 1968 as Count de Bendern, "probably one of the most colourful personalities on the contemporary scene," as the London *Evening Standard* wrote, "fabulously rich and fabulously eccentric."

The identity of the boys' natural mother has never been established: she has been variously identified as American, English and French. Arnold's name first appears in the Hirsch records as Moritz Arnold Forrest Bischoffsheim when he was nine years old, soon after the death of the legitimate Lucien.

Educated at Eton and Oxford, he was known to his friends by the wonderfully Wodehousian name of "Tootsie de Forrest." He was a fine sportsman and raced early motor cars. He was good-looking, charming, had beautiful manners and was very popular.

By the first decade of the century, he was already incredibly wealthy, with large estates all over Europe; but most of the time he lived in London, at Spencer House, St. James's. With all this behind him, Arnold was, in his early years, a political leftist, and it was as a Liberal that he entered the House of Commons in 1911. When World War I broke out, he joined the Royal Navy as a lieut.-commander. After the war he became a pacifist, disapproved more and more of Anglo-French policy, and finally left Britain in 1932.

He had relinquished his first title, an Austrian barony, in 1920. He now settled in Liechtenstein, becoming diplomatic counsellor to the Prince, who created him Count of Bendern, a village on the Rhine.

Arnold was a passionate animal and bird lover. Dr. Kurt Grunwald of Jerusalem, in a scholarly biography of Baron Hirsch, suggests that this may have been a reaction to the mass killing of birds and game at his father's famous hunting parties. On his estate on Lake Geneva he kept 40 cats and a huge aviary. When he lived in a Zurich hotel during World War II, he converted one of his rooms into another aviary, with so many birds that, ultimately, he was the only guest in the hotel. He campaigned against bull-fighting and supported foundations that cared for fauna and flora. In 1954, he donated his father's 400-acre hunting estate to the Paris Municipality for workers' housing, on condition that "no animal or bird should wilfully be destroyed, and it was apparently because of violation of this condition that he sued the Municipality, though without success."

Count Arnold had two sons by his second marriage to the daughter of an English peer. The younger, John, was a British amateur golf champion: of the elder, Alaric, all I can report is that he survived his father by only five years, dying, like him, in Biarritz as Graf von Bendern, at the age of 69.

From Alaric and Tootsie, it is a long way back to "Türkenhirsch," the hero of Grunwald's biography. He makes a strong case for a re-evaluation of Baron Hirsch's forgotten role in the history of the modern Jewish renaissance, arguing that, far from refusing to help Herzl, he preceded him in much of his thinking, and saw mass emigration and resettlement as the only solution for Russian Jewry. His attempts in Argentina also preceded Herzl's *Nachtasyl* plan for Uganda. Hirsch wanted to settle three million Jews in Argentina. The results were negligible, but many later immigrants to Israel were descendants of his colonists. His administrator in Argentina, Col. Albert Edward Goldsmid (the original of Daniel Deronda), referred to it as "a nursery for Palestine," and tried to encourage the colonists with the slogan, "From A(rgentina) to Z(ion)."

9
Black Money in a Lost Eden

I have a friend who likes to emphasize the street-name irony-gap — the artificial but entertaining contrast between a street's character and the character of the man after whom it is named. When I asked him what he knew about Lilienblum he replied, "Wasn't he a very correct *Yekke* banker?" (A *Yekke* is the affectionate, patronizing name given by Israelis to a pedantic German-Jewish immigrant.)

This was back in the days before the government introduced our supposed economic reform, and liberated what was then our lira to plunge to its true depths. In those days, Israel's foreign currency was supposed to be strictly controlled. The name Lilienblum was synonymous with black-market deals in such currency; when, lurking down there on his street (parallel to Judah Halevi, from Allenby west to Pines), untrustworthy characters used to sidle up to one muttering, "Dollars? Cheques?" in the wheedling tone associated with Feelthy Postcards. The police would turn indulgently blind eyes, and everybody gathered that the then government saw the phenomenon as a useful mechanism for exploiting the foreign currency market itself.

Moshe Leib Lilienblum was known for his personal integrity, his devotion to principles even at great personal cost, and his intellectual honesty — which can require stiffer resistance to temptation than refraining from a little financial fiddling.

Far from being a German banker, or a foreign-currency dealer, Lilienblum was an impoverished Russian Talmud-teacher, writer, critic, political journalist and leader of the early Zionist movement. He maintained a sense of humour in the face of a difficult personal life, and a flow of optimism in spite of being consistently realistic and practical.

Malal — the acronym that survives as the name of a moshav near Kfar Sava and of streets in Jerusalem and Haifa — turns out, on the basis of even superficial reading, to have been one of the most attractive of our founding fathers.

In David Vital's *Origins of Zionism,* his photograph precedes those of five other leaders (Pinsker, Edmond de Rothschild, Ahad Ha'am, Herzl and Nordau). An optimistic quotation from Lilienblum, written after the first Zionist Congress, closes Vital's book: "And who knows? We may succeed." At that point, the start of political Zionism, Lilienblum was 54 years old.

Times have changed in many ways. But not in all. Here is Lilienblum's reply to a very-angry-young-man letter from 24-year-old Menahem Ussishkin in 1887. Ussishkin was at the time "in despair" about the ineffectual, charity-based *Hovevei Zion* settlements in Palestine.

"Forgive me if I tell you that I do not know what you want. You are angry about charity in connection with the Yishuv... but what is it you really want? Do you want to leave the people in Gedera as they are?" There follows a specific description of the difficulties of buying land in Turkey; and finally, "What *Hibbat Zion* does now is no more than the beginning of the real operation... which will be performed when better days have come, days which it is beyond our power to hasten."

Lilienblum's life is a model of Russian-Jewish intellectual development of a century ago. Like so many others, he moved through three distinct phases. First, a fervent belief in the need and possibility of reforming traditional Jewish society and institutions. Next, a socialist period, when he was convinced that the whole world could be changed.

This view came to an end, as it did for so many, during the pogroms of 1881. These inspired a belief in Jewish nationalism, and in the need to "evacuate" the Diaspora and return to Zion — not, of course, for religious reasons, but because the Land of Israel was a suitable place.

There, Lilienblum felt, the Jews would not constitute a "foreign body." He did not overlook the presence of the Arabs, even then, but saw them as a small and backward group. If 100,000 Jewish families were to settle there over a period of 20 years, Lilienblum believed, they would then no longer be strangers in the land.

The son of a poor barrel-maker and the grandson of a Talmud teacher, Lilienblum was born in 1843 in a small town in Lithuania, steeped, like so many, in an atmosphere of rigid Orthodoxy. He began his *heder* studies, as was usual, as a tiny child.

"I was four years and three months old," Lilienblum wrote, "when, barely able to comprehend, I was given over to the burden of the Tora." He never forgave his parents — or, indeed, the entire Jewish tradition of the day — for making it impossible for him to enjoy the "pleasures of childhood." At these imposed duties he excelled, however, and at an early age was known for his unusual diligence and scholarship — quite something, considering the high Lithuanian standards of his surroundings. When he was 13, he organized a boys' society for Bible studies.

A year earlier, he had become engaged to a girl of 11 chosen by his parents. They were married when he was 15. The practice of child marriage — and unhappy marriage, as his was — became another point in his attacks against the social institutions of Orthodoxy. By the time he was 22, he had established two yeshivot, but had also been influenced by secular reading and the *Haskalah* movement. His development was solitary and independent, and he found himself at odds with his former friends — and his wife.

He was not afraid of making known his critical views calling for reforms of Jewish tradition — the emancipation of women, the normalization of life through work, a change in the Orthodox regulations for the Sabbatical Year. The result was that in the small-town atmosphere of his birth he became unable to earn his living as a teacher, and was declared a "heretic." Almost in danger of his life, he existed on the verge of starvation.

The name of this poverty-stricken man, high on principle but low on principal, is now associated by most of us with underhand money dealings and vast undeclared incomes. Lilienblum's principles cost him so dearly that he was persecuted by "fanatic religious elements" (the phrase is the *Encyclopaedia Judaica's*). His articles criticizing the leading rabbis of the day appeared in Hebrew journals, and his name became known to like-thinking secular intellectuals in other cities.

In 1869, at the age of 26, he moved to Odessa, where he lived for the rest of his life. He edited a Yiddish journal and wrote a series describing the grim conditions in yeshivot. His concern was the plight of the desperately poor masses of Poland and Russia; the language of the publication was Yiddish, the tongue of the black marketeers on his street. But Lilienblum, who in this period rarely had a square meal himself, saw such unproductive functions as money-changing as part of the Jewish anomaly which would disappear when Jewish life became normalized.

In 1876 his now-forgotten classic, *The Sin of Youth* was published in Vienna. A psychological autobiography, it has been praised for its utter frankness and dramatic insight into the emotional and moral conflict between a young man and Jewish tradition.

The years 1870-81 are generally considered to be his "socialist" period, coinciding with the "false dawn" of Russian liberalism. During this period, poor Lilienblum had been trying to educate himself in the secular subjects he had missed — mathematics, languages and so on — to prepare himself for higher studies, but finally realized that this was impossible.

In Odessa, he became a friend of Leon Pinsker, the prominent doctor who became famous in Jewish circles as a result of the publication of his pamphlet, *Autoemancipation,* and whom we have met at Dizengoff Circle. Pinsker's pamphlet was signed with the nom de plume, *Ein Russischer Jude.* It has been suggested that he wrote his famous call for self-help as a result of the influence of Lilienblum, 22 years his junior.

It was certainly Lilienblum who first drew Pinsker to Zionist circles, who pushed Pinsker to accept the position that the key to the solution of the Jewish problem lay in the Holy Land, in practical settlement there, and nowhere else. Pinsker personally did not believe that this location was essential, but bowed to the prodding of Lilienblum, who wrote later: "Knowing nothing of his illness, of his weakness of spirit, of his excessive modesty, and of his invariable shyness, I continued to demand that he act." Pinsker agreed to become the head of the Odessa *Hovevei Zion*, with Lilienblum as secretary — among other reasons, because his Hebrew was the best.

So began a long period of hard and discouraging work with the *Hovevei Zion* committees, and of seeing the setbacks of the projects in Eretz Yisrael. Where others became disheartened by the failures and splits, Lilienblum's good sense and measured optimism never left him. He knew how to handle political jockeying, as in the battles for power with Rabbi Mohilever, for whom both he and Pinsker were anathema by virtue of their distance from Orthodoxy.

In Jerusalem, Lilienblum and Pinsker have remained close to each other after death, in the swank suburb of Talbieh. Pinsker has been given the capital's most affluent street, sometimes known as Millionaires' Row, and sometimes as the Rose Garden, since it ends, after passing several imposing houses, in a garden of roses. Malal Street, named after Lilienblum, runs parallel to Pinsker as far as the garden — it is also lined by homes of the wealthy — and then descends a steep hill to link Talbieh with the lower classes, both financially and physically, living in the valley of the German Colony.

The association between the two writers continues in Haifa, and so does their link to more gracious living. Malal is a short street leading to the gates of the new Technion campus; Pinsker is the main street running through the better part of Neve Sha'anan. Both are lined with solid and imposing houses, many of them with gardens.

Lilienblum was a good friend of Ahad Ha'am's, although he regarded his theories as too metaphysical; he even belonged to Ahad Ha'am's semisecret group, *B'nei Moshe*, though he took little active part in it and it was really in conflict with his pragmatic approach. He approved of Rothschild's gifts of money to the Zionist cause, and was among the first to recognize the importance of Herzl as a leader.

He conducted a voluminous correspondence with the poet and critic Yehuda Leib Gordon, which was later published, and we must not forget his own literary criticism. His critique of the novelist Mapu, for instance, characteristically called for more realistic writing, free of romanticism, for "a material view of life."

By now, I suppose, I should have suggested a short walk down Lilienblum's Tel Aviv street — except that from my most recent experience I cannot really recommend it. The traffic was so dense, the surroundings were so grey and desolate, and the people were so harassed, that I didn't get much past the Herzl corner. After noting the suffocating number of

Moshe Leib Lilienblum, known for his personal integrity.

banks, plus some second-hand men's suits fluttering on a rack, I turned west again in a fit of depression. This was, of course, on a weekday. I refused to try again on a Saturday, because then the area is so gloomily deserted as to be positively creepy.

Just remember: Judah Halevi, one street over to the south, once mourned the desolation of the Land of Israel. Today, cars are double-parked on the pavement in front of the Judah Halevi banks. It is hard to believe that 30 years ago, during the War of Independence period, the Lilienblum area was one where Americans were happy to stay. For a modest "American Hotel" once existed at No. 39 Lilienblum. It had 22 rooms, running water, and central heating; the telephone number was 159. Later, it became two floors rented out as hotel-flats which were very popular for get-togethers among volunteers from the U.S.

Lilienblum's past — the street's, not the man's — thus further serves to deepen the irony gap. I am not speaking now of the contrast between seedy speculators in dollars and dirty cheques and the upright early practical Zionist of unblemished character. No: I mean that the spirit of Rehov Lilienblum, when Tel Aviv was young, was itself unblemished; the houses had character, and, while generally not as grand as those on Rothschild or Ahad Ha'am, were solidly attractive and well kept. What happens is that as the Zionists get more and more practical, they tend to devaluate their residential beginnings. By the time they wake up to the importance of revitalizing the core, it is usually too late.

The importance of Lilienblum (the man) was well recognized by the founders of Tel Aviv. When Ahuzat Bayit, that much-loved, clean and pure garden of nostalgia that grew into our metropolis, was founded in 1909, he became one of the first seven streets that made up that innocent quarter.

Another candidate was the writer Peretz Smolenskin. But several factions of street-naming philosophy sprang up at that street-naming meeting so long ago, and as a result Peretz Smolenskin was by-passed and had to wait several decades before getting his street. His reward for the delay was that he is now elegantly ensconced in the north, and appropriately set between Mapu, the first Hebrew novelist, and Y. L. Gordon, the greatest Hebrew poet of his day.

The name issue, back then, revolved around the purity of the language, which is why *Hashahar*, the name of the journal he edited, was chosen to stand for Smolenskin. Of course, Herzl's name was acceptable, and so were Montefiore's and Rothschild's, since they gave money; and nobody seemed to object to Lilienblum. Pinsker was another candidate that day, but one argument went that, if we had a Rehov Smolenskin and a Rehov Pinsker, our early Russian settlers would get confused and call them Smolensk and Pinsk, city names they knew all too well.

In any event, Lilienblum got his street close to the time of his death, which occurred in February 1910. Two of the other greats of the Ahuzat Bayit streets were still alive — Ahad Ha'am died in 1927, and robust Baron Edmond de Rothschild did not die until 1934, aged 89.

Down at the bottom of Lilienblum was Tel Aviv's first dream palace, the Eden Cinema. It was built before World War I, in 1913, by two partners, Weisser and Abarbanel, and it opened with a spectacle of ultimate relevance — *The Last Days of Pompeii.*

And we are back in our irony gap, since Lilienblum was absolutely against escapist, romantic entertainment. He believed that art (and we are using the term here very loosely, to embrace entertainment) must reflect life as it really is; that fancy style is wrong and bad; that the purpose of art is to serve society; that most love poetry is nothing but a repetition of what has been said many times before; and that we must be freed from the useless life of the imagination.

"There is no aim in life except life itself," said Lilienblum. (Yes, but what are you going to do on Saturday night?)

The name Eden, Tel Aviv's original monument to fleeting anti-Lilienblum fantasy, mostly Hollywood, was suggested by Simha (Gutman) Ben-Zion, writer, educator, a founding father of Tel Aviv, whose street, Sderot Ben-Zion, runs from Kikar Habimah down to King George.

Ben-Zion was the father of the painter and writer Nahum Gutman, which gives us a case of the father choosing a Hebrew name and the son reverting to the European original. Nahum Gutman's drawings of Little Tel Aviv are among the most attractive and evocative I know, done with humour, fantasy and love for that distant, blissful dawn.

One of Gutman's most charming sketches is of "the first concert in Tel Aviv." The romantic pair, violinist and pianist, enthrall the cultural crowd outside the hall with, almost certainly, the Kreuzer Sonata. All of us here at Ahuzat Bayit, including a well-mannered dog or perhaps cat, have gathered somewhere on Rehov Herzl, possibly at the corner of Lilienblum. This is Nostalgialand and doesn't necessarily fit any map.

In silent-film days, there was an "orchestra" in the pit — piano and violin — and later, for a really important film, two fiddles. A sound-effects man behind the screen would, for instance, bang on a sheet of tin, for thunder. Later, for a real thrill, there would be actors speaking dialogue behind the screen: Miriam Bernstein-Cohen, the famous actress, no less. And once upon a time, forthcoming attractions were advertised by a placard trundled through town on a horse-drawn cart.

During World War I, performances were given on Saturday evenings only, and the audience consisted largely of Turkish and German officers. In 1918, after Allenby's conquest, and during the brief honeymoon between the English and the Yishuv, British troops organized a party at the Eden for Passover, and a British officer with a good voice sang a Hebrew song.

Until 1923, when Pinhas Rutenberg built Tel Aviv's first electric power station on what is now the huge complex in Hahashmal Street (which means "Electricity Street") the Eden had its own generator, but old-timers also remember the projectionist, Sammy, turning the wheel by hand.

One of Tel Aviv's first Purim parties was held at the Eden; and a most memorable event was a gala performance of *Samson and Delilah* by the Hebrew Opera Company, followed by Bible recitations, in honour of Lord Balfour, when he visited the country in the spring of 1925. The main purpose of his visit was to open the Hebrew University of Jerusalem, but he also had the pleasure of opening his own street in Tel Aviv.

In Jerusalem Balfour had no street until the establishment of the State. The one he was given was in the Talbieh quarter, running between what are now Kikar Auster (Daniel Auster was Jerusalem's first mayor after Independence) and Kikar Wingate, and it was one of the few in the city where Jews and Arabs lived side by side. Known as Millionaires' Row, it had neither name nor numbers until it became Rehov Balfour: the address of the man who built what is now the official residence of the prime minister, for instance, was simply "Aghion's House, Talbieh."

To return to Tel Aviv and the Eden. From those days, the decline of that entertainment paradise has been steady. A friend who was a teenager in the '30s remembers when it was already being upstaged by uptown, as at the Mograbi. Another friend, who came in the '40s, considered it "a big barn."

Today, the Eden is a parking lot. Until a few years ago, battered and peeling, and with an ugly neon sign out of tune with its original quaint conception, it was still showing films which the flyblown posters proclaimed to have originated in Turkey or India. Then in 1975, Tel Avivians left their Eden for the last time: the seats were carried out, the cars took over.

So this is the way the city crumbles. It is partly demographic, with the "best old families" moving out and north, and new immigrants crowding into subdivided homes. Then the banks and offices take over, and the private cars: after all, the best old families must get into town. If my sources are correct, you could, at one time or another, walk along Lilienblum and find, among the stately mini-homes, the Tahkemoni School; one of the Histadrut's workers' kitchens; the Chamber of Commerce; the Nicaraguan Consulate; the Post Office; a cluster of immigrants' associations — Austrian, Hungarian, Lithuanian, Polish, Rumanian, Yugoslav — and a variety of insurance companies and banks, especially their foreign exchange departments.

Now, towering over it all from the north, where once the Herzliya Gymnasia reigned as the prince of Ahuzat Bayit, the Migdal Shalom stands as a multi-layered monument to trade, banking and government bureaucracy.

If it is true that the previous government, the socialist one, was participating from above in the goings-on in Lilienblum, the grubby street-players were merely, as it were, scapegoat and lightning-rod.

And "scapegoat" and "lightning-rod" were the words used by Lilienblum himself in his post-socialist period, after the pogroms that followed the "false dawn" of Russian liberalism. He was describing what the function of the Jews would be "if the workers came to power." It may be their function no matter who is in power; but it also seems true that we arrange our own local scapegoats and lightning-rods as each era sees fit.

Lilienblum retained the glow of optimism to the end, in spite of the harshness of his personal life and his close observation of human errors. Nurtured in the abstractions of the Talmud, he turned himself into a specialist in what was practical.

Ahad Ha'am's biographer, Leon Simon, called Lilienblum "a practical Zionist in the narrowest sense, of whom it used to be said that his heart rejoiced over every single goat" that joined the Jewish holdings in Palestine.

The man who embodied the moral opposite of illegal financial speculation and the post-control inflationary rush to easy unearned millions, wrote in his last work, *Derekh La'avor Golim — the Road for the Return of the Captives*:

"My final days are more fortunate than my earlier ones, I fully realize that my efforts were not wasted...

"The great ideal stands before us in all its grandeur... Even things great and sublime revolve upon the wheel of Time; now they ascend while the next moment they sink... Happy is the one who has hope and faith."

10
Monarchy and Murder

This time, as a reward for trooping so dutifully down the byways of Zionist history, the reader is given as a special treat a visit to a Christian king, with a murder mystery thrown in. And not just an ordinary, everyday murder, but a murder-rape case with undertones of incest.

It took place in Tel Aviv's Gan Meir on an autumn night in 1949, and it was the talk of Tel Aviv, and indeed of the whole new State of Israel, for a long time afterwards. And for a long time afterwards, women were afraid to enter the park, for some shivery doubt lingered on as to whether the accused, by then safely in jail, was really the assailant. He protested his innocence throughout the years he spent in prison.

The Gan Meir case was the first of its sensational kind. True, there had been political murders — De Haan, with its tinge of homosexuality, and Arlosoroff, with its unprinted background of jealous husbands. But the Gan Meir murder, involving a half-brother and half-sister, had the tragic plot of an ancient myth.

The road to Gan Meir is a royal one, because one entrance to the park (named as we know, after Meir Dizengoff) is the Street of King George — Rehov Hamelech George. Which of the English monarchs of that name is not specified; but everybody knows it wasn't named after mad George III, or after the unpopular profligate, George IV, but after the dutiful Fifth, grandson of Queen Victoria and grandfather of the present Queen, during whose reign the Balfour Declaration was issued.

On King George, the entrance to Gan Meir is near the famous sycamore trees and the much taller Herut building, Beit Jabotinsky, and the Jabotinsky Museum, the hard core of anti-British agitation during the Mandate. This is not entirely appropriate for one of our royal British streets. But here stood the Betar Club back in the early 1930s, when this part of the street was still called Rehov Hacarmel, when Gan Meir was only in the planning stage, and a women's training farm occupied the site, today Beit Hahalutzot, the house of the Women's League for Israel.

One lion is still left at Simtat Ploni, or maybe it's Simtat Almoni, those once charming anonymous lanes pointing east to nowhere behind the Herut building. The Gottex swimwear firm started life here, and earlier still, when this was practically the end of the world back in the 1920s, a rich American (yes, they came even more than half a century ago) wanted to develop a beautiful and luxurious neighbourhood to attract quality-of-life immigrants from the United States. Flats were built; there were illuminations at night; it was gloriously romantic. Then he died, and that was the end of that.

The Hebrew words imply anonymity: *Plonit Almonit* means an unknown, unnamed woman. As an address, they suit urban anonymity, though Hither and Thither would also do nicely for the average scurried street.

When I asked a veteran observer of the Tel Aviv Municipality's street-naming committee's deliberations what Simtat Plonit and Simtat Almonit were meant to convey, he answered: "A little joke."

Further south, King George ends in the Carmel Market and a dreary underground pedestrian passageway whose escalator is usually out of order. Even I can remember when this was considered a terrifically modern quality-of-life attraction, though it mostly attracted children who ran up and down the moving staircase when it moved, and beggars who squatted underground.

The street was named in 1935, in honour of the silver jubilee of George's coronation, the last time a Tel Aviv street was named after a living individual. A year later, George V died; the League of Nations collapsed; the Spanish Civil War began; Germany occupied the Rhineland; Italy occupied Ethiopia; and the Arab-Jewish riots began again in earnest.

The harshest criticism of our street's George that I have come across describes him as "sound but unimaginative." That description, though, adds reassuringly that he was "filled with a sense of responsibility and rigid respect for the constitution."

In character, he was certainly the opposite of his father, Edward VII, who had vigorous appetites and whom we remember as Baron Hirsch's dining-shooting-and-racing companion. Edward was rudely described by the young Rudyard Kipling as a "corpulent voluptuary." His son, by contrast, was the embodiment of personal and public duty, and thus also very different from *his* son, who spent the second half of his life as Mrs. Simpson's Duke of Windsor. Royal virtues and vices, like other phenomena, seem to run in cycles.

A quaint little speculation, which has probably rarely been speculated, is that our Tel Aviv street just missed being called "Rehov Hamelech Albert Victor." This is because George had an older brother, who died at the age of 28; historians have called his demise and the unexpected substitution of George as heir as "a merciful act of providence."

Albert Victor, or Prince Eddy as he was known, was dull-witted and unpleasant. At school he failed in all his subjects, in contrast to his younger brother, and his tutor described his mind as "abnormally dormant." What energy he had was devoted to scandalous behaviour. In recent books recalling speculations once utterly taboo in print, Jack the Ripper — the gaslight murderer of English prostitutes who terrorized the city in 1888 — is identified with none other than Eddy, the royal heir.

In January, 1892, Price Eddy died of pneumonia; or else of syphilis, according to the rumours. His younger brother George was ill with typhoid, but recovered. And that is why it was not Eddy but George who became king when Edward VII died in 1910. George had a "strong and exemplary character and robust constitution," and he "early showed promise of embodying all those domestic and public virtues the English people cherish." "strong and exemplary character and robust constitution," and he "early showed promise of embodying all those domestic and public virtues the English people cherish."

However, George tended to consider himself an "interloper" in the line of succession; he got not only Eddy's throne but Eddy's intended — Princess Mary of Teck — as well. He first wanted to marry his cousin Marie of Edinburgh, and Queen Victoria, always on the track of these matters, "thought Missy will have him." But Missy would not. She married the heir to the Rumanian throne instead, which Victoria considered *declassé*.

Docile Princess May, now seen in the tragic light of being nearly "a widow before she became a wife," spent much time with George that spring of 1892, and in the summer he had "a little talk" with his formidable grandmother. "I think dear Georgie so nice, sensible, and truly right-minded and so anxious to improve himself." Victoria wrote in her diary. Ruder descriptions have called the switch in husbands a matter of going from the bizarre to the boring, from the depraved to the dull.

George and May were duly married on July 6, 1893, during a heat wave. Their marriage was accompanied by unusual quantities of Victorian tears. George's Russian cousin Nicky, destined to be the last Tsar of Russia and the husband of George's — and his — beautiful cousin, Princess Alix of Hesse, came for the wedding. Victoria was relieved that he looked not Russian but "very like Georgie."

The royal couple lived for 18 years in relative modesty, producing children in the shadows cast by the dominant personalities of the two monarchs, Victoria and Edward. Little Princess May survived serenely to become Queen Mary, and, later, the Queen Mother, known for her quaint hats and for living to the age of 86.

George became king during an era now considered tranquil, although great parliamentary debates were raging about the power of the House of Lords, the eternal Irish question, an epidemic of strikes and industrial strife, the revival of socialism, and the women's rights movement. Suffragettes were being brutally force-fed by the police. Still, in retrospect it is considered a golden period. It ended in World War I.

The king often visited war zones and came under fire. Once his horse, startled by the cheers of the troops, reared and fell, crushing and mangling the king. When Winston Churchill, some months later, had to give up his post as First Lord of the Admiralty after the Dardanelles disaster and went to take leave of the king, he was shocked by the poor condition of his health — borne resolutely, and of course hidden from the public, something which could never happen today.

In July 1917, King George, whose background was so richly German, renounced all German titles for himself and his family. The royal house, he proclaimed, would no longer be known as Saxe-Coburg-Gotha or Hanover or Brunswick, but as the House of Windsor.

For our purposes, we might select out of all the pomp and pageantry a scene eight months later, on a Saturday morning in March 1918, when Chaim Weizmann was supposed to have an audience with the king at Buckingham Palace. Weizmann was not sure he ought to go, "since we were setting out on a long and difficult road." It might be wiser, he thought, to wait. But British friends prevailed — Arthur Balfour, Sir Mark Sykes — so Weizmann put on his top hat and set out for the Palace, via the Foreign Office.

There he met Sykes, confused and apologetic. "I have just received some very disquieting telegrams from Cairo," said Sykes, a sentence destined to be repeated many a time in the years to come. "The Arabs are beginning to ask uncomfortable questions. Perhaps it would be better to cancel the interview."

But now, under such circumstances, Weizmann would not agree. Then Balfour arrived; there were long, nervous discussions, and finally Balfour telephoned the Palace to explain that it was all his fault because he was late. The meeting was set for the following Monday.

King George, on meeting Weizmann, said "You know, Mr. Balfour always *does* come late to the office. I quite understand." (The trait would have made him an honorary Israeli). His Majesty then spoke about Palestine, "showing great interest," and also knowing that his guest had been born there; about Russia, where the Revolution was in full swing. "I always warned Nicky about the risks he ran in maintaining that régime, but he would not listen." King George then returned to the purpose of the meeting, "and wished us success in our endeavours."

The colonial echoes of royal social events, which rolled around each year in the backwaters of Palestine during the Mandate, were viewed with superior suspicion by most members of the Yishuv, although a minority found the ambience of such events as the king's birthday celebrations madly attractive.

Those festivities in 1923 were fixed officially for Saturday June 2, and thus brought a typically local complication. Lt.-Col. Kisch, just starting his stint as chairman of the Palestine Zionist Executive, noted that at the garden party at the Governor's House in Jerusalem the only Jews attending, other than officials, were four representatives from Agudat Israel "whose participation is, I consider, proof that their ultra-Orthodoxy is essentially political. Had the community in general attended, I have no doubt that Agudat Israel would not only have abstained, but would have accused us Zionists of violating the Sabbath."

During George's 50th birthday celebrations, there was "trouble about flags," Kisch noted — the Arabs were upset that the Star of David was flying together with the Union Jack. In 1930, after attending the parade of the troops for the royal birthday, Kisch observed that the honours list for the Palestine government officials included three "whom we would ourselves have selected on account of their conduct during the riots." Afterwards, at the garden party, "for the first time since August, there was a thoroughly representative gathering of Jews and Arabs together with English officials mixing freely, a point on which a member of the Arab Executive came to speak to me in friendly comment."

Six years later, George V was dead. Socialist Kingsley Martin said, "He had become the perfect father figure." By the time his very different eldest son and heir Edward had abdicated in favour of his brother, who became George VI, the Arab riots were in full swing.

On all this, and much else, the sycamores of Tel Aviv's King George Street have looked down — but fewer and fewer of them. Threats to the remaining gnarled giants by the march of progress (i.e., traffic) have, from time to time, inspired protests by concerned Tel Aviv citizens. A little lane going briefly east to nowhere off King George, at Beit Jabotinsky, is called "Lane of the Seven Sycamores." Tchernichowsky, whose street skirts the other side of Gan Meir, wrote fondly nearly 40 years ago of the six sycamores of King George. The most I can count these days is five, there in the centre of King George between two streams of cars. I am deeply grateful for this remaining island and try when possible while poised for the leap across, to remember the prophet Amos, whose profession it was to puncture the sycamore-fig fruit.

Pausing at the entrance to the park to read the sign enjoining us to keep it clean, to keep our dogs on a leash, and to refrain from taking photographs on the Sabbath, we finally arrive at the sensational Gan Meir mystery.

Some time after midnight on the night of August 21, 1949, a passerby — had there been one — might have seen the bloodied figure of a young man staggering out of the dark shrubbery of Gan Meir and on to nearby Rehov Bograshov, making desperate efforts to get to the flat where his mother lived. He was taken to Hadassah Hospital, where he died the next morning.

Meanwhile, back in Gan Meir, his half-sister was still trying to get away from the assailant who had attacked them both with a heavy club. After a long struggle — according to the girl's subsequent testimony, it went on for over an hour — the man said, "I will 'have' you even if you should die." He threw her to the ground, beat her, told her he had a knife, and raped her; she was too frightened to call for help.

Afterwards (according to a summary eight months later, in court, by the State Attorney, the late Erwin Shimron) "some compassion awoke in the assailant" and he brought her a red-and-white housecoat (stolen from one Miriam Ernst, who lived nearby). The rapist then offered to take the girl to the edge of the park, but she groaned "Magen David Adom." So he woke the watchman of Beit Hahalutzot and with his help called the police; when they arrived, he gave them his name and address.

What had happened earlier that fatal evening was something like this. On Rehov Allenby, the young man who was killed, a 24-year-old music teacher at a left-wing kibbutz, married and the father of a baby, had by chance met his half-sister, a 21-year-old girl — and an unusually composed and intelligent one, all agreed as the trial dragged on. (We will call her Ruth and her brother David, since I have no wish to embarrass anybody by dragging out this ancient case, even though all the names are on record in the local newspapers that covered it, and the court was thronged with eager sensation-seekers during the long months it was in session.)

Ruth and David had known each other only three weeks before he was murdered. "On the fateful evening," as *The Jerusalem Post* reported the testimony in one of its 82 accounts of the case, they had arranged to meet later after bumping into each other on Allenby. They visited David's mother (they had the same father), and "walked aimlessly in the streets until they reached Gan Meir. Since the gate was locked, they climbed over the fence, sat on the grass, walked about the park, and sat down again facing each other, when suddenly she received a blow on the head... and saw a man standing above her swinging a club."

Because the trial, after two preliminary inquiries, involved 54 witnesses in 44 sittings, whose evidence ran to over 1,000 pages, I cannot even begin to cover the material. It might be mentioned, though, that the defence argued that there had not been one attacker but several, and that these in fact had been "friends of the murdered man's former girl friend." To support this, his mother's early testimony was recalled: she "allegedly told the police, shortly before her son's death... that he was unable to speak after the attack, but nodded affirmatively whenever she asked him if his former girl friend was involved in the attack."

The defendant was convicted of murder and sentenced to death by the District Court. The Supreme Court reduced this to a 15-year sentence for manslaughter. The Supreme Court judgement ran to 78 pages, the longest ever delivered until that time. Justice Agranat found it difficult, for a num-

George V broadcasting to the nation.

ber of reasons, even to accept that the accused was the offender. The accused himself steadfastly maintained his innocence. He was released in 1959, after serving 10 years and being an "exemplary prisoner," and was met at the gates of the Ma'asiyahu Prison by his wife's employers.

What I think may be revealed here is that his real name — not the one in those recurring headlines — turned out to be Christoff Nicolaides. He was a Cypriot and a deserter from the Cyprus army, although he insisted that he was born of Jewish parents in Salonica, and had left the Cyprus army legally.

The defence produced an alibi to show that the accused was elsewhere on the night in question, but it did not stand up under cross-examination. The prosecution, after dealing with the "psychological riddle" of the accused's behaviour in getting a housecoat for its female victim and helping to call the police, also claimed that he had been in the habit of attacking "isolated couples" in the park, "scaring off the male escort and assaulting the girl." There had been other cases of couples attacked in Gan Meir late at night (yes, even 30 years ago) and the evidence pointed to the accused.

Today Gan Meir is an unexpected oasis in the concrete — a bit dusty-looking, and not really as beautiful as an English park, which is what it can look like when skilfully photographed. Boys play basketball, smaller children sport on swings and slides, elderly men and women stroll about and sit on the benches. Mostly the very young and the old seem to come here — those, perhaps, who prefer not to cope with the doings on nearby Dizengoff. The older contingent was certainly born well within the reign of George V. The younger ones, who have not heard of him aside from the street, get all the sex and violence they need on television.

Jerusalem's King George V Street is a powerful monarch of the roads, a street without which no life of any kind could take place in the capital. Together with Ben-Yehuda Street and Jaffa Road, one section of King George forms the famous "Triangle," where all the night life of Jerusalem such as it is, is concentrated. Whenever any great event occurs, such as the Jerusalem soccer team winning the cup, crowds throng King George in spontaneous celebrations, during which the street is closed to traffic.

Not that King George at this stage in its career has such a royal look. It is lined by felafel kiosks, pizza bars, steak bars, ice-cream parlours, gift shops, and so on. One enterprising clothes store calls itself "King," which is fair enough. There are two well-known restaurants, Fink's, and The Gondola.

As soon as the "Triangle" ends, at Ben-Yehuda, King George becomes more majestic. First there is the Hamashbir department store, Jerusalem's largest, which brought the Holy City its first indoor escalator, and close by a new skyscraper, which has brought it its first outdoor one. Just behind is the building which housed Israel's parliament, the Knesset, when it was first moved up from Tel Aviv in 1949. Many great fights took place here between David Ben-Gurion and Menachem Begin: on one occasion, over the issue of whether Israel should accept German reparations, the building was besieged by stone-throwing would-be rejectors of German gold.

All ended satisfactorily, and the reparations were accepted. In due course the Knesset moved to its permanent home, an impressive new building in the government complex known as the Kirya, and its old quarters were taken over by the Ministry of Tourism.

King George Avenue now ends at Paris Square. It used to go right down the hill to what in the old days was Julian's Way, but now, by an ironic twist, has majestic status as King David Street — because that is where the famous King David Hotel is located. King George's dominion was clipped because the Keren Hayesod clamoured for equality with the Keren Kayemet, which already had its street near the Jewish Agency; the lower part of what Jerusalem old-timers still insist on calling King George Avenue accordingly became Rehov Keren Hayesod.

Had King George V still been alive then, it is doubtful whether this would have caused him as much distress as hearing that Princess Mary Avenue would in future commemorate, not his beloved only daughter, but one of ancient Israel's royals, Queen Shlomzion, than which a less euphonious name would be hard to find in any language.

In Haifa, His Majesty was subjected to even harsher treatment. There, the main street through the lower town, running past the port, was Kingsway in Mandatory times. But "Red Haifa," so called because of the city's allegiance to the Labour Party, celebrated statehood by changing its name to Independence Street.

11
Gossip about the Motzkins

Upstairs in the Palace's visitors' gallery, a little man with a little beard sat busily scribbling. Downstairs were the VIPs — Goebbels, Austria's chancellor Dolfuss, Poland's Colonel Beck. Suddenly the little man jumped up and ran down to where Eduard Beneš, the Foreign Minister of Czechoslovakia, was approaching the speakers' rostrum; for Dr. Beneš, it had just been announced, would be the next speaker.

As he met Beneš, the little man gave him the paper on which he had been scribbling. Then Dr. Benes took his place at the rostrum. Watching it all was Ezriel Carlebach, a young journalist who was to found *Ma'ariv*, Israel's largest newspaper, 16 years later. The place was the palace of the League of Nations in Geneva; the year was 1933; and the little man with the beard was Leo Motzkin.

"And then unfolded a performance I was never to forget," Carlebach recalled in 1953. "Beneš put aside the speech prepared by his Foreign Ministry assistants and began to read an oration he had never seen in his life..." It was the speech Motzkin had scribbled upstairs, the message the defender of minority rights everywhere would have delivered if only his title, Chairman of the Committee of Jewish Delegations to the League of Nations, had entitled him to a voice.

"I have seen many of our greatest leaders in their contacts with others," Carlebach continued, "but never have I seen one who, purely through the power of his personality, inspired such unqualified confidence as Motzkin did."

This is one of the Motzkin stories that abound in memoirs and a few memories. Most of us, though, would score poorly in identifying Leo (Aryeh Leib) Motzkin, who was born in a village near Kiev in 1867 and died in Paris very soon after that dramatic scene in Geneva, on his 66th birthday. Yet *The New York Times* gave him a 30-inch obituary, noting that in his constant travels he "circled the globe many times" — in an area when travel meant bumping through the night in an upper berth in a train, or long ocean crossings.

A favourite Motzkinism of mine in this connection is that he always travelled third class, because a first-class ticket seemed to him a shameful waste of funds. Considered eccentric in Zionist circles 50 years ago, today I suppose it would be unthinkable.

Another favourite and hitherto unpublished story concerns his underwear. I have it from the source's mouth, who used to buy replacements for threadbare Motzkin on his visits to London, and at Jaeger's, no less. This horrified Motzkin, because of the expense. "Don't worry," my source used to reassure him, "in the long run they wear so much better and they're *so much easier to darn.*"

Motzkin's family moved to Kiev when he was 14, in 1881, on the day the pogrom started. It made a lasting impression: Motzkin was to become the "pogrom expert," publicizing the problem extensively and defending victims of false accusations.

But the impact of 1881 did not throw the boy off his studies. He attracted the attention of Professor Max Mandelstamm, who was to become a close associate of Herzl. (On the Tel Aviv street map, Mandelstamm's little street is parallel to Motzkin's, on the other side of Dizengoff; in Herzl's *Altneuland* he appears as no less than the President of the Jewish State, "President Eichenstamm.")

In 1882, on the professor's recommendation, Motzkin was sent to high school in Berlin. He finished brilliantly, entered university, and, in addition to mathematics, studied history, literature, philosophy and psychology.

With the Berlin student days began Motzkin's 44-year career of uninterrupted Zionist activity, in place of the predicted brilliant academic life. Always a great organizer, he was one of the founders of the "Russian-Jewish Scientific Society," a group of students in Berlin that included Nahman Syrkin, Shmaryahu Levin and Chaim Weizmann. In 1892, five years before the First Zionist Congress, the group was calling for "Eretz Israel as the centre for a national and spiritual home."

The origin of the affectionate relationship with Weizmann — on his side it became almost hero-worship — is disclosed in the first note the young man from Pinsk wrote to Motzkin in the spring of 1894, a few months after enrolling at the Berlin Polytechnic.

"I shall be able to come for a lesson on Saturday... Be so kind as to have the two marks ready for me... I desperately need the money.

And there was a postscript: "Perhaps you could lend me some money as well... I shall repay you on the first."

I have not been able to discover what subject Motzkin was being coached in by Weizmann, seven years his junior, but the plea for a loan or the return of some money owed was a recurring theme over the next three years. By the summer of 1897 things were becoming desperate for Weizmann. At the beginning of June, he was requesting help because "I am in bed without a pfennig, and I am in dire need."

A day or so later there was a peremptory note: "Mr. Motzkin, I am still without a reply to my letter. My need for money increases every day, and I urgently *insist* on some kind of an answer."

Leo Motzkin — a 44-year career of Zionist activity.

On the 29th, with his landlady to be paid and money owing to "several persons who are causing me unbearable unpleasantness," Weizmann's situation was intolerable, and he was begging for 30 marks at least. "...I am in terrible straits and in fact depend entirely on you. I have nothing to pawn."

At the beginning of July, having been "driven to extremes," he left a visiting card at Motzkin's lodgings, threatening that should the money he was expecting not be forthcoming by eight the following morning, "I shall be forced to seek another solution, which may result in serious unpleasantness..."

On July 31, a few days before leaving Berlin for good (he was going to Switzerland at the beginning of the next academic year to work for his doctorate), Weizmann was formally cool: "I need 30 marks before my departure... I am awaiting an immediate satisfactory reply... this is my last appeal to you..."

This is the last time the subject of money appears in Weizmann's letters to Motzkin; but a second theme was to continue to the end of the friendship. Motzkin may have been a good organizer, but he must have been one of the world's worst correspondents. In the first volume of Weizmann's published letters, in more than seventy that he wrote to Motzkin over the seven years from 1895 to 1902 there is evidence of no more than half a dozen replies. Weizmann's complaint early in 1896 that he is begging for a reply "for the sixth time" becomes increasingly familiar over the years.

Towards the end of 1901 the one-way flow of letters has become a torrent: from November to the following July there are no less than 46, most of them long screeds full of reports on Zionist affairs and requests for information that is never supplied. But on August 11, 1902, he has — wonder of wonders! — heard from Motzkin, and sits down immediately to reply.

In a letter unusually long even for Weizmann, he brings Motzkin up to date with news about the Democratic Fraction — the breakaway from the mainstream of the Zionist Organization they had helped to create a few months earlier to assure the democratic nature and advance the cultural aspects of the movement; reports on the position among the students at Heidelberg; refers to the forthcoming Zionist meeting at Minsk; and informs him that he has obtained the first 1,000 roubles of the 10,000 they will need if they are to go ahead with the project for establishing a Jewish university, if possible in Palestine.

That is the last of a series of letters that become increasingly impersonal since the beginning of the year. At the end of the previous October Weizmann had been writing, "I haven't forgotten my sacred duty to write to you not only as to a friend — one doesn't write to a friend out of duty —

but as to a teacher to whom, to a considerable extent, I owe my ability to work." But less than three months later, after the Fifth Zionist Congress in Basle, the tone changed radically.

There had obviously been trouble at the Congress with the other members of the Fraction, partly due to the fact that Weizmann had acted independently in consulting Herzl without them. On January 14 he wrote: "I do not understand a thing. Can everything have changed so much? Is everything forgotten, scorned and destroyed?" Two weeks later, in reply to one of Motzkin's rare letters, which he describes as being "full of very bitter reproaches, partly undeserved and cruel," he says: "I had a feeling at Basle that you were not quite at ease in my presence, that you sensed something hostile in me..." And in his few remaining letters there are references to "friction" and "ill-feeling" between himself and all the Berlin colleagues.

But if the change was due mainly to political differences, there was another cause too, which had nothing to do with Zionism: it was a matter of chivalry. And to trace its source, we must go back several years, with Leo Motzkin at Berlin University, "frittering away his days and nights," as Weizmann later put it so critically in *Trial and Error*, "in innumerable little student gatherings among the bright young things."

Among the brightest was a group of friends who had been close since high school in Russia and were to remain a close circle later in Palestine. They included a girl called Sophia Getzova, who was studying medicine and was to become the first professor of pathology at the Hadassah-Hebrew University Medical School in Jerusalem; another girl, Helena, who was to marry Shmaryahu Levin; two boys who were to be professors in this country; and Paula Rosenblum, Motzkin's future wife.

Chaim Weizmann and Sophia Getzova became engaged — and an engagement, or "betrothal" in the spirit of the times, was a profoundly serious arrangement, even in emancipated bohemian student circles. One enquirer into this episode in Zionist courtship historiography insists that the two actually "lived together." We shall never know, and it does not matter in the least: the whole issue merely seems to me a blessed relief from political speculation.

But Weizmann went off to continue his studies in Geneva, and there, at the turn of the century, he fell deeply in love with another medical student, Vera Katzman, the woman who was to become the redoubtable First Lady of Israel. In the summer of 1901, he finally wrote to tell his fiancée that he was breaking off their engagement and intended to marry Vera.

The Berlin circle thought he was behaving very badly toward Sophia. And when, in December, Chaim arrived at the Congress in Basle with Vera on his arm, Sophia, in her seat in the gallery, realizing fully at last the extent of his betrayal, fainted dead away.

For Sophia's friends, the sight was unforgettable. Was this the behaviour of an honourable man?

And so a "Comrades' Court of Honour," headed by Motzkin, was formed by six of his friends (Shmaryahu Levin was one) to rule on Weizmann's complex love life. The members deliberated, and decreed that Weizmann must marry Sophia to do her justice; then, if he wished, he could immediately divorce her and marry Vera. They felt that Sophia deserved at least a token marriage after all these years of betrothal.

Weizmann refused. Motzkin considered it dishonourable of him not to accept his comrades' verdict. He also considered it a serious revelation of Weizmann's character. I know, because I heard it from a friend of Motzkin's who had heard it from his own lips a mere two decades after the event.

The story, has, in fact, had a long and healthy life. Motzkin considered it so good a conversation piece that he brought it to friends in London "in place of a present" when he came for dinner, and it was endlessly retold in the Motzkin family, all definitely "on Sophia's side," as Weizmann's parents were also said to have been.

It is just possible that a lingering resentment in this "Court of Honour" affair played its part, on both sides, in subsequent political antagonisms, not to mention the low grades Weizmann passed out to Motzkin many years later. Weizmann wrote of Motzkin that his "great gift" had never been given a chance because of his "muddled" education; he could have done much more for the movement had he completed his education properly — though yet another mathematics professor could hardly compete with an applied chemist and a lucrative, well-timed discovery.

When Herzl's Zionist activities became known, Motzkin immediately supported him. He described his first meeting with Herzl as "filled with glory," and he himself made an instant impression on the First Congress. Yet he objected to Herzl's aims and methods, and headed the "radicals" who called for a clear and decisive statement of principles in the Basle Programme, which he helped draft.

Herzl nevertheless sent Motzkin to Palestine in 1898 to report on conditions, which he did with fulsome statistics. He wrote that the existing settlements were a grave disappointment to anybody expecting either a "biblical or a socialist basis," except for the Biluim at Gedera, and that "the Baron's representatives were not Hovevei Zion."

At the Second Congress, together with Martin Buber, Weizmann, and Berthold Feiwel (his street runs north from Arlosoroff), Motzkin founded the Democratic Fraction as a counter-weight to Herzl's steam-roller tactics.

After all this (and this is only a hint of the man's contributions), there may be a simple but unusual reason for Motzkin's obscurity today: he was a very nice man. Both Socialists and Revisionists liked him and got along with him — a curious but understandable basis for neglect. Motzkin was neither ruthless nor an egomaniac, and has therefore been described as "not cut out to be a leader." But at many a Zionist Congress, the first act of business, traditionally, was to elect Motzkin chairman unanimously and then to get on with the squabbling.

At the same time, his principles, both private and public, were rock-like. Perhaps paradoxically, for one known for his decency, he sacrificed not only himself but his family for those principles. He dearly loved his wife and two sons; yet he became, as Miriam Yalan-Stekelis wrote, "a guest in his own home."

In Tel Aviv, Motzkin's little street is unexpected, almost secret. It is tucked away in a fine neighbourhood near the hotels and embassies, but many Tel Avivians are not sure exactly where. And then, suddenly, the wanderer near the Hilton will find that a narrow side-street widens almost magically into a tree-lined square, almost a brief boulevard. Motzkin is between Ben-Yehuda and Dizengoff and cradled, as it were, in the arms of Jabotinsky and Nordau. This is not inappropriate, because the Revisionists, who saw themselves as the true heirs of Herzl's political Zionism, liked to claim Motzkin.

The back entrance to the Dizengoff police station is on Motzkin, and a friend who has lived practically next door for years assures me that, in the past, terrible shrieks used to be heard from the building, something that would have broken the heart of a liberal Social Democrat like Motzkin.

In Jerusalem, Motzkin's street is also small and charming, although it comes to a dead end. It is located in Kiryat Hayovel, a suburb just beyond Mount Herzl, on the road to the Hadassah Hospital, and was established in the 1950s to provide cheap housing for new immigrants. Motzkin consists of ten attractive little cottages with old-fashioned gardens set off by vines and shrubbery — one of the few streets of this type in the whole of Jerusalem.

Near Haifa, Motzkin's name was also commemorated in the cause of cheap housing for the mass immigration. But here he got a large, bustling suburb in Haifa Bay that has its own municipal council. Kiryat Motzkin was founded in 1934; but far from being a dead-end street of flower gardens, it expanded in the Fifties to absorb two nearby settlements, one a workers' village and the other named after a religious leader.

Here Motzkin's name is commemorated clearly, but for a really secret Motzkin street we go to Ramat Gan, where, until a few years ago the street now named Krinitzi, in honour of that town's late mayor, was called Yahalom. This was not, as one might think, because of any connection with diamonds, although that is the meaning of the word and Ramat Gan is the home of Israel's Diamond Exchange. This Yahalom was supposed to be an acronym for Motzkin, on the argument that his name was really Yehuda Leib Motzkin, the name Aryeh, Hebrew for lion, always being linked with Yehuda, because the lion was the symbol of the tribe of Judah.

The two interests that always conflicted in Motzkin's own life — mathematics and an academic existence versus incessant Zionist and public activity — worked themselves out in the next two generations in an unusually satisfying pattern.

Motzkin had two sons, Theodore Samuel and Gabriel. Theodore (1908-70) was a mathematician who taught at the Hebrew University from 1936 to 1948 and thereafter at Harvard and the University of California — not, as his eldest son assured me, because he wished to live out his life abroad, but simply because "it worked out that way."

Theodore's three sons are all supremely academic in character. I mean this in the kindly sense that they seem to have been born and bred to function within universities, which is more than can be said for many of the people who spend time in them. Dr. Aryeh Leib Motzkin, named after his grandfather, is an expert of mediaeval Jewish history and philosophy. Elhana, the middle grandson, is a professor of mathematics in France, and the youngest, Gabriel, is also a philosopher.

Gabriel was named after his uncle, who died of typhoid at Moshav Moledet in 1942, at the age of thirty-two. He was an unusual boy — sensitive looking, blue-eyed and curly-haired, but with an iron will and a huge dose of idealism. Those who die young, I know, run the risk of being over-eulogized; but I trust the glowing essays written after Gabriel died, in which his resemblance to his mother is stressed — the same quiet manner, aristocratic certitude and complete self-control.

In Germany he first studied mathematics, switched to medicine as being more socially useful, but finally decided that he must come to Palestine and do agricultural work in some new social framework — not the kibbutz, he concluded after intensive ideological analysis, but the newly developing *moshav shitufi*. He prepared for his new life at Be'er Tuvia and Nahalal, and at courses in Rehovot; in the few years he had at Moledet in Galilee, he came to love nature and the land.

It was the young Aryeh Leib Motzkin — the mediaeval Jewish history grandson — who described to me the last flicker of the antique embers of the Weizmann-Getzova-Katzman triangle that he himself witnessed as a boy of about ten.

One day in the mid-Forties, he was walking along a street in Jerusalem with his widowed grandmother and her close friend Dr. Sophia Getzova, who never married, and was by then retired from the Hadassah Hospital. Suddenly the two women stopped in their tracks. Walking toward them

was Chaim Weizmann. He and Sophia had not seen each other for nearly 50 years (although in 1925, when Dr. Getzova was trying to get an appointment to the about-to-open Hebrew University, she appealed to Weizmann to help her with a little "pull").

"I couldn't understand what was happening," recalled Dr. Motzkin. "Suddenly, nobody moved. I kept saying, 'Nu, let's go.' My grandmother and Sophia muttered to each other. Finally, after what seemed to me a very long time, everybody managed to make the passage and get across the street..."

This scene from over 30 years ago, retrieving an episode of half a century earlier is, I confess, more vivid and understandable to me than some of the splits to which it may be connected by however tenuous threads — such as the 1931 vote removing Weizmann from the presidency of the Zionist Congress, and substituting Sokolow, with Motzkin pulling the strings. That, of course, was because the Russian Zionists were openly furious with Weizmann for having, as they saw it, betrayed the principles of political Zionism as set forth in the Basle Programme: in a famous speech in 1929, Weizmann had said that an independent Jewish state was not the immediate aim of Zionism.

The scene also brings to the stage, for the first time, Motzkin's wife Paula. Miriam Yalan-Stekelis, who loved her and observed her closely, felt compelled to rescue her friend from the anonymity she seemed to crave.

After Paula's death, she published an essay about this intellectual girl with the aristocratic character, an example of total self-restraint and modesty, although entirely emancipated by the standards of her time and indeed by the standards of our own day. Paula's field was psychology, and in her student days her papers were published by a leading German psychological journal.

And yet, wrote Miriam Yalan-Stekelis, "it was as though she stopped living her own life when she married him," and as though "her own life was not really a life." Perhaps freeing her husband from all home responsibilities and becoming both a father and a mother to the boys was Paula's chosen form of Zionism. Perhaps the little man with the beard, famous for having more decency and intellect than charisma, nevertheless gave his wife a powerful and romantic centre for her life.

Paula Motzkin, née Rosenblum, was born in Bobruisk, near Minsk, in 1872. She was one of five unusually talented, charming and intelligent sisters (and one brother), in a home noted as a centre of warmth and culture, with fascinating guests always arriving, and an emphasis on learning — in short, everything for which a liberated girl could ask. In high school, she was the leader of that group of young Zionists who were to be lifelong friends, eventually in Palestine.

In 1894, Paula went to Berlin University, and met there the brightest lights of its intellectual life, among them Leo Motzkin. It was, according to legend, "love at first sight" for both, though they did not marry until five years later. She helped Motzkin in his work, including the massively researched two volumes on the Russian pogroms, until the birth of Theodore in 1903. After Gabriel was born, two years later, she devoted herself entirely to the children — and to a constant moving of house, trying to keep up with Motzkin.

Theodore was already at the Hebrew University when Motzkin died in Paris in 1933; his death brought Paula and Gabriel to Palestine, for the burial and for their separate ways here. Paula lived in Jerusalem with Theodore and his family, uninvolved and almost in seclusion, until her death in 1950 at the age of 78. This was eight years after Gabriel was buried at Moledet. Paula, at the graveyard, was stoic as always.

A final Motzkin story, an apocryphal one, again from Ezriel Carlebach, who opened this chapter.

The Zionist Congress was meeting for the first time after Motzkin's death. His old friend Menàhem Ussishkin, the new chairman, eulogized the deceased and then went on to the factionalism at hand.

Suddenly — pandemonium! Motzkin appears. Everybody is thunderstruck. Ussishkin exclaims, "But Motzkin, what are you doing here? You're dead!"

Motzkin, smiling shyly: "That is indeed correct. But today's agenda was so important, one simply had to come."

145

12

The Chelouche Saga

In 1838 or thereabouts (nobody is absolutely sure of the date) a sailing vessel was chartered in war-torn Algeria to bring several Jewish families to the Holy Land. They were headed by 26-year-old Avraham Chelouche and his wife Simha.

According to family tradition, Chelouches had settled in Algeria in 1490 after their expulsion from Portugal. Tradition also tells us they left Oran to help build Jewish settlement in this country. They certainly came to live and work, and not to subsist on charity and be buried here, as most Ashkenazim were then doing.

Disaster overtook the four-masted ship — on the medallion struck by the family a few years ago she bears a strong resemblance to the Mayflower — and she capsized off the rocky coast near Haifa. Little boats put out from shore to rescue the passengers, and about 20 were saved. They included Avraham and Simha Chelouche, their nine-year-old son Aharon, and their two daughters, Hannah and Rika. But 18 were lost, probably when one of the rescue boats overturned. Among them were the two younger Chelouche boys, Eliahu and Yosef.

After a year in Haifa, a village of about 2,000 souls and thus too small for a merchant of Avraham's expectations, the family moved first to Nablus and then to Jerusalem. They stayed there for a very short time, finally settling in Jaffa, probably in 1840 or soon after.

There were exactly 123 Jews in this walled town of perhaps 5,000 Arab Moslems and Christians. The Jews included 113 Sephardim, nine Ashkenazim, and one lonely Yemenite. We know all this, and their names and ages and occupations, because Sir Moses Montefiore ordered a census in Jaffa in 1839; and since our Chelouches do not appear in it, we know they must have arrived later.

Montefiore's statistics make an interesting point about Jaffa's Jews. A quarter of them were craftsmen and 40 per cent were "in business" — a far healthier situation than in holy Jerusalem. In Jaffa, only 19 per cent were "occupied with religion," and the rest were in that useful catch-all, "miscellaneous."

These Jews were in Jaffa in spite of the *herem*, the ban that Jerusalem's rabbis had placed on the port city centuries earlier, in order to keep travellers from being "tempted" to settle there. The ban was finally lifted in 1841.

For the Chelouches, as for all new arrivals, the nearest approach to a hotel was the Jewish Hostel, founded a few decades earlier by a wealthy Jew from Istanbul. Soon after, they moved to permanent quarters above what had been, at different times, the Turkish Governor's palace and a soap factory and is now the Archaeological Museum, and over the adjoining *hamam*, the Turkish baths.

Of Avraham's two daughters, Rika, the younger, married Nissim Carasenti,whose family, known as "the tobacco kings of Algeria," had arrived in Palestine not long after the Chelouches. Hannah married Alter Luria, whose father was a Safad rabbi descended from the renowned Ari. The rabbi was killed in the disastrous earthquake of 1837, the year Alter was born. His widowed mother took him to Jerusalem, where she married a goldsmith who taught the boy his craft. When Alter grew up he moved to Jaffa, one of the first Ashkenazim to settle there. Soon after marrying Hannah he opened a jewellery shop and began teaching his young brother-in-law Aharon gold-and silver-smithing.

Aharon acquired his own little shop in the Street of the Money-Changers, an alley behind Jaffa's picturesque clocktower. He soon branched out into exchanging coins; and being an astute businessman who understood the difference between the exchange rate and the gold-content value of a coin, he prospered.

And as he prospered, he started buying land around Jaffa from Arab owners — first alone and then with friends prominent in the Sephardi community,Haim Amzalag, the British vice-consul, and Yosef Bey Moyal, and later on with his sons. Land in those days was measured by the distance covered by a rock thrown by the purchaser. Aharon had a strong throwing arm and a strong reason for buying land among the dunes and groves around Jaffa. For he was among the first to have the vision of an enormous Jewish city that would stretch far past the horizon north of Jaffa.

Before his arm tired, he had acquired more than 800 dunams — 200 acres — in various sectors. In one of them, in 1887, he built a house for himself, solitary among the dunes, with a view of the sea. The house was a small community in itself. In its eight rooms lived Aharon and his wife Sarah, the daughter of a Baghdad family named Matzliah whom he had married in 1859, their two daughters and three sons, and the sons' wives and children. Aharon's grandchildren grew up "like brothers" in the old house. But despite this extended clan system, the women complained that they were lonely and eventually "went on strike" and insisted that, somehow, neighbours should be provided.

So, offering plot around his own house at very low prices, he attracted others wishing to leave the confines of Jaffa. And that was the start of Neve Tzedek — "Habitations of Justice" — two decades before the metropolis of Tel Aviv was founded.

If you walk down to Neve Tzedek today, you enter another world the moment you step across the southern end of Lilienblum or Judah Halevi. The streets are narrower, so the traffic is immediately vastly diminished. Judah Halevi suddenly becomes Shimon Rokach Street — Rokach, with Chelouche, was a founder of Neve Tzedek.

Rokach Street is very short, ending at Chelouche Street, which is still dominated by the old mansion, now Number 32, in which Aharon lived until his death at the age of 91. The other houses are one-storey, some lived in, others now serving as small workshops — a carpenter's, a printing shop, a candy factory. These are the buildings which, when they were first erected, were admiringly referred to by the Arabs of Jaffa as the "Parisian houses," the last word in European elegance. Number 7 is embellished by a pair of Roman columns, which gives it an air of slightly mad classic grandeur. Nearby is a children's playground — like so much else, built on land given by the Chelouche family to the city.

Where the railroad used to run to Jaffa, the deep gully is filling up with trash. But it could be a garden. Indeed, one house built near the bridge has a country-squire look, with a dovecote and geraniums in huge pots. The bridge here, built by Chelouche, used to be the sporting centre of town, with the neighbourhood boys gathering to watch the train come by, or to jump off the bridge down into the gully, or best of all, to gather a store of rocks on Saturday in order to throw them at the boys of the nearby German Templar community to the south, towards Jaffa.

The vanished railroad marked the border between "Valhalla" — the German Templar colony, with its population of about 350, its handsome houses and gardens, and the best hotel for miles around before World War I — and the Parisian houses of Neve Tzedek in its prime.

Off Chelouche Street is the obscure Chelouche Lane, dwindling into an unpaved area of garages and workshops. It has no proper street sign; the name appears only on a plastic disc swaying from the side of an elderly house.

The third street named for the Chelouche family is a long way north of Jaffa, near the Mann Auditorium, and actually a continuation of Huberman. Only one of the street signs along the two blocks that make up Yosef Eliahu Street explains that his full name was Yosef Eliahu Chelouche. He was the second of Aharon's three sons, named after the two little brothers who had died in the shipwreck.

Yosef Eliahu and his elder brother, Avraham Haim, a modest and hard-working man, were partners in Chelouche Frères, the building factory established next door to the family mansion, which built much of the early city of Tel Aviv. Today it is a plastic bag factory.

Aharon's youngest son, Ya'acov, went to Beirut to study commerce, Arabic literature and Middle Eastern history. In 1903 he was appointed

The Chelouche mansion 1829 (above). Twin houses of the Chelouche brothers (below).

treasurer of the Anglo-Palestine Bank, where he worked until his death 41 years later. Ya'acov, who helped to establish Tel Aviv, also found time to be the city's first inspector of kindergartens, was a member of the board of the Habimah Theatre and of Beit Bialik, worked tirelessly for understanding between Ashkenazim and Sephardim and between Jews and Arabs, and wrote poetry in both Hebrew and Arabic.

There was a strong poetic streak in his eldest brother too.

"This girl has skin as white as marble, as white as crystal, as smooth as silk! By Allah, she will find favour in your eyes!" So began a letter written by Avraham Haim to Ya'acov, for whom the time had come to find a bride. Avraham had undertaken the almost two-day journey to Jerusalem to be taken by a friend to the home of Rabbi Shlomo Baruch, father of the prospective bride.

"What a family!" he wrote. "What serenity and quiet! What an atmosphere of honour! When the rabbi speaks, nobody opens his mouth. The women sit together to one side, speak among themselves about women's concerns. My friend requested a glass of water for me. And then Perla came in, and she is beautiful and pure, with a skin as white as crystal.

"'How is the water?' my friend asked me. And I answered, 'There is no water so pure and beautiful as the water of Jerusalem.'"

And that was how, once upon a time, brides were found for young men.

Avraham Haim himself had married his wife, Sarah Elbaz, when she was a mere 12 years old; a year later, she bore the first of her six children. This early child-bearing did not affect her looks: one of the family legends is about the disbelief of the hotel clerk when she accompanied her eldest son to Paris and checked in as his mother.

Chelouche descendants still cultivate their family legends. One is about the night, nearly a hundred years ago, when burglars attempted to break into the Chelouche mansion to steal the cash for the new railroad, which for some unexplained reason was kept by Aharon. The burglary was unsuccessful; but the Turkish Governor stationed 12 soldiers to guard the house from then on. They ate so well, courtesy of the Chelouche household, that they were heartbroken when orders came for them to depart.

On another occasion, Aharon was woken up by strange sounds in the house. He got out of bed, went into the synagogue which he had built as a wing of the house, and started praying. The sight of the patriarchal figure in his long nightshirt, grasping the Bible in prophetic style, so terrified the intruders that they ran away without stealing anything. He was better than any burglar alarm.

Then there's the legend about the kidnapping of Yosef Eliahu when he was six years old. He was leaving his father's shop one noon, dressed as usual in silken finery, when he was accosted by a mysterious Arab who lured him away and walked him out of Jaffa — out past the orange groves

150

and the sand dunes into the desert. Late at night, after a search party of Turkish soldiers had been sent out, he was found — by whom, I was not able to discover. Nobody ever understood the motive. Possibly it was the legend of the Green Vein — for young Yosef Eliahu had a green vein between his eyes, which, it was said, could bring great treasure...

But perhaps the best of the legends is the one that began one bright morning at the turn of the century, when Aharon was walking from his carriage down the narrow Street of the Money-Changers to his little shop. Noticing a teenaged Arab boy crying bitterly, he stopped to ask what the trouble was. His camel had been stolen, the boy answered, and all his money too.

"My father, Sheikh Samara, sent me to Jaffa from our village, to sell the camel. I slept in the khan here, and during the night thieves stole all my money, and the camel as well. And now, how can I show my face at home?"

Aharon Chelouche took a coin from the pocket of his long jelabia; it was a Turkish mejida — not a trifling sum. "Take it, my son," he said. "Your father will forgive you."

The boy was overwhelmed. "But you don't know me at all. I come from Kafr Jamal, which is far away. How will I be able to repay this debt? And — who are you?"

"My name is Aharon Chelouche," said the old gentleman. "Now return to your village, and may Allah bless you."

Like other veteran Sephardi families in this country (and long-established, Arabic-speaking Ashkenazi families as well), Chelouches down the generations have had close personal and business ties with Arabs here and in the neighbouring countries: for a family that has lived in the Arabic-speaking world for 500 years, it would have been peculiar otherwise.

These encounters began on a natural and innocent human level, if anything in the Middle East is ever innocent.

A year before the outbreak of World War I, Yosef Eliahu went to Egypt to conduct industrial espionage. His idea was to learn how to make bricks of a kind Jewish workers could work with, for only the Arabs knew how to deal with the soft sandstone blocks then used. After much correspondence, he learned that an Egyptian factory was making such silicate bricks. The owner, he also learned, was a freemason, and so Yosef Eliahu, armed with a letter of introduction from a masonic friend in Jaffa, went off to Egypt. The owner welcomed him kindly, but it soon became clear that there was no question of obtaining the manufacturing process.

At the suggestion of an Egyptian friend, Yosef Eliahu therefore put on tattered workman's clothes and turned up at the factory, where he worked for 10 days as an ordinary labourer and soon learned what he needed to know. (The owner of the factory, whose hospitality Yosef Eliahu abused, was in fact not an Arab at all, but a Greek.)

In the end, Yosef Eliahu could not set up his long-dreamed-of brick silicate factory. It is a sad story, as he tells it in his memoirs: a group of Ashkenazi entrepreneurs put up a plant that was "far too grandiose, and unsuited to our conditions." It does not look all that grandiose in a photo of the times; but then, we have often erred on the side of grandeur and inappropriateness. Certainly, what stands today on the old "silicate" site, near Dizengoff Circle, is a multi-storeyed parking garage.

Many of the Chelouches have been critical of the attitude adopted towards the Arabs by Jews who immigrated from Europe, and from whose ranks the official Jewish leadership was drawn. This attitude, almost one of contempt and certainly one which showed a lack of understanding, was based on ignorance of the Arabic language, Arab culture, Arab aspirations, Arab pride and Arab customs. Would the course of history have been changed if the veteran Sephardi families, like the Chelouches, had been able to determine policy? A grandson of Yosef Eliahu, Aviezer Chelouche, who served at one time as a high-ranking Foreign Ministry official and is also a university vice-president, has described speculating about such a question as "an exercise in futility."

With World War I and the expulsion from Tel Aviv in 1917 of all Jews who were not Turkish citizens, the status of the Chelouches (who had always maintained their French citizenship) changed rudely, and like everybody else, they became refugees.

Yosef Eliahu emphasizes the help and kindness offered by Arab friends, who gave money and food with no arrangement for repayment. The Jews of Petah Tikva, on the other hand, were interested in high rents from the homeless. Worse still, they discriminated against the Sephardim — and still more against the Yemenites — in distributing aid. Meir Dizengoff, writing of the same period, observed that everybody was "like one family." Not so, says Yosef Eliahu, who took his complaints to the Central Committee and insisted that ethnic discrimination end.

In 1918, with the approach of the British Army, the exiles were ordered to leave Petah Tikva. Yosef Eliahu, ever critical of the moshava leaders' lack of comprehension of Oriental ways, believed that they did not deal intelligently with the Turkish commander. In any event, hungry and ragged, and with only occasional help from Arab friends, the once prosperous Chelouche clan — some 40 souls — finally arrived at an Arab village called Kfar Jamal, near Kfar Sava.

A small comic scene is recalled by Margalit Havatzelet, the daughter of Ya'acov Chelouche.

"When we got to the village, we arranged to rent a tiny Arab house for our family — my mother, the five children — and yes, a maid too." (War

152

is war, exile is exile, but in the old days one travelled with servants.)

"My mother took everything in her stride until the man who was renting us the house said, 'And of course, the camel will sleep here with you.' That was too much for her, and she burst into tears. Though from the Arab's point of view it was logical, since the camel was his most valuable possession."

Finally, a bit more money was paid and the camel slept elsewhere.

The war rolled on. Food and money became increasingly scarce. Then one day — Margalit remembers — a little caravan of five camels led by an Arab on a donkey appeared. The Arab dismounted from the donkey and asked, "Is there here a man called Chelouche?" Old Aharon, now a venerable 89, presented himself, and the stranger said, "You don't remember me. My name is Hadj Ibrahim Samara, and I am the boy to whom you once gave a mejida in Jaffa. I will never forget that kindness as long as I live. Now I have heard that you are refugees here..."

And the man began to unload his camels and give the hungry Chelouches sacks of flour, and jars of oil, and containers of carob honey, and delicacies they had forgotten existed.

And then the sheikh invited Yosef Eliahu to his home, and began measuring the wall, and broke the plaster, and took from a certain spot a red cloth that contained 500 gold sovereigns. And he gave them to Chelouche, insisting that he himself had no need for them at the moment. When, Allah willing, the war ended, the family could repay him.

The details, as Yosef Eliahu recalled them, are marvellous. "But what if we should die before the war ends?" he asked the Arab. The man replied, "Well, then neither of us will need the money."

The debt was paid soon after the war ended; and warm relations between the families continued for years. Regularly, a wagon of sugar cane, watermelons and the finest fruits of the season came from the family in Kfar Jamal to the Chelouche homes in Tel Aviv. It was widely believed that one of Sheikh Ibrahim's sons wanted to marry pretty Simha, Avraham Haim's elder daughter. She married a Polish dentist, as it happened, but she used to go riding with the young Arabs in the carriage that came from the village, because it was obvious that she was absolutely safe with them.

In May 1921, serious Arab riots broke out in Jerusalem, Jaffa and other parts of Palestine. In the newly formed municipal council of Jaffa-Tel Aviv, the conflict between Jewish and Arab members burst into a dangerous confrontation. In an attempt to prevent bloodshed, Yosef Eliahu went from Tel Aviv to Jaffa, through streets crowded with club-swinging Arabs. Just as one was about to attack him, "one from a village who didn't know me," he was saved by another Arab who shouted, in the nick of time, "Don't touch that man! He is a son of this country!"

While the violence raged in the streets, the three Moslem members of the Council sat cheerfully watching when Yosef Eliahu arrived at the council building. They hated each other, Yosef Eliahu knew; this was the first time he had ever seen them united. "It's all the fault of those Bolsheviks of yours, who came from Moscow," shouted one of the effendis.

This time Yosef Eliahu defended the Ashkenazi newcomers. "My brothers have come to build this country, not to quarrel. You simply do not understand them." If this conflict continued, he warned, both sides would suffer — the Arabs as much as the Jews.

One of the members of the present generation of the Chelouche family who has very strong feelings about the relationship between Jews and Arabs is Aharon Luria, a son of old Aharon Chelouche's younger daughter Sultana and her husband Yeshayahu, a grandson of Aharon's sister Hannah Luria.

Aharon Luria became manager of El Al's Haifa office, and lives in a Spanish — i.e. Sephardi — villa on a hilltop near Haifa, which one sees through a series of romantic Oriental arches. It was built by Arabs from the West Bank. Aharon feels vehemently that Arabs must be treated with friendship and respect.

"That is the way I was brought up," he told me. "For years now I have been arguing with Jews who say that Arabs understand only force and a heavy hand. These are Jews who've come here only fifteen, twenty or thirty years ago..." His voice trails off with a kind of contempt.

"The walls of my cellar are 30 centimetres thick, instead of the 20 specified. When I asked the Arab workers why they built the walls so thick, they replied, 'Because we like you.'

"My mother, Sultana, always used to bring matzot to her Arab friends during Pessah," he went on. "The Arabs looked upon it as bread with a special blessing. And they, in turn, always brought us a lamb for Pessah, and gifts of green olives and honey and a little bundle of wheat at the end of the festival. My father would hang the wheat over our door, and we would pray, and the Arabs would pronounce the blessing *Santak hadra* — May your year be green."

Another remarkable repository of the purely Middle Eastern way of life that once prevailed here is Julia Chelouche, the widow of Avraham Haim's son David. In her richly detailed memoirs she has recalled literally hundreds of vignettes of the life of her own family, the Moyals, as well as that of the one she married into. Julia has total recall, not only for events, but for a remarkable series of predictions in dreams. Thus, as a girl, she foresaw her engagement to a Chelouche when she dreamt of meeting her future father-in-law on the street in Jaffa and being presented by him with a string of expensive pearls.

Actually, it was Avraham Haim's eldest son Marko whom she nearly married. The Chelouche and Moyal families both thought a match would be an excellent thing and that Marko, as the eldest, ought to have first choice. But Marko was in Paris at the time, so Julia was photographed by Tel Aviv's pioneer photographer, Soskin, and her photo was sent to France. "Father, I cannot decide by mail," Marko wrote back. "Let David decide." David was only too happy to do so.

In the *dolce vita* tradition of Tel Aviv in the Twenties, Julia's trousseau came from Paris, her lingerie was hand-embroidered in Jaffa, and other purchases were made in Cairo. At the wedding party in October 1921, held at the Eden Cinema, the British Army band played, and many Arabs were among the guests, the first time Arabs attended a big Jewish event since the riots of May that year.

Despite their friendship with the Arabs, the Chelouches were inevitably drawn into the conflict, as it became ever more intense and bitter. In 1948, during one of the few periods when the IZL, the dissident underground movement, and the Hagana, the official Jewish resistance, were cooperating, a Chelouche house served as IZL headquarters. This was one of the remarkable "twin" houses on Pines Street, opposite the old Eden Cinema, that Aharon had built for his two older sons in 1910. The houses were identical twins, but Aharon had the brothers draw lots to decide who would get which, so no quarrel could possibly arise.

By 1948, Zaki Chelouche, Avraham Haim's second son (an architect, educated in France and Switzerland,active in public and engineering circles here) was living alone in the house, a solid two-storey building filled in the Chelouche manner with beautiful Oriental rugs, silverware and everything needed for gracious living. The IZL commander approached Zaki in great secrecy and asked if the house, which would fit in beautifully in any bourgeois French suburb of the day, could be turned over to his men for planning the attack. Certainly, said, Zaki, who packed a small suitcase and went to stay with one of his numerous relatives.

Two weeks and much bloodshed later, the key was returned to Zaki Chelouche, and he moved back to his house to find that every item, down to the smallest silver spoon, was exactly where he had left it.

But we must be even-handed in our treatment of the Chelouches and their attitude to the rival underground military organizations. If Zaki's house was used by the IZL, Ya'acov Chelouche's big house on Rothschild Boulevard had long been secretly used by the Hagana: Ya'acov's younger son, Shlomo, was a Hagana officer.

Ya'acov, the Arabic scholar who wrote poetry in Arabic and had for decades worked to promote Arab-Jewish understanding, had at first been reluctant to be drawn into any activist Jewish underground movement.The murder of his eldest son Gabriel in 1938 by an Arab ambush on the road to Jerusalem changed his attitude.

Gabriel, killed at 32, was an engineer trained in Alexandria and Paris, active in civic projects for the city of Tel Aviv. The big house on Rothschild was filled with hundreds of mourners after the funeral — Arab as well as Jewish. Neither Ya'acov nor his wife ever recovered from the tragedy.

To close one cycle of the story of old Aharon and the mejida: in 1950 his great-grandson, Aharon Chelouche, a senior police officer, encountered a son of the boy — by then a sheikh — who had received the coin. He was a villager living illegally within the old Green Line, for Kafr Jamal was now on the Jordanian side, and he pleaded with Chelouche to be allowed to stay with relatives in Israel. The two men, now officially enemies, confronted the past in a dramatic scene.

"In my mind's eye, I saw those camels which brought food and help to my family," the present Aharon Chelouche later recalled. He said to the Arab, "You don't know me, but your father once saved my family," and proceeded to obtain special permission for the man to remain in Israel.

The last link occurred a few years ago, when Aharon Chelouche was working as academic secretary at Tel Aviv University. Among the virulently anti-Israel Arab students on the campus, one of ths most active turned out to be — yes, a great-granddaughter of the kindly sheikh from Kafr Jamal. The story of the past emerged in Chelouche's office, and the girl invited him to visit her village, "though I wouldn't say that she turned into a Zionist."

The day of the patriarch is over in this land, but the children of past patriarchs will continue to meet here, and exotic old debts which seem irrelevant in an era of power politics nevertheless deserve to be remembered.

Let us end the Chelouche saga, as we began, with the shipwreck. Margalit Havatzelet, eldest daughter of Ya'acov, Aharon's youngest son, was born in the big house in Neve Tzedek, and she remembers vividly the stories told by her grandfather, the old patriarch, to his ever-growing circle of grandchildren.

Margalit says: "Even as a very old man, when Aharon came to the part of the story when he watched his two little brothers, Yosef and Eliahu, drown in the storm — he could never help crying."

13
A New Historical Jesus

In what I like to think of as a Chagall-style vision, the ghost of the historical Jesus can, without too much difficulty, be made to float problematically over the street named in honour of the writer, philosopher and historian, Micha Josef Berdyczewski.

There is a good basis for this notion, startling though it may be to the residents and shopkeepers, and most especially to the members of Agudat Israel, the ultra-Orthodox political party, whose building is at the Rothschild end of Berdyczewski Street.

For although Micha Josef Berdyczewski, who was born in Russia in 1865, is best known for his stories of Jewish life in Eastern Europe, he himself considered his research into early Jewish history, the Samaritan tradition and the origins of Christianity to be his most important contributions to literature, history and philosophy.

One result of this research was a radical theory about the man who became the Christ of the New Testament: Berdyczewski dealt with the subject at a time when doing so was even less acceptable in Jewish circles than it is today.

Berdyczewski's theory, based on a passage in the fifth chapter of Josephus Flavius' *The Jewish War*, was that the "real" Jesus was not Jesus of Nazareth at all, but another one entirely. Berdyczewski's Jesus was Yeshu Ben Hanan, who lived nearly 40 years later than Jesus the son of Mary; in this account, there is no legend-like virgin birth in Bethlehem, no descent from the line of David, no crucifixion. Berdyczewski's Jesus wandered around Jerusalem before and during the Roman siege for about seven years, crying "Woe to the City, the people, and the Sanctuary!" and predicting its destruction. The Romans scourged him; then they released him, on the grounds that he was mad. He reacted neither to torment nor to comfort. This Jesus was killed accidentally, by a stone from a catapult during the siege, in the year 70.

Another reference by Josephus to Jesus, this time in the *Antiquities*, fits the spirit of the New Testament version; it has been much discussed by scholars and is widely thought to be a latter insertion by another writer. But then, as Israel's most irresistible and distinguished Bible scholar, David Flusser, pointed out in a negative critique of Berdyczewski's theory in *Ha'aretz* in 1959, about 20 people called "Yeshu" are referred to in Josephus' voluminous writings.

157

In his article, Professor Flusser arrayed a mass of scholarly data against Berdyczewski's revolutionary theory. The bemused reader is introduced to such assumptions of Berdyczewski's as, for instance, that the figure of Judas Iscariot in the evangelical account of Jesus Christ is really a legendary symbol for Brutus as the betrayer of Julius Caesar. But the real difficulty, says Flusser, is that Berdyczewski's Jesus dies in the year 70, three years after the death of Paul, which is inconsistent with the early history of the church.

Flusser gallantly apologized for attacking the thesis of an author no longer alive to defend it. He recalled Berdyczewski's position in Hebrew literature and hoped, as well, that the book would send readers back to Josephus Flavius.

Berdyczewski's little street in Tel Aviv (between Marmorek and Crémieux, from Judah Halevi to Rothschild) leads us through some very remarkable intellectual scenery. It makes us consider the competition between Jerusalem and Samaria; the problem of rewriting history; and the much-discussed conflict, if any, between Judaism and "humanism."

But before we start scampering down the bylaws, I want to insert the following typically paradoxical anecdote. "What brought me to this country," a founding member of a Jordan Valley kibbutz told Berdyczewski's son some years ago, "was not the Zionism of Ahad Ha'am, but the anti-Zionism of Berdyczewski."

The street is short and straight, but Berdyczewski's intellectual path to Zion was a complex maze of ambivalence and tensions. It is not only Agudat Israel that should feel uncomfortable about Berdyczewski, and for reasons transcending the problem of Jesus. Today's secular malaise and our atmosphere of crisis of ends and means can take us right back to Berdyczewski, who believed that the Jews themselves are to a great extent to blame for their oppression. None of the variously proffered solutions to their problems could succeed, he believed, because they were not radical enough.

The Jews had to build a new nation in their own land. But it would have to be based on the values of pre-rabbinate Judaism, and all Jewish tradition, scholarship and religion of the Diaspora would have to be overthrown. This is a tall order, as he himself realized, and he was deeply pessimistic about any ultimate solution.

A prodigiously educated scion of 13 generations of Hassidic rabbis, Berdyczewski attacked such abstractions as the static values of institutionalized religion, public consensus, history, and, yes, ideology too. He opposed not only Ahad Ha'am, who esteemed him and for whom he worked briefly, but Herzl as well. A "spiritual centre" without material reality was impossible; but, on the other hand, political Zionism did not go far enough; it was wrong to try to graft new ideas on old ones, and

158

political Zionism had become trapped in "religious romanticism."

He never visited Palestine; but then, he could not have afforded the trip, for he and his family lived in poverty while he worked prodigiously. He also opposed the well-meaning activities of Rothschild and Hirsch, although he knew that only visible, concrete facts could accomplish anything. But these facts would have to be preceded by that change in morality and ethics. In any analysis of Berdyczewski, the name of Nietzsche often crops up, although his son believes that the influence of Schopenhauer was more relevant.

I have not discussed any of this with my friend Hinde, the reigning fishmonger of Rehov Berdyczewski, for she has troubles of her own. Inflation, for one thing; also, what she considers the perfidy of the government. "What will be the end?" she asks, cleaving a carp. "Remember, not long ago, when *kasif* was IL8 a kilo? Now it goes up every day. And do you know, nobody cares! And there's no control. The members of the government are liars, all liars."

Berdyczewski's son Emanuel Bin-Gorion, is a scholarly writer, editor, and former librarian, who translated (from Hebrew into German), and published posthumously, many of his father's works.

Much of what I learned from him is, I think, unfamiliar even to many who know his father's fiction, with the exception, of course, of those hundred or so who have written, or are now writing, doctoral theses on Berdyczewski, because of his current academic revival.

Because Berdyczewski devoted 'his writing to both fiction and history, he was considered for some time as having fallen between two stools. And this, so one doctoral candidate suggested to me, may partly account for the long neglect of his works. But his anti-establishment-and-all-other-sacred-cows attitude certainly contributed to his falling into disfavour. Things are now changing; in the late Seventies 5,000 copies of his fat anthology of Jewish legends were published in, of all places, East Germany.

Rehov Berdyczewski ought, strictly speaking, to be called Rehov Bin-Gorion. That is how, from 1912 onwards he signed his works, and in 1918 he adopted it legally as his name. Emanuel always refers to his father as "MJB," and from now on I shall do the same.

The street might well be called Rehov Josephus Flavius, or the Hebrew version of the great classical historian's name, Yosef Ben-Matityahu, for it was in his honour that MJB chose his new name. But why Bin-Gorion? Because — and even this simplified version is complicated — a history of Josephus and the wars of the Jews and the Romans, entitled *Sefer Yosifon*, was written in Italy around the 10th century. The unknown author refers to himself as Yosef Ben-Gorion Hacohen. The book was once attributed to Josephus Flavius himself, and in it a Ben-Gorion also appears as a Jewish general. This rare work attracted MJB, and he adopted the name, changing "Ben" to "Bin."

Among other controversies into which MJB plunged, he questioned in his historical research the eternal centrality of Jerusalem in Jewish history. We are invited to recall the early conflict between Shechem (Nablus) and Jerusalem, and to consider two distinct trends in Jewish tradition. The one which prevailed as history came to be written in the Bible, involved Moses, Mt. Sinai, and the Ten Commandments. The other involved Joshua, Mt. Gerizim and Mt. Ebal, on either side of Shechem, and the Twelve Curses. Here MJB's references are to Deuteronomy 27 and Joshua 24. We are now in a region famous for purification rites and covenant renewals. It is also the most controversial part of the West Bank, which excites political passions both in Israel and abroad.

MJB finished a novel, *Myriam,* on November 16, 1921, and the following day he told his wife that he considered his uncompleted historical analysis so important that perhaps his belief in it would give him the strength to survive and finish it. But that was not to be; he died the very next day, at the age of 56.

The outline of MJB's rather threadbare external life is more easily sketched than that of his intellectual life, which was richly studded with contrasts and antitheses. He was born in Podolia, in the Ukraine. He was married off by his family when he was 17, but two years later, his rigidly Orthodox brother-in-law forced him to divorce his wife, and banished him from the house, because he had been caught reading a Hebrew book by Nahum Sokolow.

Single again, he entered the famous yeshiva at Volosnov. Attracted by the Enlightenment, still deep in the rabbinical world, he began to write; by the time he was 25, he had published 100 articles. In search of more intellectual freedom, he moved to Odessa, but in 1891 he went to Germany, and never again returned to the restraints of Eastern Europe, except for a brief trip so that his father could perform his second wedding ceremony. He studied philosophy and political science at the universities of Breslau, Berlin and Berne; at times he was so poor that he read by the light of the street lamp. It was not until 1901, when he was 36, that he remarried, this time a young dentistry student, Rahel Ramberg, who helped him professionally, and supported him financially, until his death at the age of 56. She and Emanuel came to settle in Palestine in 1936.

MJB's subject-matter was always Jewish (or Samaritan), whether he was dealing with the *shtetl* experiences of his youth in his fiction, or using biblical or talmudic or aggadah sources for his research. Yet he chose to live a modern, secular life, and opposed the organized religious life of the synagogue.

One of MJB's great admirers was the Hebrew writer Yosef Brenner, whose own pessimistic, ambivalent, and in the end probably suicidal

160

views are now also enjoying a revival in academic circles. He first visited MJB in Breslau in 1908, and it is not surprising that he came to regard him as a kindred spirit. They corresponded until Brenner's murder by Arabs in the Jaffa riots in May 1921, just six months before MJB's death. Their letters were edited by Shlomo Bertonoff and published by Kibbutz Me'uhad.

At their first meeting, described in MJB's diary, they discussed the Jewish question, and he wondered later "why Brenner suffered so, why he returned to the Judaism he had left," and to the Zionism he considered so empty. Brenner "looked like an escaped criminal," but he immediately "made friends with the child and gave him a little carved boat to play with in the bathtub."

The child was the five-year-old Emanuel, and it was he who, 70 years later, read me the passage. Emanuel Bin-Gorion is married to the dancer Devora Bertonoff. One room in their Holon flat is dedicated to the memory of her father, Yehoshua Bertonoff who was one of Habimah's most popular actors. Next to it is a room containing books and mementos of MJB. Together, the two rooms make an impressive conjunction of intellectual and cultural history.

David Ben-Gurion, whose original name was Gryn, was apparently very anxious to reassure himself that he was first to pick the new name, for he twice raised the matter with Emanuel. In fact, he beat MJB to it by about two years, for he first adopted it — curiously enough, also as a journalistic *nom de plume* — when he joined the editorial staff of the *Poale Zion* journal, *Ahdut,* in 1910.

It was not until nearly forty years after MJB's death that B-G learned of MJB's research regarding the two mountains on whose peaks rests the core of Jewish tradition — Sinai and Gerizim. This was when, having turned to his own historical musings following the 1957 withdrawal from Sinai, he announced his view that Mount Sinai was in a sense less crucial to Jewish history than Mount Gerizim. At this point, Emanuel Bin-Gorion sent Prime Minister Ben-Gurion the relevant portions of his father's six-volume work: *The Life of Moses, The Stations of the Law in the Pentateuch; Sinai and Gerizim; Judah and Israel; Jesus, Son of Ananos*; and *Saul and Paul.*

B-G was obviously looking for biblical justification for a political act. MJB's motive, if I understand it correctly, was just the opposite: a concern with historical truth, and, precisely, the wish to correct what he took to be the "editing" of the Bible by interested political parties.

By the time B-G was relishing the confirmation he found in MJB so long after its first publication, archaeologists with no axe to grind, from such American universities as Vanderbilt and Drew, had been at work excavating Shechem, the "uncrowned Queen of Palestine." They emphasized its early religious and political supremacy; they pointed disparagingly to

Hebrew writer Micha Josef Berdyczewski (Bin-Gorion).

the Bible's "Jerusalem bias" resulting from David's political successes.

When Emanuel Bin-Gorion was a boy, he asked his father why in the world he had picked the name of a man generally regarded as a traitor to his people. His father answered that the boy ought not to believe everything he heard. Besides, he pointed out, not only was Josephus Flavius an important historian without whose writings we would know far less of the past, but he himself and his writings are the only sources of all that is held against him.

Josephus wrote with astonishing frankness about his own conduct during the wars of the Jews against the Romans. He was appointed by the Jewish leadership to lead the revolt against the Romans in Galilee, and despite the fact that he was an able strategist, his forces were routed; he was captured and taken before Vespasian. Convinced of the hopelessness of the Jewish cause, he switched sides, a move which paid off handsomely in material benefits. Vespasian rewarded him with honours and gifts, also insisting that he divorce his wife, and marry a Jewish woman from Caesarea. Later, Josephus, "displeased at her behaviour," divorced her and married a rich woman from Crete.

Thus, during his lifetime, his view that Rome was all-powerful proved to be accurate. He wrote brilliant histories of the time, which are the main sources of knowledge of the first century C.E., and have been confirmed by archaeological findings. But, spiritually, he has remained for Jews a symbol of treachery, as Judas Iscariot is for Christians.

Strange as it may seem, the Jerusalem Municipality apparently agreed with MJB about Josephus, for he has been given a comparatively important thoroughfare in the capital, Yosef Ben-Matityahu Street, which links Jaffa Road to Malchei Israel (Kings of Israel). The inhabitants are mostly Orthodox, and will throw a stone at anyone who drives through it on the Shabbath, but they do not seem to mind giving Josephus' name as their address.

In Tel Aviv, MJB's street is an elderly part of town, so the experienced street-walker can indulge in a bit of street-sign archaeology. There are several generations of street-signs here, put up at different stages of the city's development. Some were put up before the State was founded: these are lettered blue on white, and appear in Arabic as well as Hebrew and English. The next generation, also blue on white, has dropped the Arabic and put vowel-points on the Hebrew, no doubt a concession to the mass immigration of the fifties. These signs begat a white-on-blue generation, and on some corners there are brief descriptions of the persons commemorated. The very newest street signs, which are not in this area, are a kind of luminous plastic which light up at night, and are easily broken.

On the map, Berdyczewski's street appears to be one of a little quartet, with Marmorek to the north and Cremieux and Lunz to the south. Each is just two blocks long, and it is usual to cross all four, which takes less than ten minutes, without giving the slightest thought to the four very different personalities they represent and the nearly 150 years they span. Four men who lived in different worlds are now permanent residents in a pleasant little corner of Tel Aviv; they never met, but I think they might have had much to discuss. One of them, Lunz, did in fact publish an essay on the 120th anniversary of the birth of another, Cremieux. Since the neighbourhood is so companionable, I am adding to MJB's story these notes on his sidewalk associates.

Starting from the north, the first and by far the busiest street is named after Alexander Marmorek, eminent biologist and intimate of Herzl, who was born in Galicia in 1865 and died in Paris in 1932. Marmorek studied in Vienna and worked in Paris at the Pasteur Institute. He is credited with the discovery of an antidote against puerperal fever and an anti-tuberculosis vaccine, and he initiated the study of serum which lead to the modern treatment of typhus and diabetes. With all this, he found time to attend Zionist Congresses. After World War I, he opposed Weizmann by proclaiming that "the Palestine Mandate is not the fulfilment of Herzl's ideas."

Alexander had two brothers, Isidor and Oscar, both also close friends of Herzl. Oscar, an architect, was a member of the Zionist Executive and a co-founder of the newspaper, *Die Welt*. He accompanied Herzl to Constantinople on his visit to the Sultan in 1901 and appears in Herzl's *Altneuland* as "Architect Steineck."

So does our Alexander, as a browse through *Altneuland* quickly reveals. In fact, he appears in the lobby of a Tiberias Hotel, following one of Herzl's little love-interest scenes: "'It is truly the garden of Eden,' said Fredrich softly, and feeling Miriam close to him, he involuntarily took her hand and pressed it..." At this point in the novel we are introduced to "Professor Steineck, brother of the architect," who fills the role of a dynamic scientist building up the new state.

The imaginative and elaborate centenary edition of *Altneuland*, published in Haifa in 1960, includes a photograph of Dr. Alexander Marmorek, "Professor Steineck in this book," with moustache, pince-nez and all, posing behind his beakers, test-tubes, and retorts at what may well be the Pasteur Institute.

"A jolly, absent-minded and hasty person, who always shouted as if his hearers were deaf," is how Herzl introduces Alexander Marmorek, who has a big scene guiding tourists around his Tiberias laboratory, where he is working on cholera, diphtheria, hydrophobia, malaria, refrigeration, cheese production and tobacco curing, for a start.

Alexander Marmorek always quarrelled with his brother Oscar (who did not get a street — and I hope this was not because he committed

164

suicide in 1909). But, Herzl tells us, "they were exceedingly fond of each other." In Herzl's book, both saw nothing but the golden glow of rational progress in the future ahead.

Oscar appears as a cheerful extrovert in an earlier scene in *Altneuland*, in which an amiable Arab explains why the Arabs were so pleased to have the Jews arrive, why "Jewish immigration was a blessing for us." At this point, Oscar Marmorek roars, "Civilization is everything! We Jews have brought civilization to the country."

Altneuland includes several lyrical expositions on the delights of transportation, expressed again by the Marmoreks' friend, the amiable Arab. "Yes, travelling is a real pleasure," he says, meaning the railroad, and specifically the electric train, which is less polluting. True, Architect Steineck travelling with a party to Tiberias to see his brother, is driving by private minibus, but the advantages of the railroad for mass transportation are made clear to all.

Poor Oscar Marmorek designed synagogues in Austria. What would he make of the unplanned synagogue that juts out from Marmorek at Huberman? The Tel Aviv traffic screeches around it; and I had so hoped that the Begins, who live nearby, would have a much-needed traffic light installed, as it is practically impossible to cross Marmorek here.

How would Alexander himself, "Professor Steineck," feel about the wonders of technology, since the cars parked on Marmorek make the people walk in the street "exactly as we did in Poland, with the pigs!" as I heard a woman mutter.

And how could Herzl have ever foreseen that Rehov Marmorek would become the scene of a small battle between a British armoured unit and an armed Palmah platoon?

This happened on a night in March 1946, when Tel Aviv was flooded with Hagana and Palmah units during an operation intended to bring to safety illegal immigrants from the ship "Orde Wingate" (his street is over toward Yad Eliahu). The British caught the ship long before it reached the Tel Aviv shore, but there was no way of letting the roving units know that the operation had been aborted.

At Marmorek, a British armoured car fired on a Palmah platoon, wounding the commander, a girl of 19. She died on the balcony of a house a little to the north. Her name was Bracha Fuld, and she was born in Berlin. The little street which runs from Bilu to Ibn Gabirol, and where she died, is named in her honour.

Parallel to Berdyczewski to the south is Crémieux, who appears on the street sign as Yitzhak Moshe but was more generally known as Adolph, distinguished French lawyer and statesman, he was born in Nimes in 1796 and died in Paris in 1880. He was Minister of Justice in the provisionary revolutionary government of 1848, and again in 1870.

Crémieux was descended from a Jewish family of Portuguese Marranos, who had long been established in France. He was one of the first Jewish students admitted to the Lycée Imperial. Very active in Jewish affairs, he defended the rights of the Jewish communities of North Africa. He secured the franchise for the Jews of Algeria by a decree known as the *Décret Crémieux* and, as we know, accompanied Montefiore on a trip to the Middle East and helped free Jews imprisoned in Damscus. He was also president of *Alliance Israélite* and was tirelessly active on behalf of Moroccan, Rumanian and Russian Jewry.

At the same time, he lived an extremely assimilated life, and his children were baptized. If he himself had taken this step, we would never have had a Crémieux Street, because one of the street-naming rules is that converted Jews are excluded.

In Jerusalem, Crémieux has a short street running from a main artery, Emek Refaim (Valley of the Ghosts) Road to come to a dead end in the railway line, a rather dismal fate, which he shares with such illustrious gentile friends of the Jews as Lloyd George, Emile Zola, Josiah Wedgwood and Jan Masaryk.

In our Tel Aviv tour, the street south of Crémieux is Hahashmonaim, which is Hebrew for the Maccabeans. We will simply cross it, without looking back 2,000 years; for this street would take us right back again to the period of MJB's research, which is simply too exhausting for a short stroll in historical biography. So we merely pause here, at Hahashmonaim, noting with pleasure a very unpretentious park, with some welcome, if dusty, trees, benches and slides for children.

A moment later we are at the street of Avraham Moshe Lunz, who was born in Kovno in 1854 and died in Jerusalem in 1918. He was one of the first and most important researchers in the history and geography of Eretz Israel. He wrote guide books, published the annual *Calendar of Events* between 1898 and 1912, worked with Israel Dov Frumkin on the newspaper *Havatzelet* and was the author of hundreds of articles on Talmud, etc., over a period of 40 years. All this is impressive enough. What makes it even more remarkable is that Lunz became blind when he was 25, yet continued his enormous output at a time when blindness generally meant inactivity. He was a founder of the Education Centre for the Blind.

He was known as a child prodigy in rabbinical circles in Kovno, and was brought to Jerusalem when he was in his early teens. According to legend, this was because his mother had vowed to bring her child here if she finally had a boy. Young Lunz wanted to study abroad to become a "modern" rabbi, but mother was against this, and quickly married him off to a rabbi's daughter.

Nevertheless, he moved in "progressive" circles, organized *Tiferet Yerushalayim* with other like-minded young men, and began his studies of secular history and geography, which till then had been investigated only by non-Jewish scholars.

Lunz's streets in Jerusalem and Haifa are more mercantile than literary. The one in Jerusalem is famous as the street of the *sherut* taxis, many of which begin their journeys from the geographer's road. In Haifa, Lunz Street is the main market-place.

Another Lunz legend makes him responsible for the fact that Israelis speak modern Hebrew with a Sephardi rather than an Ashkenazi pronunciation. According to this story, once upon a time Lunz and his friend Eliezer Ben-Yehuda, "the father of modern Hebrew" were recuperating from an illness in the same hospital, and they naturally discussed the question of speaking the language. In another bed in the same room was a recent arrival from Russia, who did not understand a word of Hebrew. The two masters of the language agreed to let him decide which pronunciation sounded better — the Ashkenazi which Ben-Yehuda knew from Russia, or the Sephardi which Lunz knew from the Sephardi Jews of Jerusalem.

Lunz's pronunciation, appealed to the uncomprehending arbiter far more than that of Ben-Yehuda, who from then on based his dictionary of the language on the Sephardi accent. And that is why, today, we speak Hebrew the way we do.

14
A Long Line of Poets

Awake, O my love, from your sleep,
Let me see your face as it wakes.
If you dream someone kisses your lips,
I will interpret your dreams for you.

These lines, written in Spain nearly 900 years ago, begin a poem by Judah Halevi, who was born in Toledo in about 1080, and died on his way to the Holy Land, probably in Egypt, some 60 years later.

His street in Tel Aviv, one of the first six to be named, starts down south, below Herzl, and meanders up to Marmorek. At this corner there is an abrupt change in style and name, and Judah Halevi becomes another slightly earlier Spanish Jewish poet, Solomon Ben-Judah Ibn Gabirol, whose exact dates are also unknown, but who is believed to have been born about 1020 and died about 10 years before Judah Halevi's birth.

"Where is the man who has been tried and found strong and sound?" wrote Ibn Gabirol in a poem called "The Degenerate Age." It went on, "Where is the friend of reason and knowledge? I see only sceptics and weaklings, I see only prisoners of their senses..."

These little excerpts are not intended as characteristic samples of either of our two Neoplatonist philosopher-poets. Both Judah Halevi and Ibn Gabirol wrote secular as well as religious verse, and major philosophical works as well as poetry. Scholars consider Ibn Gabirol to be the chief representative of Neoplatonism in Jewish literature, and find "traces" of it in Judah Halevi.

By those who grade these matters, Halevi is considered the most outstanding poet of the age. He was also the first to put into action the religious and intellectual "longing for Zion" by actually packing his bags, getting on a boat, and making for the Holy Land.

Down from the academic clouds to the pedestrian pavements, it is in Tel Aviv that the two poets together make up one of the city's longest north-south thoroughfares; so we begin with this epic strip — a traffic-jammed city's tribute to creativity in the Moslem Empire's Golden Age.

Over 800 of Judah Halevi's poems are known, and about 300 works are attributed to Ibn Gabirol. Therefore, if Tel Aviv's streets were paved with lyrics, this would make about one poem per five metres of their roughly 5.5 kilometre joint length (if my calculations are correct, which I always doubt, in Platonic recognition of the unattainability of perfection in our daily world). At its source, Judah Halevi is actually the continuation of Rokah, named after Shimon Rokah, a founder of Neve Zedek, while Ibn Gabirol flows north across the Yarkon river to meet Shimon's son Yisrael, the third mayor of Tel Aviv; all of which is not bad, either, as a form of Platonic order.

Judah Halevi's street, though jammed with modern traffic, is lined with elderly little all-purpose shops, clothing outlets, kiosks, and, of course, the omnipresent banks. The old, i.e., convenient, railway station for Jerusalem used to be about halfway up Judah Halevi. Then brilliant planning turned this into a parking lot. In the really old days, when the start of Judah Halevi ran along the really old railway, to Jaffa, it was flanked by solid, well-kept houses — and an absence of traffic to gladden the heart of the most progressive town-planner.

These days, No. 1 Judah Halevi is the office of a tax adviser, while until recently the last enterprise on its west side, at Marmorek, was Herly's café; but the management took up Transcendental Meditation and sold the premises. The place is now a furniture shop, an apparent attempt to meet the modernity of Ibn Gabirol, beckoning just beyond the traffic light, because the change at this corner is instant and unmistakable. There are those who say that the action is moving from Dizengoff and that Ibn Gabirol is becoming our swingingest street, with ice-cream parlours crowded in the evenings, South American sandwich shops, Chinese restaurants, glittering expanses of electronic appliances; the supermarket, Shekem, the Municipality and a square for demonstrations; and much appeal to Prisoners of their Senses.

What do you remember about Judah Halevi? When I tossed this unpleasant question at interviewees — not exactly the man in the street, but people who have been exposed to Hebrew literature — the answers were mostly groans. The more successful respondents, when pressed, did come up with, "I am in the West, but my heart is in the East" — Halevi's famous cry from "Zionides." One high-school student with a greater than usual interest in literature confessed that while she didn't like studying the poems for examinations, afterwards she did. And she pointed out with enthusiasm that this poet was, after all, "the first Zionist."

Some juicy biographical details, enough to perk up a high-school class, appear in a best-selling American popular history. In this version, Judah abandoned his wife and children to become a wandering poet. He got to Cordoba, "the Paris of that age, an immoral, luxurious, cosmopolitan city, the home of every vice and virture," and "abandoned himself to its pleasures." He composed poetry in the spirit of *The Rubaiyat of Omar Khayyam* and Shakespeare's sonnets, till the pleasures of the senses palled. Then he became a "troubadour of God," craved only the love of

God, and warned the Jews not to be seduced by rationalism:

And let not the wisdom of the Greeks

Beguile thee. Which hath not fruit but only flowers.

No such scenario exists in Yehuda Burla's charming little book on Judah Halevi. Burla, the 20th-century Jerusalem-born novelist, traced the poet's travels through Spain, with illustrations from the poems, emphasizing that the secular ones are "real love poems, not stylistic exercises," with emotional expressions of friendship and loneliness and, as the years go by, "time as the enemy."

For immigrants to Israel, some of the most understandable of Judah Halevi's many letters to friends are in a long correspondence about whether he really ought to make the difficult and dangerous trip to the Holy Land. It took him years to make up his mind. In elegant verse, friends tried to discourage him from this wild notion, because of Crusaders, unstable conditions and so forth. "But is there any place, either east or west, where we have peace?" answered our poet. Except for the literary level of such debates, not much has changed.

Hakuzari, Halevi's great philosophical poem modelled on the Book of Job, deals with the conversion to Judaism of the Tatar Khazars under their king, Bulan, in the 8th century. (Hakuzari, the street, is south of Bloomfield Stadium.) In the poem, a Mohammedan and a Christian argue on behalf of their faith; then a Jewish scholar explains to the questing Khazar king the nature of Judaism, "complete and final": the visible presence of God is everywhere but His invisible presence is found only in Jerusalem. And so, after converting Bulan, the scholar in the poem goes to Jerusalem. Halevi himself set out for the East soon afterwards, but there is no record of his journey beyond Damascus, at which point he mysteriously disappears from history.

Burla also wrote an imaginative *Journeys of Rabbi Yehuda Halevi* based on a folk legend that the poet did in fact reach the Holy Land. Burla describes Yehuda Halevi's fictional travels here, and pulls off the virtuoso trick of composing poems and letters in the master's style. In a scene in Elijah's Cave near Haifa, the poet has a mystical experience with the prophet himself, and with time past and future flowing together. Transcendental Meditation, via the vanished café at the end of Judah Halevi, is the best subliminal connection I can suggest.

In Jerusalem, his street is really a sweep of handsome steps, and they are based on another legend entirely — the widely accepted one that Halevi was murdered by a horseman just after he finally arrived in the Holy City, and was on his way to "the uttermost East," the Western Wall of the Temple Mount.

But anybody looking for his street in the capital, and relying on most of the popular street maps available, is in for a frustrating experience. Accord-

170

Statue of Ibn Gabirol by Reed Armstrong.   Yehuda Halevi (right) with Maimonides.

Yehuda Halevi Street, Tel Aviv, in the old days.

ing to these, Judah Halevi Boulevard shown clearly near the western extremity of the city, linking Herzl Boulevard to Agrippas Road, with a passing nod at Nordau Plaza. This would make it a noble four-lane highway, passing right in front of Binyenei Ha'uma, Jerusalem's central congress hall.

But the street signs on the spot are unequivocal: this is Zalman Shazar's Boulevard; and after his death, the Municipality disposed the 11th-century Sephardi poet to accommodate the Russian-born writer, socialist leader, and third President of the State of Israel.

However, Judah Halevi has received a magnificent and imaginative alternative to his former boulevard. After the Six Day War reunited Jerusalem, some very handsome steps were built to link the Old City's Jewish Quarter with the Western Wall. The Municipality's street-naming compound in front of the Western Wall.

And so his steps, *Ma'alot Rabbi Yehuda Halevi*, link Misgav Ladach one of the main streets in the revived Jewish Quarter of the Old City, to the compound in front of the Western Wall, the gate to El Aqsa Mosque, and the Dome of the Rock.

As you walk down the steps, you see the silver dome of El Aqsa, the Intercontinental Hotel, the onion spires of the Russian Church, and behind it the graves on the Mount of Olives — a supremely encompassing portrait of Jerusalem. Descending further, you see the golden roof of the Dome of the Rock (popularly known as the Mosque of Omar) and at one side the Western Wall, with the archaeological dig of David's city alongside it.

The flights of steps are separated by a series of landings. At the final one there is usually a cluster of tourists, some often sitting on the steps with their shoes off, to rest their conscientious feet. From this point, their guide can explain the entire geography of one of the most revered spots on earth.

At the bottom of the steps is a sentry, who may want to search visitors. Above him is a sign: "Respect the Sanctity of this Holy Site Refrain from Smoking on the Sabbath Do not Photograph on Sabbath and Holidays." These demands do not seem excessive.

In total contrast, Haifa's Judah Halevi Street, right down at sea level, must be one of the worst slums in Israel. This is hardly the romantic and spiritual East for which his soul yearned when he was in the intellectual and well-developed West of Moslem Spain.

More or less parallel and slightly up the hill from the sea is Ibn Gabirol Street. It is also a slum, though slightly better than Judah Halevi, if one can work out gradations in slummery. There is talk that the Haifa Municipality plans to redeem both streets by turning them into an artists' quarter, which would be a change for the better, and certainly more appropriate to the illustrious names.

Back again in Jerusalem, the matter is once more handled more felicitously. Ibn Gabirol Street is in Rehavia, one of the nicest old-established residential quarters in the city. It is a short street but has great historical chic. What was the Prime Minister's Office, in the days of Ben-Gurion and Sharett, is here, and also the Bialik Institute, the Jewish Agency's publishing house. So, too, are some of Rehavia's choicest apartments. The Prime Minister's Office has been taken over by the Ministry of Transport, which fights a continuing battle to keep parking places for its own automobiles on the narrow street.

Ibn Gabirol is spelled and pronounced many different ways on our streets. Scholars also know him as Avicebron or Avencebrol; a shopkeeper on his street has spelled him "Even". I suppose we should be grateful he hasn't been turned into "Ivan": Ibn is, of course, the Arabic equivalent for the Hebrew "Ben", as in "son of".

A modern statue of Ibn Gabirol in his birthplace, Malaga, shows him in a pensive mood, turbaned, in a long flowing robe. The thumbnail biographies tell us that he was the first to popularize Arabic metres in Hebrew; that his lyrical compositions include *Keter Malchut* ("Crown of The Kingdom"), and that his chief philosophical work, translated from Arabic to Latin as *Fons Vitae* ("The Fountain of Life"), was ignored by Jewish thinkers because of its non-religious attitude and Neoplatonic notion of God as unknowable and transcendental.

The most scholarly volume ever written about our Neoplatonic street figure — *Ibn Gabirol — ostwestliches Dichtertum*, is by the late Prof. Frederick P. Bargebuhr (an architect by training who settled in Palestine in 1934, and who taught Islam at the Dormition Monastery on Mount Zion). The book runs to 800 pages and I haven't read it, but I am in a position to observe that, for instance, Ibn Gabirol advocated not having children, probably never married, went through a period of disparaging the whole world, suffered from megalomania, and was often sacrilegious.

Yet Prof. Bargebuhr sees in *Keter Malchut* "the most authentic religiosity, the most penitent poetry ever written by this poet." Elements of heresy may be found elsewhere, though, and the Jews of Saragossa accused Ibn Gabirol of Hellenism and forced him to leave the city.

But this earnest approach will never popularize our early and great poets. They cry out for a Judah Halevi and Ibn Gabirol Pop Festival, and all that is required is a slight re-doing of some of the hundreds of love lyrics they left us. Here, for instance, is Judah on the pangs of separation. The translation, by Emma Lazarus, lacks pzazz; but simplified for a strong disco beat, we might still turn it into a top hit:

> "And so we twain must part! Oh, linger yet,
> Let me still feed my glance upon thine eyes.
> Forget not, love, the day of our delight,
> And I our nights of bliss shall ever prize..."

There is another Judah or Yehuda Halevi, and he, too, is commemorated in a street in Tel Aviv, although obliquely. He was the first rabbi of Jaffa, and he deserves attention for a number of reasons. Not the least of these, as far as I am concerned, is that when he travelled from Jaffa to Egypt in 1873 on a fund-raising mission for a Talmud Tora school, he was 90 years old, so he must have been quite an unusual type.

His street is in Jaffa, where he headed the Jewish community for 54 years, but not everybody will connect the man with his street. It had to be explained to me because, although it is a wide thoroughfare not far from the old port and in the neighbourhood of other rabbinical streets, it is named Yehuda Meragusa, without any Halevi to help one out. Ragusa, to make things a bit more confusing, is the Italian name for the Yugoslav city of Dubrovnik, where his father was rabbi. He himself, however, was born in Sarajevo, came to Jerusalem at the age of 18, in 1801, and became an outstanding scholar.

Jerusalem's Sephardi community sent him to Istanbul to raise money for a yeshiva; and in 1825, apparently having proved himself a good rabbi-diplomat, he was sent to Jaffa to act as the Jerusalem rabbis' representative and to deal with all the problems of Jews arriving in the port town, organize their caravan travel to the Holy City and see to it that the rich ones paid the "travel tax" to subsidize the poor ones.

After the ban on living in Jaffa was rescinded in 1841, the Jewish community increased, and Rabbi Yehuda Halevi served as its spiritual father for over half a century.

He believed in an agricultural future for Jews around Jaffa. He helped to supervise Sir Moses Montefiore's orange groves north of the city's walls and encouraged Karl Netter in his plans for the Mikve Israel agricultural school.

His photograph shows a wise, aristocratic face, a beautiful white beard, and a turban. The hard-working rabbi lived to the age of 96, a few years short of Montefiore's record; like him, say the books, he kept full possession of all his faculties till the day he died. Perhaps the secrets of a long life are activity and sanctity.

15
Three Gordons

Which Gordon is the Gordon of Gordon Street?

This is not a question on which national unity is about to shatter. But the quest of the answer leads down such scenic byways that this tour (not for inexperienced hikers) is a triple-trip through Gordonia, about which more later.

I must confess that I've had it wrong till recently. For years, the name "Gordon" used to produce a rapid change of slides in my mind, colourful but inaccurate. First on the mental screen flashed an image of Scottish Highlander, bagpipes and all, a hero of the British Empire, who was killed in Khartoum by the Mahdi Mohammed Ahmed, and his fanatical "fuzzy-wuzzies." And then, with the embarrassment of getting a slide from the wrong country in by mistake, on would come a saintly man with a beard, the patron prophet of the kibbutz movement.

Wrong Gordons. Tel Aviv has three streets named after three different Gordons, though two of the names, to avoid confusion, are no more than hints to the wise; not to mention other Gordons in other cities here, and settlements and institutions as well. But which Gordon?

Rehov Gordon, the street of the art galleries, which runs from the Municipality to the sea between Ben-Gurion and Frischmann, is named after Yehuda Leib Gordon, "Yalag," the greatest Hebrew poet of the Enlightenment, who was born in Vilna in 1831 and died in St. Petersburg in 1892. He had no beard; his chin was bare, in the fashion of a century ago, with a little fringe at the jaw.

The saintly man with the beard is, of course, Aharon David, A.D. Gordon, (1856-1922), the spiritual mentor of that pre-hippy wing of the Zionist labour movement which believed in individual self-realization through work on the land. He was born 25 years after Yalag, but his free-flowing beard makes A.D. seem either much older, or else far-out contemporary.

His romantic story has left a more lasting impact on many Israelis than any other Gordon; this, I suppose is why an idler in Tel Aviv's most important Gordon Street automatically, but incorrectly, assumes that it is named after A.D. I am afraid that Yalag, whose street it rightly is, left less of an impression on recent generations of students here, who studied his writings at school, than A.D. Gordon has done.

A.D does have a street in Tel Aviv. But since Yalag's street was already in possession of the name Gordon, it is called "Aharon David." On street signs and house numbers, "Gordon" occasionally follows in parentheses. It runs the short distance between LaSalle and Arlosoroff, parallel to Bernstein.

This was originally a neighbourhood of Histadrut officials, now turned into a pleasant little area handy for hotels and embassies, a bit north of Atarim (Namir) Square, which makes it a sorry site for the mystical philosopher of productive labour.

As is known to an inner circle of connoisseurs, there is yet a third Gordon among our streets — "Shalag," commemorating another writer, Shmuel Arie Leib Gordon (1865-1933), known for his multi-volume biblical commentary.

Shalag, the smallest of the Gordon street trio, runs parallel to Yalag's Gordon, curving off Ruppin and dropping briefly down to the sea. It is a wise passerby who knows the Gordonian acronym here, since the street signs give no inkling of Shmuel Leib Gordon, let alone that he has been called a direct literary descendant of Yehuda Leib Gordon who, in turn, happened to be the brother-in-law of the Yiddish poet, Mikhel Gordon.

Gordon-wise, this is pretty confusing. It could have been even worse, for we do have a welter of Gordons, enough to form a proper clan with its own tartan plaid.

This essentially Scottish but also persistently Russian-Jewish name appears 75 times in the Tel Aviv phone book, not counting taxis and cinemas. There are 11 Gordons in the *Encyclopaedia Judaica*, and, in an almost entirely different list, 15 in Tidhar's *Pioneers of the Yishuv*.

This does not take into account such exotic ineligibles as the English General Charles George "Chinese" Gordon, who spent an archaeological sabbatical here in 1884, before going to his death at Khartoum, and is commemorated in "Gordon's Cavalry," the skull-shaped hill north of the Old City of Jerusalem, which he identified as Golgotha.

We might also remember Lord George Gordon, the third son of the Duke of Gordon, if only because he converted to Judaism. He was imprisoned for libelling the Queen of France and died in Newgate prison, an Orthodox Jew, in 1793. His name, I am sorry to say, is commemorated in the Gordon Riots. These occurred when, while still a Protestant, he led a London mob against the Catholics which became "an orgy to destruction and plunder."

Yet another exotic Gordon brings us to Russia, the home of many of our Gordons. For *Patrick* Gordon, raised in Aberdeenshire, was a famous *Russian* general who fought for Peter the Great; and when Patrick died, it was Peter who "with his own hands, closed his eyes."

Nor can I resist dragging in Lord Byron, whose little street is not far from Rehov Gordon, and whose name I have seen listed on the index to a local map as "Byron, George Gordon."

But back to our own medley of Gordonia, a word reminiscent of the name of the pioneering Zionist youth movement set up in Galicia in 1923, after A.D. Gordon's death and named after him. At its height during World War II it had nearly 40,000 members, in Eastern Europe and the U.S. Its heroic exploits in the ghettoes during the Holocaust are documented in the movement's archives at Kibbutz Hulda. After a confusing series of splits and mergers, at which Zionist movements are so good, Gordonia was finally dissolved when the kibbutz federation, Ihud Hakvutzot Vehakibbutzim, was founded in 1951.

Gordonia's principles included "building up the homeland, education in humanistic values, creation of a working nation, the renaissance of Hebrew culture, and the labour of the individual." This is quite a mouthful, and we will return to it and to Aharon David. But first, a little tour of our two other Gordons.

At the foot of Yalag's street, the old Gordon Beach is now obscured by a wall of hotels. The sands here were, not too long ago, the site of the Mahlul Quarter shacks — squatters of the Forties who kept the insides of their shacks immaculately clean (according to my informants) although the general area looked squalid. This part of the beach was thick with Tel Avivians one day in September, 1939, when the "illegal" immigrant ship Tiger Hill ran aground with its 14,000 refugees, some of whom managed to swim ashore and escape in the crowd.

A hundred years earlier, Yehuda Leib was a scholarly little boy of eight, well on his way to becoming a prodigy at Bible, Hebrew grammar and Talmud: he was recognized as such by the age of 14. By 17 he was studying European culture, French, English, Polish, German, and Russian. Not that he was limited to the humanities, for he later became science editor, as well as literary critic, of a Russian Jewish monthly.

"Be a Jew at home and a human being in the street." This quotation from Gordon, which is usually what I come up with when I ask former students about him, became a motto of the maskilim, the members of the Enlightenment movement; but it represented only the early period of Gordon's thinking, when he believed, in the spirit of liberalism, that education and reform could solve the Jewish problem. When Russian liberalism gave way to pogroms, Gordon, disillusioned, advocated emigration to the West, especially America. He was not enthusiastic about the Holy Land under the Turks; and, anyway, as he wrote in the spirit of Ahad Ha'am, "our redemption can come about only after our spiritual deliverance."

Yalag's troubles with his fellow Jews, especially the religious establishment, were more bitter than those with the Tsarist authorities, who once imprisoned him because of accusations by the Hassidim. He considered inflexible rabbis the source of much evil, and they returned the compliment.

It has been suggested that Yalag was the anonymous author of a pamphlet published in Vienna in 1877 (also attributed to Disraeli), proposing a Jewish state in Palestine under British sovereignty; but it has also been suggested that Gordon was "more afraid of theocracy in a Jewish state than he was of the Sultan."

He fought for the poor and the oppressed — including women in traditional Jewish society. His poem *Kozo shel Yod* (The Point on Top of the Yod) is a cry for the liberation of women from rigid Orthodoxy:

Hebrew woman, who knows your life?
In darkness you came and in darkness shall go...

At the same time he warned against the total rejection of Jewish values, which he feared might include discarding the Hebrew language. "Perhaps I am the last of Zion's poets," he wrote, "and you the last readers." How differently it all turned out, up where Gordon crosses Dizengoff, dotted with boutiques whose names are written in Hebrew.

Near the sea, where Gordon crosses Ruppin, we jog to the left and find ourselves at Shalag. This is a tiny street with an enormous villa enclosed by a wall and the "Technocrat" painting contractors.

Shmuel Arie Leib Gordon came to Jaffa from Lithuania in 1898, taught at the *Hovevei Zion* school, returned to Warsaw and journalistic work, then came back to settle here in 1924. His translations include *King Lear;* his *Olam Katan* was the first Hebrew children's newspaper, and his biblical commentary is in every pupil's school bag. His own children became on integral part of the local scene — one son was the director of Mossad Bialik, another was chief physician of the Ministry of Defence, and the third a member of Kibbutz Mishmar Ha'emek.

Shalag is intimately connected with other Tel Aviv streets: Frischmann and Ahad Ha'am printed his poetry, and Rehov Yehoash, which runs into him from the south, commemorates his brother-in-law, the Yiddish poet Yehoash Bloomgarden, who settled in the U.S.

Moving a bit north across Ben-Gurion, we come to A.D. — saint, rebbe, guru, impractical old duffer, a burden to his friends, but also an inspiration. His life is the most richly romantic of our Gordons. He is the best remembered in theory, the most sinned against in practice.

He was the prophet of the Second Aliya, the group of pioneers that created the kibbutz, produced such leaders as David Ben-Gurion and Itzhak Ben-Zvi, and provided the philosophical background for the Zionist Socialist movement which dominated Jewish life in this country for so many decades, before and after the creation of the state.

Gordon believed that a Hebrew culture could be created only if it rested on foundations of self-labour. He attached to physical labour, particularly agricultural work, a mystic, almost religious quality. As a corollary, he loathed the very idea of hiring somebody else to do one's "black work," as he called it.

His thinking inspired members of moshavim and kibbutzim. When the mass immigration of the Fifties took place, Premier Ben-Gurion demanded that the Zionist Socialists give the newcomers a chance to work by hiring them. The disciples of Gordon suffered agonies of conscience, but in the light of the national need, eventually gave in.

Despite the fact that his principles are now more honoured in the breach than the observance, Gordon is still regarded with reverence by Israel's Socialists.

Vegetarianism; pacifism; back to nature and simplicity; a fanatical devotion to manual labour; nights singing and dancing, philosophical discussions and literary work; self-education, but for its own sake and never for the degree; a mystical concern for the relation of the individual to the cosmos — some of A.D.'s principles are still with us, others ebb and flow as ideological fashions come and go.

The world's last round of hippies and communes faded fast; vegetarianism, though, is "in" among many of our young, and quite a few want to get away from our polluted cities, though not to menial labour but to power lawnmowers; settlements on beautiful beaches, yes, but subsidized, and equipped with stereos and Coca-Cola.

Gordon's idea of "quality of life" was far from suburbia. Scraggly beard, Tolstoyan tunic, benevolent blue eyes, he came here at the age of 49, in poor health, determined to do the hardest physical labour. Man could "regain his sanity," and become "one with the cosmos" only by working the land, and he did not mean rooftop gardens. When man left the soil and moved to the city, Gordon believed, he deteriorated in the same measure that he grew alienated from nature. All this, of course, was thought out in Tolstoy's day, long before urbanization became a modern crisis, even in the empty land Gordon walked through on foot 75 years ago.

Most philosophers who exalt manual labour come from reasonably comfortable backgrounds, and Gordon was no exception. His family had a very rich relative, Baron Joseph Günzburg of St. Petersburg, who offered to finance a medical education. Young Gordon politely turned this down because he had purist ideas: he wanted no education for utilitarian purposes, but only learning for the love of learning. He already had a traditional Jewish education with private tutors, and had studied secular subjects on his own.

As the only surviving child of his parents' five children (his mother, incidentally, was the daughter of one Shimshon Gordon), he could have avoided military service, but insisted on presenting himself for examination. He was found physically unfit. Thirty years later, he exposed himself

Yehuda Leib Gordon.

Shmuel Arie Leib Gordon.

Charles "Chinese" Gordon.

A.D. Gordon, "the saintly man with the beard."

180

to physical hardships that defeated much younger and stronger men. He also was unenthusiastic about the Jewish Legion in World War I (and about the Balfour Declaration too), because he believed that little good could come of military actions or political efforts. Salvation was possible only through the individual's efforts to change himself.

For over two decades, Gordon worked as financial manager of Baron Günzburg's estates. He also established a workers' library and did community work among youth, teaching "Hebrew, humanism, and Zionism." He badly wanted to study agriculture to prepare himself for life here, but family responsibilities prevented such self-indulgence.

Gordon had become engaged at the age of 15 — by parental arrangement, of course — to a cousin, and had married soon after. Seven children were born, of whom only two survived. In the face of a long series of personal tragedies, perhaps the most bitter concerned Gordon's one remaining son, Yehiel Michael. Having been taught solely by his father in true Tolstoyan style, he walked out on his parents, cut off all ties, turned his back on the world of "liberalism and progress" and chose to enter, of all things, an Orthodox yeshiva. He and his father never met again.

In 1904, the year after his son's defection and his parents' death, and the point generally taken to mark the start of the Second Aliya, Gordon arrived in Jaffa. He left his wife and his daughter Yael behind. Five years later he scraped together enough money to bring them to the country, though both were ill; his wife died within a year.

All such private afflictions, according to observers, were less difficult for Gordon than the ideological splits among the Jewish settlers and their tendency to despair and compromise. Who knows which was more exhausting, the work in the hot sun for a sickly man — or all that ideology, as discussed nightly with such friends as Brenner, Berl Katznelson, Ben-Zvi, and others?

A.D. Gordon was the spiritual leader of a whole generation of pioneers from the moment of his arrival until his death 18 years later, but they certainly never all agreed, and disputes raged between *Hapoel Hatzair*, for which Gordon wrote, and *Poalei Zion*, on such issues as whether to join the *Hashomer* defence organization — considered by the real pacifists to be "too militaristic."

He cheerfully applied his principles about physical labour to himself. He turned down the easy job of librarian at the Jaffa workers' library, offered as soon as he arrived, and for nearly two decades worked, when not sick in bed with malaria, exhaustion, bruises, etc., in the orchards and ditches of our tiny labour enclaves — Petah Tikva, Rishon, Sejera, Migdal, Yavniel, Kinneret, Tel Adashim.

181

A.D. is the only one of the Gordons to have a street in his name in Jerusalem. It is in Kiryat Hayovel, essentially a workers' suburb, and is a very pleasant little turnoff off the street of Borochov, an even earlier believer in the pioneering spirit. Gordon is lined with small cottages, around which the inhabitants have planted their own little gardens. This modest street would probably have been considered ideal by Gordon, had he not been convinced that nobody should live in a city at all. But there is evidence of a possible danger to Gordonian principles. Some richer Jerusalemites have discovered this island of greenery in a sea of concrete; they have purchased two little houses, and combined them into rather luxurious villas.

This has not happened in Haifa, where Gordon's street is also a quiet dead-end road of small houses with little gardens in the mixed suburb of Neve Sha'anan, where there are both handsome edifices and workers' dwellings.

But he is accorded his greatest honour at Kibbutz Deganya Aleph, where he lived for a time, and where his daughter lived till her death. Here, numerous bodies have cooperated to build Beit Gordon, an Agriculture and Nature Study Institute, which includes a museum, a meteorogical station, and a library. The museum contains 30,000 stuffed birds and other specimens of animal, bird and insect life, with special emphasis on the Kinneret area. The plant collection has 7,000 specimens, and the inorganic collection of minerals, fossils and soils more than 2,000 specimens.

Gordon did agree to go abroad twice on Zionist business — to Basle for the 11th Congress in 1913, and to Prague in 1920 for the *Hapoel Hatzair* conference. I like to think though, that he was not as eager for these "free trips" as his disciples are today. Perhaps (to speculate wildly) he secretly enjoyed the beauties of the old cities, but was doubtless overjoyed to get back to his white-cheese-and-tomatoes living conditions.

One Gordonian issue — Arab labour — has never stopped rearing its head and its dimensions increase as our living standards rise. For A.D., it was a very real problem in the orange groves. In Petah Tikva, together with a group of hungry and penniless Jewish workers, he quit in protest against Jewish farmers hiring Arab labour.

The issue was, of course, part of the "Arab problem," which Gordon knew at close hand — close enough to be beaten up by Arabs on one of his walks to Jaffa from Petah Tikva. It took him months to recover, during which he worked on translations — and looked forward to returning to physical labour.

In spite of the painful specifics, Gordon saw the Arab problem, philosophically, as the test of the moral nature of the Jew. Jews must treat Arabs "with moral courage on the highest plane, even if the behaviour of the other side is not all that is desired. Indeed, their hostility is all the more reason for our humanity," for no people may ever "place itself above morality." So much for pragmatism.

The sorest test of this view must have come when his close friend and disciple, Yosef Hayim Brenner, was murdered by Arabs in the 1921 riots. Brenner, 25 years younger than Gordon, was known for his bouts of despair: they practically never affected "the old one," who at the blackest of times always insisted that "we must not become discouraged."

Gordon recognized the economic threat of cheap Arab labour and the physical threat of Arab hostility, but most dangerous for him was the cultural threat of what happens when people do not do their own productive work.

"Let us assume," Gordon wrote one night nearly 70 years ago, "that a dense Jewish settlement were to come into being." Would this change the Jews' age-old detachment from nature, from productive work? "Will not our Jews continue to prefer mercantile pursuits, financial transactions, all the callings in which others work and they assume direction? What we need today is... not an academic culture but a culture of life itself...

"All that we desire in Palestine comes to this: that we create with our own hands all that constitutes life; that with our own hands we perform all the work needed, from the highest and most complicated down to the coarsest and most contemptible... Only when we do that will we possess a culture, because only thus will we have a life of our own."

The end, for Gordon, came in Degania, after a trip to Vienna to diagnose his fatal disease. He decided to live out his last year among his friends; his daughter Yael gave him injections to ease his pains, borne with his usual fortitude. He was delighted by "the wonderful young people now coming to settle"; he refused to accept the medically-prescribed food because it was not vegetarian, or "natural," and he continued to write essays in bed in his famous "clear, pearl-like handwriting."

A description of Gordon's last days, in Shimon Kushnir's *Anshei Nevo*, contains a segment from his writing. The moral human striving for immortality, Gordon wrote, usually takes the form of "leaving behind" books or paintings, scientific discoveries or projects of some sort.

"How insignificant and superficial!" Gordon wrote with his fading strength. "For the individual personality is nothing but a wave passing over the eternal sea of life and experience; and to the extent that a human being helps to increase the renewing and creative spirit in life, what he leaves behind after death can continue to exist only to the extent that it has not yet totally emerged from its receptacle."

An analogy, he continues, might be that of a man who dies leaving a pregnant wife; or more broadly, like those distant stars whose light

reaches us long after they have ceased to exist...''
Or like street signs.

16
Whither?

Few cities in the great world outside are likely to have a street "Whither?" Tel Aviv does not have merely a lane called *"Le'an?"*, complete with question mark. No; being highly organized, we have a *"Le'an Aleph"* and a *"Le'an Bet"* — "Whither A" and "Whither B." They are parallel offshoots, leading west to nowhere, from Feuerberg (which runs parallel to Ahad Ha'am between Balfour and Bar-Ilan).

Mordechai Ze'ev Feuerberg was born in Russia in 1874, and died there 25 years later. His short, tragic life was filled with intense literary activity in the face of equally intense paternal opposition. He died a few months before his major work, a story called *Le'an?*, appeared in print.

Most of his brief life, like his writing, was a bitter personal conflict between those famous "two worlds" that polarized so many Russian-Jewish writers of his generation, so many of whom became Tel Aviv streets. This was the dichotomy between Orthodox Jewish life and secular modern European existence, between the Jewish community and life outside, between "loyalty to the spiritual ascetic tradition and the natural life of the senses."

Feuerberg's father, a devout Hassid, beat his son and on occasion threw him out of the house because the boy, sickly and physically weak though intellectually unusual, began reading the Bible and modern Hebrew literature under the influence of the Enlightenment.

Still hoping for the best, his father arranged an engagement to the daughter of a *shohet*, a ritual slaughterer, and set Mordechai Ze'ev up as a grocer. But the shop became a *Hovevei Zion* centre and the engagement was broken off when the young man was discovered to have tuberculosis.

In 1896, aged 22, he went to Warsaw and showed his poems and stories to Nahum Sokolow, who encouraged him to stick to fiction. Ahad Ha'am arranged for a stipendium from Wissotzky, who means Tea to Israelis, but who — in addition to being a rich merchant — supported *Hovevei Zion* and Hebrew literature. Feuerberg was now free, in the less than four years remaining until his death, to concentrate on his literary ideology and his central theme. It was to influence, among others, Bialik and Berdyczewsky, and was to be analysed in articles by Brenner and Fichman.

The tragic hero of *Le'an?* is Nahman, "the sensitive, thinking individual who detaches himself, and is cut off from, the historical Jewish community." Scion of a rabbinical dynasty, Nahman "searches for a way."

The way leads from alienation through Messianic longing, through the Enlightenment and loss of faith in Divine Providence, to a total rift with his father and the community. Nahman's final outcry before his death is a speech at a *Hovevei Zion* gathering, in which he calls for a national renaissance "and a return to the East."

Feuerberg's street has a certain dichotomy in that there are both palms and pines, although it is generally solid and relatively quiet, with three- and four-storey residences and the kind of balconies people once sat on.

Le'an Aleph and Le'an Bet are, properly and symbolically, much more problematical. Aleph is grander, unpaved, dead-end, with bigger houses, only two on each side, and in better repair; Number One Aleph, which is Feuerberg 23, is quite a good example of how a large house can be maintained. At the end of the lane is a big tree, and we hear, but can never reach, the presses of the newspaper *Davar*. The sign on one side says "Le'an Lane"; a tiny apostrophe between the E and the A is not enough to demystify the non-Hebrew loiterer. The opposite sign says "Simtat Le'an," which isn't much help either.

Feuerberg ends at Bar-Ilan, named for the leader of religious Zionism known for most of his life as Meir Berlin. Born in Russia in 1880, he spent many years in the United States as head of the Mizrachi movement and died in Jerusalem in 1949. Bar-Ilan University is such a magnificent memorial that he could hardly take umbrage at his modest little Tel Aviv street. It, too, has some rather good examples of polarity and dichotomy in the sense of a synagogue facing an insurance loss adjuster.

What the "Whithers?" are really yearning toward, frozen in an eternally hopeless striving (these Russian writers begin to affect one) of a few impenetrable metres, is Lord Melchett. And what a different world we have here, though the two streets don't look all that dissimilar. Melchett is longer than Feuerberg, more elegant in spots, and appropriately equipped with, for instance, a management and efficiency consultant. The streets are parallel; the two men's lives were anything but.

I realize that to compare poor doomed Mordechai Ze'ev Feuerberg with wordly and successful Alfred Moritz Mond, 1st Baron Melchett (1868-1930), is a pointless exercise based on an arbitrary and artificial parallel on a map. Having said this, I still think a brief comparison can also help us remember a little about each, just because they are such an odd couple.

Feuerberg goes with Ahad Ha'am, his parallel partner to the east. Lord Melchett goes rather well with King George, not far west.

Feuerberg, we have seen, was a victim of his time and place, of family circumstances, and of poor health. Melchett, who has been described as "a giant in body and spirit," was a chemist, law student, industrialist, statesman, and jet-setter of his day, and got nearly everything he wanted — except becoming prime minister of England.

And while the elder Feuerberg, a devout Hassid, was beating his son and trying to marry him off to the *shohet*'s daughter, successfully assimilated papa Ludwig Mond (born in Germany, became an English subject in 1867, chemist and industrialist whose scientific methodology led to enormously profitable discoveries, especially in gas manufacture) sent his son to Cheltenham. There he, too, was certainly also beaten, but in the chic English public-school style, and he went on to Cambridge and Edinburgh universities, and Ludwig lived to see him elected a Liberal Member of Parliament, and watched with satisfaction as he married a Christian wife.

Alfred Mond was an M.P. from 1906 to 1928. Created a baronet in 1910, he served as Commissioner of Works under Lloyd George and later as Minister of Health. When he crossed the floor of the House to join the Conservatives in 1926, because he disagreed with Lloyd George's land policy, it was front-page news on both sides of the Atlantic.

Where Feuerberg's central theme always remained that of the Jew wavering between two worlds, in the style of the "confessional lyric short story" and as "poetic prose fragments," Sir Alfred was known as "solidly realistic, unconcerned with abstractions, energetic, never given to despair, and above all pragmatic." He has been compared to American tycoons like the Morgans, and no wonder: he became head of Imperial Chemical Industries (ICI), which controlled the chemical industries of the British Empire. Considered to be the wealthiest man in England, he was also regarded as one of the wisest: in a poll of "The Best Brains of England" conducted by *The Spectator*, he was voted number seven.

In parliamentary debates, Mond was a brilliant opponent of Socialism. But his own business was never afflicted by strikes or walkouts, and he believed in real cooperation between capital and labour, a partnership that became known as "Mondism." (The process developed by his father for extracting nickel is still known as "the Mond process.")

In 1928 he was raised to the peerage and became Lord Melchett. His daughter Eva married the son of the Marquess of Reading (born Rufus Daniel Isaacs), Viceroy of India, whom we have commemorated not only with a power station but also with a street in Ramat Aviv. This does not seem fair, because the Marquess of Reading was always considered a distinguished example, together with Edwin Montagu, of an outstanding elegant assimilationist. To the Marquess of Reading, Chaim Weizmann once made the stinging comment: "All the intelligence you have you give to the British, and the little 'stupidity' that is left you give to us."

The Marquess of Reading was "induced," as Weizmann put it, to

become chairman of our Electric Corporation, and is therefore commemorated in our controversial Reading Dalet; while Pinhas Rutenberg,
who almost single-handedly founded the Electric Corporation, did not —
as far as I can see — get even the leanest lane.

Melchett's daughter Eva, Marchioness of Reading, and her brother
Henry, 2nd Baron Melchett, converted to Judaism after the rise of Hitler
and became supporters of Zionism. Henry was president of Maccabi; Eva
was active in the World Jewish Congress and continued to visit here, and
stay at the Villa Melchett, for many years. George Bernard Shaw was
among her guests there, and young Edwin Samuel, who took him swimming in Lake Kinneret, was impressed by the bard's beard, sticking up like
a periscope from the mystic waters.

Eva's daughter married Sir Solly Zuckerman, now Lord Zuckerman, the
famous scientist, but her only son, the 3rd Marquess of Reading, married
Margot Irene, daughter of Percy Duke, OBE, of the Island, Walton-on-the-
Hill, Surrey.

This antiquated name-dropping shows how far we have come from poor
Nahman in the story *Le'an.* His "unbearable tension" snaps in the synagogue
on Yom Kippur: he extinguishes the candle, and the last rift between him
and his father and the community, breaks out into the open. The community considers him mad.

Here we can return to stable, practical Alfred Mond, because the one flaw
in his rewarding progression through life lay in the anti-Semitic attacks on
him by his political enemies, who insisted that both his virtues and his
shortcomings sprang from his Jewish ancestry.

For the first 50 years of his life, Alfred Mond remained consistently
silent about his origin. Then, during World War I, "his foes practically forced him into the Zionist camp, though as the son of assimilated parents he
could not really see himself in that environment." It is not unlikely that his
"conversion" was influenced by such British leaders as Balfour and Lloyd
George.

In a periodical called *Plain English,* edited by Lord Alfred Douglas (one-
time "boyfriend" of Oscar Wilde), Sir Alfred Mond was abused as a "German Jew." He brought an action for libel against the paper on the grounds
that he was neither a German nor a Jew, having been born in England,
and having been baptized as a member of the Church of England at the age
of 10.

The case aroused much public interest at the time; but its conclusion
was still more interesting. Mond was awarded something like £20,000
damages. Thereupon, he announced that he was donating the whole
amount to the Keren Hayesod!

In 1918, he joined Sir Herbert Samuel's advisory committee for the

Sir Alfred Mond (Lord Melchett) ''a giant in body and spirit.''

economic development of Palestine, and three years later, after meeting Chaim Weizmann, he came here to see things for himself. "I have never lived so intensely as a Jew before," he said after this visit.

Once among the Zionists, he threw himself into the new cause, rejuvenated and vigorous. He made speeches, attacked anti-Zionists in high places, and in 1928 became president of the Zionist Federation of Great Britain. When the Jewish Agency was created in 1929, he was elected chairman of its Council, together with Louis Marshall, and from the time of his discovery of Zionism, he donated large sums for the rebuilding of Palestine.

Although he never reconverted to Judaism, there can be no doubt about his Zionist convictions. "I do not consider myself to be an Englishman," he once said. "I am a Palestinian. My heart is in Eretz Israel. This is my electorate. These are my people."

He bought large tracts of land at what is now called Tel Mond, near Ra'anana, for farm settlement. And for his own family, on the shores of Lake Kinneret, he built the "pink villa," a fairy-tale palace with a great deal of marble, a huge fireplace, priceless Persian rugs, a hothouse, and avenues of flowering trees.

"It was paradise on earth," I am assured by a friend who lived there as a child, when his family lived in the house except when the Monds came on holiday, and who farmed the nearby banana groves. During the War of Liberation, the pink villa was occupied by the Palmah and the rugs somehow disappeared. It is now owned by Israel's richest industrialist.

A few months before his death in 1930, Melchett, together with Felix Warburg, followed Weizmann in resigning from the Jewish Agency in protest against the Passfield (Sidney Webb) White Paper suspending the immigration of Jews to Palestine.

On an evening in December, 1930, Gershon Agronsky telephoned Lieutenant-Colonel (later Brigadier) F.H. Kisch, chairman of the Palestine Zionist Executive, with the news of Lord Melchett's death, and asked him to write an obituary for *The Palestine Post.*

"I did so somewhat inadequately, I fear," Kisch wrote in his diary "but with an endeavour to stress the fearlessness of Melchett's support of our movement, a quality which sometimes led him beyond the limits of discretion. Any movement is, however, healthier for having within its leadership an outspoken advocate who, at a crisis, will ignore considerations of tact and tactics, and who is big enough to do so with effect. Such was Melchett."

Closing the entry on Melchett, he adds that Ronald Storrs visited him that evening and, "after mentioning his regard for Melchett, rather characteristically dwelt at greater length on Melchett's regard for him."

Kisch was killed on active service in World War II, at the age of 55. His

Tel Aviv street, in the suburb of Yad Eliahu, runs, appropriately, into that of an Australian officer of World War I, Eliezer Margolin, who commanded the Jewish Legion, the Jewish volunteer battalion of the Royal Fusiliers.

In Haifa, Melchett's street is in the downtown central area known as Hadar, the main commercial centre of the city. But the street itself is curiously quiet, secluded and aristocratic, as befits its lordly name.

17
Were We Happier Once?

Five orchestras played through the night for the throngs of laughing guests. Masked and wearing exotic costumes, they danced and flirted till dawn as coloured lights flickered and paper streamers flashed over them. The non-stop orchestras included a big Sudanese group with a tom-tom section; a Persian orchestra playing Afghanistan hits; a brass band; a police band; and a large jazz orchestra.

Such, such were the joys of Purim in Little Tel Aviv in 1929, the year that brought the Great Depression to America and new Arab riots to Tel Aviv. Here, though — annually, briefly, conscientiously, and often very earnestly — the accent was on "joy," and on the birth of a brave new tradition.

That "large jazz orchestra," to bring things into proper local focus, was made up of players from the Tel Aviv Workers' Council. The police band was from Jerusalem, and the brass band was a military one from Ramallah, under a British conductor. The festivities took place far north of the city, close to the Yarkon River, in the Exhibition grounds of the Levant Fair.

The papa of those famous Purim parties was Baruch Agadati, who also designed Purim as a "happening" to engender an "ecstasy of joy." The Purim Carnival, which later became the *Adloyada*, was said to have been the invention of Moshe Halevy of the Ohel Theatre.

Agadati, who never married, was also the father of two Israeli art forms. First, he developed a dramatically ethnic Jewish avant-garde ballet (he considered the Inbal his successor), toured Europe as a soloist in the Twenties, and was a wild success. In 1934 he suddenly stopped dancing and turned to cinema, producing the first Hebrew talking film *Zot-hi Ha'aretz* ("This is the Land").

Despite these contributions to the performing arts, his first art, and his last, was painting. Born in Benderi, Bessarabia, in 1895, he came to this country alone, at the unlikely age of 15, to study at the Bezalel art school in Jerusalem. Thirty years later he returned to painting, embarking on a long and lonely search for new techniques and images. The last decades of his life were solitary, spent with paints (water colours on silk) in his famous hut on Rehov Yitzhak Elhanan, in the shadow of the Shalom Tower.

Three years after his death in 1976, the street signs of Rehov Baruch Agadati went up on a pleasant new thoroughfare in Zahala, hitherto known as Rehov 2098.

The question naturally arises, why didn't Baruch Agadati get his street where his hut stood so long, on the border of Neve Zedek, and where his long and flamboyantly varied career so uniquely — and atypically — spanned the romantic part of the city's own history? Why, instead of planting Rehov Agadati irrelevantly in Zahala, which has a present and a future but no past, could not Rehov Yitzhak Elhanan have been subdivided, to accommodate the street's most famous resident? Such subdivisions occur here from time to time, which partly explains our shorter-than-average streets; and in any case, Yitzhak Elhanan is a little longer than other streets in that old area.

One reason why Yitzhak Elhanan (Spector, revered Russian rabbi and commentator, 1817-1896) cannot be trimmed involves the religious connection and municipal coalition considerations. Streets commemorating religious leaders may not be tampered with, even though Rabbi Spector already has the Nahlat Yitzhak neighbourhood named after him, not to mention a large yeshiva in New York.

I am afraid not many people walking down Yitzhak Elhanan could identify Rabbi Spector, but here is a short questionnaire that might be put to residents of Rehov Agadati:

Who was 1) named in the presence of Bialik; 2) applauded on the stages of seven European capitals; 3) hung in London; 4) a shining light in bohemian circles here, yet always dressed like Beau Brummel; 5) holder of the local record for being asked by journalists the classic question, "Were we happier once — or does it just seem that way today?"

Explanations:

1. Agadati's original family name was Karushansky. One day long, long ago, Ya'akov Fichman (poet, educator, writer, whose street is in Ramat Aviv not far from Baron Hirsch), took young Baruch to meet Chaim Nahman Bialik. Fichman introduced him by saying to Bialik, "I'd like you to meet *Baruch ha'agadati*," which means, "the legendary Baruch." He was so pleased with how this sounded that from then on, it was his name.

2. His European dance tours during the years 1922-1927 were extremely well, sometimes rapturously, reviewed. From the Swiss *Basler Nachrichten* of September 11, 1927, for instance:

"The dancer seemed at first more Russian than Jewish in style but then Agadati's expressiveness, mirroring the life and spirit of different Jewish types, became more fascinatingly original with every dance... The marvellously colourful and tasteful costumes strongly enhanced the work of this distinguished dancer..."

And in Vienna a month later, the *Telegraph* reported on the "dancing philosopher Baruch Agadati," who with his "totally proportioned giant figure and his passionate yet cultivated style entranced an enthusiastic

Agadati, patron of the arts.

Baruch Agadati — the legendary Baruch.

The papa of those famous parties.

194

audience and roused it to stormy applause" in a hall filled to capacity, with "hundreds who could not buy tickets being turned away, calling for a repeat concert." And so it went, in Paris, Warsaw, Berlin, Amsterdam, Budapest...

3. Some 50 years after these European dance triumphs, an exhibition of Agadati's paintings, done on silk by a special technique which he never let anyone watch, was hung in London at the Alwyn Gallery, and had exceptionally good reviews. (In London at the time of the Six Day War, Agadati began — paradoxically — to paint flowers, his last theme after earlier landscapes and his famous "Hora" series.)

Like other Israeli artists, Agadati enjoyed a better critical success abroad than at home, a fact that caused him much pain; he seems to have wished for understanding and approval more than for financial rewards. I have friends who, on trying to buy paintings from Agadati, found that he was more attached to his art than to what it would bring in; it was not easy to part the paintings from the painter.

4. Although Agadati moved in bohemian circles, among artists and journalists (not that our journalists are, so far as I have noticed, all that bohemian), he was spectacularly unbohemian in his dress. Elegant and fastidious, he wore beautifully-cut suits and jackets fitted to his tall, loping frame. ("Nearly two metres" burbled a Viennese newspaper; actually just over 1.80 m.)

In his fashionably colourful clothing, Agadati stood out in Tel Aviv over a sea of sloppy shorts and white shirts. But we ought not to forget that Tel Aviv always had its super-bourgeois side, with quite a few young blades trying to live up to British standards of dress. Apolitical and non-ideological, except in the sense of being pro-Schönberg and Bartok in the early Twenties and under the spell of "revolutionary art," Agadati was definitely a pioneer in natty masculine dress, to the extent of a gold jacket 50 years ago.

I myself remember the inevitable little felt hat — it always seemed a size or two too small, perhaps to accentuate his height — moving along up my street when Agadati came to call on my next-door neighbours.

These were his brother and sister-in-law, Yitzhak and Tzila, to whom he was devoted. He never married, and they had lived with him in the old hut before they came to live in my street — indeed, in my very flat, for they preceded me as tenants before they moved to a bigger apartment next door.

Baruch's life-story has appeared countless times in the local press. It made good copy, and those pilgrimages to the hut for a chat and a glass of brandy were always a magic change from the world outside. The English reader, by the way, is spared the corny headline *Ha'agada shel Agadati* (The Agadati Legend), re-used so remorselessly that one blushes for the inventiveness of our bohemian journalists.

He first arrived in Jaffa in 1910 and was accepted at Bezalel, where his classmates included Reuven Rubin and Ziona Tagger. During alternate months he worked in the Petah Tikva orange groves. Expelled by the Turks in World War I, he returned to Russia, studied dance and joined the ballet of the Odessa Opera. With the world in flames and the revolution raging, Baruch had his mind on new forms of art: music, costume, dance.

In 1919 he came back to Palestine with the rest of his family — his parents, two brothers and a sister. They came to Jaffa on the famous "Ruslan," the first ship from Russia to arrive after the war, and now a street in Jaffa (but originally, of course, the beloved of Ludmilla in Pushkin's romantic poem, and Pushkin Street is not too far from Ruslan Street).

The family moved into the second floor of a house in Neve Zedek, in which Agnon lived when the neighbourhood was in its prime. It was on Rehov Rokah (Shimon Rokah, 1863-1922, a founder of Tel Aviv. The street of his son Israel, 1896-1953, the second mayor of Tel Aviv, is a spacious stretch north of the Yarkon running to the Exhibition Grounds, where those old Purim parties took place. Between the two Rokahs, father and son, stretches all the history of Tel Aviv in both time and space).

One day in 1920, Mayor Dizengoff took Agadati by the hand and walked north to the outskirts of Tel Aviv, to about where the Migdal Shalom now stands. Pointing to a stretch of sand dunes a few hundred metres from the sea, Dizengoff said, "This land is ownerless. Build your home here, be a pioneer. Help protect the north flank of our city."

It turned out, years later, that the land was not legally without an owner, and a long-drawn-out court case was to ensue. But that was decades in the future. In 1920, Baruch and his younger brother Yitzhak, with the help of a carpenter, built their hut, and the whole family moved in. "Hut" is hardly the right translation for *tzrif* in this case, since although the structure had a tin roof, it was over 200 sq.m. and stood solidly for 65 years. It served later as a film studio — Baruch was proud of the acoustics — and as a private art gallery; in time, the press came to call it a "Museum of the Past."

When Yitzhak married in 1939, he brought his bride to the hut, and Tzila kept house for the brothers for 15 years. Compared with a great number of the shacks which served as Tel Aviv residences, the place was a many-roomed splendour, with bucolic charm. There were well-tended flowers, white doves, a dog called Notara and a pet chicken called Carmela. It also had, Tzila assures me, its housekeeping advantages — hard to imagine as, today, I look from my kitchen across to her well-equipped one.

"There was the outhouse, of course," she recalls dreamily. "Baruch put

196

in an indoor toilet after we left. He imagined, I think, that we might come back..."

Back now to the early Twenties. The first of the famous Purim parties was held in 1921, at the Eden Cinema in Lilienblum. Masks were obligatory. Ussishkin at first refused to wear his, then agreed to. Identification under the masks was checked at the door — by Yitzhak — for security reasons. Parties ran in two series: at 7 *grush* a ticket for the poor, 15 for the rich. And around 3,500 tickets were sold each year.

At this time Agadati was also teaching dance at the Herzliya Gymnasia, Tel Aviv's famous high-school; holding private ballet classes; touring Europe and putting on the first avant-garde opera, also at the Eden, with music by Schonberg, to the distress of very conservative audiences.

Half the income from the Purim parties always went to the Keren Kayemet. But it was still a long way from adhering to proletarian values, and at one point a loosely organized "drinking club" of working types called *Hevra Trask* accused Agadati of profiteering from the events.

He took them to court; Bialik testified on his behalf, and the *Hevra Trask* was found guilty of libel. And Baruch Agadati went on organizing everything, including our first beauty contests, each year presenting the lucky girl to Mayor Dizengoff as Queen Esther.

Meanwhile, there were Arab riots, economic crises, a sudden large immigration from Poland, the start of the Hagana. Yitzhak enlisted in the underground defence force going on to do photography, at Moshe Sneh's request, for the Hagana and, later, the Palmah. Baruch remained with his muse and dreamed up bigger and better carnivals each year. While he danced, he encouraged Yitzhak's interest in sports, and the younger brother boxed and cycled for the Maccabi Club.

In 1934, there occurred an event of no public importance whatsoever, though it was crucial for Baruch. It took place during a revolutionary dance recital in Tel Aviv, at which Agadati introduced a Hassidic dance in modern dress, without music. Agadati lost his audience: nobody liked it.

"I will never dance again," said Baruch Agadati. In an interview with *The Jerusalem Post* in 1962, he claimed that the dance had been successful but the audience was "cold," and they had applauded with their hands, not their hearts."

It so happened that at this time an Italian film company which was making a movie about the Holy Land went bankrupt: cameras and equipment were to be had for a song. And so Baruch Agadati began to make *Zothi Ha'aretz*, a documentary shot on momentous locations and featuring, among other things, Meir Dizengoff wearing a dark moustache to make himself look younger. A very young-looking Raphael Klatchkin also appeared in the film.

Yitzhak Agadati, who went on to found Geva Films and to train several generations of film technicians, was in charge of getting things done, of keeping the crew happy, and in general of translating into reality his brother's grand ideas — as he also did for the Purim parties and carnivals.

The first Hebrew talkie was the hit of 1936, playing for eight weeks at Tel Aviv's biggest theatre, the Mograbi and even making a little money. Baruch made a few more films, some of which lost money. By the end of the Thirties he began to remove himself from the social scene to paint in solitude, especially at night; and he grew increasingly tired of being asked over and over again for his views on Little Tel Aviv, its parties and its carnival, weary of those profound questions on the Nature of Happiness.

In a 1942 interview with the Hebrew daily *Yediot Ahronot,* the theme is already nostalgia (and we think we have only recently invented the mood). No, he was not "bitter," said Agadati, though he was often reluctant to answer a knock on the door of his hut. But people had not understood him. Part of it had to do with the provincialism of Tel Aviv compared to the wider vistas of Europe; but beyond this — who is to know what is "really" understood, ever, anywhere? A catalogue of one of his exhibitions suggested that "his dance was painting in motion, his painting static choreography," if this makes things clearer.

In an enigmatic statement to another journalist, Agadati said that he had no regrets. He had seen much and done much, "things that are permitted as well as things that are forbidden, and some day I shall no doubt have to pay for them."

In 1962, Tel Aviv's journalists to a man — certainly all those who counted — rallied to help him to fight a court order evicting him from his hut so that it could be torn down. The pendulum had swung all the way from "pioneering" under Dizengoff to real-estate realities several mayors later. Agadati was embittered by the attitude of the Municipality. To *The Jerusalem Post* he said:

"I believe in progress, but progress can never mean tearing down my hut... to build a multi-storey office devoid of any feeling except the rapacity of businessmen. Does progress mean destroying the very emotional roots on which progress is founded?"

However, towards the end of his life he relented, and even invited Mayor Shlomo Lahat and his secretary, Zvi Avigai, to dinner at the hut, for the mills of the law ground slowly, and it outlived him.

Yitzhak and Tzila had the gloomy task, for months after his death, of sorting out the accumulation of Little Tel Aviviana that he had kept there. This was right after Yitzhak's production of a remarkable film on his brother's life, directed by Ilan Tiano for the Ministry of Education and Culture. Every day, Yitzhak took Baruch from his sick-bed to a final stint

198

with the cameras; Baruch died during the filming. Yitzhak outlived him by four years.

At last we come to the fifth and last component in the Baruch Agadati riddle, which keen-eyed readers may have noticed was left open-ended — that question, set at the start, which poor Baruch was asked for over 30 years: Were we happier once, back then when those Purim festivities were born, when Tel Aviv was young and there was nowhere to look but ahead? There is, of course, no answer. Agadati tried manfully for journalist after journalist to produce the obvious one: that we all get older, that nostalgic old-timers are simply mourning their lost youth. Those who are young today will, presumably, have their innings of retrospection in due course, when today will seem blissful. Still and all, Agadati used to say, there *was* something special about his parties that never happened again.

That happiness question is a futile one, though everyone will have an answer to contribute. It encompasses a whole bundle of elements — lost innocence, the end of beginnings, the price of achievement and development. Why did no one think of asking the few oldsters then around in Little Tel Aviv whether everything had been better in *their* youth? The answer might well have been a resounding No, because Tel Aviv is unique in that, within living memory, it was perceived as a bright and shining hope of the future.

Quite a few Street People were terribly earnest about evaluating Purim as an Instant Tradition (the festivities came to an end more than a decade ago). For instance, Moshe Beilinson "whom we met with Dizengoff, between Pinsker and Ben-Ami," pointed exultantly to the "purity" of Tel Aviv's Purim. Compared to the riotousness of Latin American carnivals, we had the "unequalled situation in which a woman can walk along the streets at night without the faintest danger of coarseness or hurtful jokes..."

Asher Barash (1889-1952, writer and educator; his street is up north, off Reading) wrote a long and loving description of the happy throngs on "the day that was all joy." Barash's daughter spoke on the radio not long ago on the subject of nostalgia, on "whether it really was all so wonderful" in the Little Tel Aviv in which she grew up. Her conclusion was that the physical environment was certainly more pleasant and attractive than it is today, but that the human scenery was just about the same, with some nice people and some not nice at all.

Bialik's article on the 1933 Purim celebrations, "The *Adloyada* Justifies Itself," sounds more like the comments of a dull civic commissioner than of a national poet.

"The event must become a tradition," Bialik wrote the year before his death, and many years after giving Agadati his name. "The parties and the decorations were very good. But the words of the play didn't get to people far from the stage... We must try, for the *Purimspiel*, to devise something very Purim-ish... The dances this year were somewhat weak and the music disappointing, and there was a noticeable absence of audience participation. Graphic design was very good, better than ever... Between the sections of the parade we ought to have groups of dancers, to spread the feeling of joy. This year we didn't have enough orchestras, and ought to have more next year..."

Baruch Agadati claimed even in his last years that it *was* still possible to orchestrate public happiness by magically tapping the inner personal springs. He maintained this even in our era of television and plastic hammers, used to hit people pointlessly on the head in modern Independence Day celebrations. These hammers are preferable, I suppose, to complete passivity; but they hardly signal that "ecstasy of joy" Bialik wanted.

For permanent success, Agadati might have been very pleased at his triumphant role in a million-dollar art theft not long after his death. In a haul from a private local collection, including world-famous impressionists, the only Israeli picture taken was an Agadati.